HACKISH
PC
Pranks & Cracks

Michael Flenov

A-LIST, LLC
295 East Swedesford Rd.
PMB #285
Wayne, PA 19087
702-977-5377 (FAX)
mail@alistpublishing.com
http://www.alistpublishing.com

This book is printed on acid-free paper.

All brand names and product names mentioned in this book are trademarks or service marks of their respective companies. Any omission or misuse (of any kind) of service marks or trademarks should not be regarded as intent to infringe on the property of others. The publisher recognizes and respects all marks used by companies, manufacturers, and developers as a means to distinguish their products.

Michael Flenov. *Hackish PC Pranks & Cracks*
ISBN: 1-931769-42-7

Printed in the United States of America
05 7 6 5 4 3   First Edition

A-LIST, LLC titles are available for site license or bulk purchase by institutions, user groups, corporations, etc.

Book Editor: Thomas Rymer

Contents

Preface

This book describes the innards of the Windows operating system, as well as some interesting methods for configuring both it and the computer, on which it is running.

You will learn how to use the computer to play practical jokes on your friends or coworkers, as well as learn some Internet secrets that will let you spend your time on the web more productively. At the same time, I will share many of my own computer practical jokes, funny and unusual situations, and a number of other (I think) interesting things.

The book focuses on three basic elements: the computer, the Windows operating system, and the Internet.

These are really the fundamentals of our modern life and, therefore, it is these that we will consider from the Hacker's point of view.

In particular, you will learn how to tune up (optimize and accelerate) your computer, Windows, and Internet resources, how to break into them, and how to protect yourself against break-ins.

What makes this book different from others on this subject is that it provides useful knowledge while making it fun and entertaining. You will learn to make your computer work better while making it more interesting, effective, and secure.

Introduction

Computers are becoming an inseparable part of our lives; I personally carry my notebook with me wherever I go. I can't even imagine my life without it. Any time I have a free minute, the notebook screen comes up and starts glowing different colors as Windows XP is loading. Now I can work anywhere, any time, as long as there is juice in the battery.

But work should be fun. Plugging away all the time at the same workplace is tiresome. After all, you do rearrange the furniture at home from time to time, redecorate the interiors, and so on, so as not to go bonkers within the same four walls, don't you? The same process is important with regard to your computer. The monotonous nature of windows generates boredom, and merely changing the desktop wallpaper and windows colors fails to produce the desired relief. You want something grander and more exiting.

Fig. 1. Windows XP can load with flair

You will learn how to embellish Windows and its application programs to make the time you spend at the computer more pleasant. In the first chapter, we will look at simple tuning techniques using specialized utilities to make the job simple. In the second chapter, we will look into what Windows XP themes, loaders, and programs for entering the system are made of and how you can edit them directly.

But the computer today is not simply an element of fashion. I personally use it to earn my living, to rest and relax, to gain information and knowledge, and, of course, to express myself. It allows me to do anything I want to. In this book I will pass along the most interesting things I know from the user's point of view about Windows' internal workings. The knowledge you gain will allow you to devise new computer jokes, to squeeze the most out of your hardware, and to simply make life more fun.

You will learn how to make program interface more handy and pleasant to look at. Personally, I often decorate my favorite programs with garlands for the New Year and plant flowers in dialog windows in the summer. It helps to brighten things up.

After buying a new car, the first thing many people do is start adding their own bells and whistles. This allows them to express their individuality and to stand out in the surrounding world. Why not do the same with your computer? We have every right to do the same to stand apart from the masses.

Some hackers go in for redesigning and decorating the actual system block; often with impressive results. But the system block is often stashed out of the way under a desk, where it cannot be admired in all its beauty. Further, you don't spend eight hours a day looking at the system block. You spend it looking at your monitor. For this reason, we will first turn our attention to decorating Windows. But we will not stop here, as we will also learn some universal techniques for making changes to other programs. These, as you might have guessed, will not work with all programs, but are effective in most cases.

I spend 10 to 12 hours a day at the computer and, before I got married and had kids, I spent up to 16 hours in front of the monitor, the largest part at night, when all is quiet and peaceful. I would only leave the computer to grab some sleep, and ate most meals while glued to the keyboard. Since I almost never play computer games, most of the time was spent programming and exploring the internal workings of the system. But all work and no play makes Jack a dull boy. To avoid this pitfall, I started playing practical jokes on my friends and coworkers.

Most of these were conceived and played out at work, where there are always guinea pigs for new ideas. It's in man's nature, sometimes unfortunately, to prove himself better than others, and jokes are one of the best ways to do this. Even more importantly, there are a large number of computers on the corporate network at work, meaning many potential targets for my pranks. The network provides the opportunity to make these jokes more interesting, so the fact that the number of computers that are connected to each other and surrounding world continues to increase is one that only fills me with gladness.

I got lucky with my former department's (I've since changed jobs) assistant supervisor, because he was also not averse to playing the occasional joke on fellow coworkers. One day, he played a rather original prank on me: My monitor would not work and, for the longest time, I couldn't figure out why. As it turned out, the monitor was working just fine. My assistant supervisor had simply happened to be passing by it (the specifics of this prank are provided in *Chapter 3*). This, of course, triggered an all-out war between the two of us. At least, a part of most days was spent dreaming up new and interesting ways to play tricks on each other. And every day the pranks became more creative and interesting.

Some of the things that we will consider in the book might violate the license agreements of some of the application software, operating systems, or computers being used. Therefore, before getting down to the action, you should read these carefully. You will, for example, learn how to modify program resources (windows, menus, icons, etc.), which violates the software license agreements from the majority of large developers. Small software development companies and individual programmers generally make their license agreements more flexible, or don't even bother with them at all.

I personally don't understand why we are forbidden to change something in a program, for which we have paid our own, hard-earned money. Television manufacturers do not forbid you from painting the set a different color; you can also do anything you want to your car (except for the fact that the warranty may be voided). Why can't we do the same with Windows?

You should be aware that by violating the license agreement you can lose technical support for whatever product you are fiddling with. For myself, as well as others who don't use these support resources, this is not an issue, so we simply change anything we want to.

Nevertheless, remember that most of the information in this book is provided only for information purposes, so as to enhance your understanding of computer hardware and software. The author and publisher are in no way responsible for any illegal use of your newly-acquired knowledge. I have always maintained that even the most harmless item can be fashioned into a tool of destruction.

Later, when we consider computer overclocking, applying the theory discussed in practice with your machine will void the manufacturer's warranty. If your computer ends up frying out because of something you've done to it, no one will repair it under the terms of the warranty. If you don't have enough experience working with computer hardware, use the information provided here for intellectual pursuits only. Most beginners end up burning something out when attempting extreme overclocking (usually, the motherboard or the processor). Since replacement can only be carried out at your own expense, gaining practical experience can end up being costly. If you have the money to burn, go ahead and practice.

For my own part, I generally overclock machines that have outlived their usefulness and won't be a great loss if something goes wrong. At the same time, new, fast, and stable computers don't need to be overclocked.

Because the Internet has conquered the hearts of most computer aficionados and significant time is spent on the web, we will provide you with some secrets and advice concerning net travel and use. Since the lion's share of time spent on the Internet involves the use of a browser, the greater part of the Internet chapter will be devoted to this application.

Throughout the book, I will provide many recommendations on the use of the computer, Windows, and the Internet. They will allow you to make the most out of these three technologies, which have taken over the world and become a part of our everyday life.

Everything presented in this book is based on my own personal experience, acquired over long years of work with computers. When you have finished reading this book, you will see the computer, Windows, and the Internet in an entirely different light. I hope that you will like what you see and discover for yourself an entirely new world.

In conclusion, I want to stress that all information presented in this book is provided for educational purposes only. The author bears no responsibility for any inadvertent computer destruction or breaking of the law.

Well then, let's get down to studying Windows the way I see it. I hope that seeing it from my point of view will be to your liking and that you will learn new things that will be useful in your everyday life.

Who Are Hackers?

This is a question that has long been a topic of debate. Let's consider the notion of the hacker in the context that I am using it in this book. First, however, we have to take a trip down memory lane.

The concept "hacker" was born when the first computer network — ARPANET — was just being established. In those days, the term was used to denote a person knowledgeable in computers. Some even considered a hacker to be someone who didn't care about anything but computers. The notion was associated with a free computernik, a person striving for complete freedom in everything that involved his or her favorite toy. It is this striving for computer freedom and the striving for free information exchange that gave rise to what is now the rapidly expanding world-wide net. Hackers made a great contribution toward Internet development. For example, they created the Fidonet. Thanks to their efforts, UNIX, at the inception a special purpose-oriented operating system, has evolved into a widely used open-source operating system, under which a large number of internet servers run. Many large corporations entrust this system with their data, stability, and success.

There were no viruses in the early days of the Internet, nor was there the practice of breaking into networks or individual computers. The image of the hacker appeared somewhat later. But this is only an image. Real hackers never have anything to do with system break-ins and their actions directed towards destruction are sharply disapproved of by the virtual society. Even the staunchest freedom fighters do not like having others spy on their personal lives.

A real hacker is a creator, not a destroyer. Since there are more creators than destroyers, the real hackers have distanced themselves from those carrying out break-ins, labeling them as crackers, or simply vandals. Both hackers and crackers are geniuses of the virtual world. Both are fighting for free access to information. But crackers break into sites, confidential databases and other information sources for personal gain or with malicious intent, while hackers do this to satisfy their need to exercise their minds and sharpen their skills. If a cracker breaks into a system for the sole sake of the freedom of information, he or she can be forgiven. However, if he or she does it for money, some other form of personal gain, or a minute of glory, the cracker can only be persecuted as a criminal, which is the actual case under the law.

If you break a program to see how it works, then you are a hacker. But if you break it with the intention of selling it or putting the crack on the Internet, then you become a cracker and a criminal. If you break into a server and inform the administration of the system's vulnerabilities, you are a hacker. If you, instead, destroy information and run away, you are a cracker and a criminal.

It's too bad that many specialists do not recognize this distinction and consider hacker explorations as criminal actions. A hacker's interest in computer security is motivated by the desire to improve it and make it more reliable, while crackers are driven by the lust for lucre or destruction. Some countries have already started to pass laws stating that, unless someone has actually broken into a server, no crime has been committed. Indeed, if a person is interested in learning how the security system of a server works simply for educational purposes, why should this be considered a crime?

To summarize the above, crackers are the following:

- ❑ Virus writers: people who apply their knowledge to writing destructive programs.
- ❑ Vandals: those who are bent on destroying systems, deleting files, or disrupting the work of the server.
- ❑ Computer and server breakers: professionals who break systems for profit. They can break into systems to steal information, but seldom use their skills to destroy anything.
- ❑ Program crackers: individuals who remove protection from software and make the compromised programs available for everyone. These people deprive software companies of their just compensation, and governments of tax revenues. Programmers must be paid for their labors and Caesar must be given his due.

The difference between a hacker and a cracker can be seen in their respective approaches to breaking programs. Many think that software companies charge too much for their products. A cracker will act upon this belief by breaking the protection, while a hacker will write his or her own program offering the same functionality, but at a lower, or even no price at all. Thus, Open Source movement participants are hackers, whereas those breaking closed source software belong to the cracker grouping.

Simply to know the computer is not enough to be a hacker. Any hacker must be versed in programming. When we consider attack methods used by hackers, you will see that most of these attacks cannot be carried out without solid programming knowledge and skills. If you are interested in raising your proficiency level and learning more about programming, I (humbly) recommend my own title: *Hackish C++ Pranks & Tricks*. This book will teach you how to create your own prank programs and hacker software. You do not need to have deep knowledge of programming to understand the material presented in this book.

The computer practical jokes that will be considered in this book are effective. But wouldn't you like to be able to create your own prankish program and then slip it into the computers of your friends?

I think that the confusion regarding who is a hacker and what a hacker does is caused by the media's lack of understanding of the subject. Popular mass media attribute any computer system break-in to hackers, although there is a huge difference between criminals and real hackers.

So, as you can see, a hacker is simply a person with some degree of genius who has directed his or her intellect toward computer exploration. Those who think that hackers simply engage in destructive activities are badly mistaken. Real hackers never use their knowledge to cause harm to others. This is the principle that is advocated in this book, so you will not find any specific advice on how to break into computers or write viruses. All you will find is useful and intellectual information that can help increase your knowledge.

How Can You Become a Hacker?

This is a common question, to which there is no exact answer. I will try to provide some advice, but this will be rather general, as everything depends on the specific area, in which you want to achieve perfection.

Let's compare a computer specialist with a construction worker. Both a bricklayer and a carpenter can achieve perfection in their corresponding trades. But even though both trades are construction jobs, they involve different specializations. In exactly the same way a UNIX specialist, a software-application writer, or a web site developer can all be hackers. It all depends on your interests and requirements.

So, here are some recommendations that will help you achieve recognition as a real hacker by your friends and colleagues.

❑ You must know your overall computer system thoroughly and be able to control it effectively. As a bonus, knowing every components of its hardware will only serve as a significant plus to the hacker grade you achieve.

What does it mean to control a computer effectively? It means that you must know all of the possible ways to perform any operation and how to use the most optimal of these in a given situation. In particular, you must learn the hotkeys instead of bothering your rodent for every trifle. Pressing a key takes less time than even the slightest mouse movement. Simply get into the habit of using hotkeys, and you will discover all of the joys of working with the keyboard. I personally seldom use the mouse, trying always to use the keyboard instead.

Here is a little example on this subject. My boss always copies and pastes data using toolbar buttons or context menu commands. But if you also do coping this way, you probably know that not all toolbars or context menus have **Copy** and **Paste** buttons. In these situations, my boss enters text by typing it manually. Instead he could use the <Ctrl>+<C>/<Ctrl>+<V>

or <Ctrl>+<Ins>/<Shift>+<Ins> hotkeys for this purpose. These are present in virtually all modern applications — even in those that do not provide for buttons or menus.

Copying and pasting in the standard Windows components (such as input lines or text fields) is done by the operating system itself and requires no actions on the part of the application to work. Just because the application programmer has not supplied the appropriate buttons does not mean that these actions cannot be performed. They can, using the hotkeys.

Here is another example. At one time I was working as a programmer for a large company (with over 20,000 employees). I was given a task of writing a cost-accounting database. A large volume of parameters had to be entered into the database manually by operators. The first version of the program did not use hotkeys and required 25 data-entry operators. After hotkeys were added to the program, productivity increased and the number of data entry operators dropped below 20. The savings the hotkeys produced were manifest.

❐ You must thoroughly learn everything about computers in your particular field of interest. If you are interested in graphics, you must study the best graphics packages, how to draw any scene using them and how to create the most complex worlds. If you are a network enthusiast, then try to learn whatever you can about networks. Just in case you decide that you already know everything about a particular area, buy yourself a book on the given subject and you will soon realize how badly mistaken you are. It is impossible to know everything about computers.

Hackers are, above all, professionals in any area, not necessarily in computers or programming. In this book, however, only computer hackers will be considered.

❐ A hacker must know at least one programming language. Knowing several programming languages is even better. I personally recommend all aspiring hackers to learn Delphi or C++ for starters. Delphi is a sufficiently simple, fast, effective, and, most importantly, powerful language. C++ is the world renowned standard, but is somewhat more difficult to master. This advice does not, however, mean that you can learn programming only with these two languages or that, having learned them, you should not learn others. You can learn programming using any language, even Basic (while I do not recommend using Basic for serious practical work, it will not hurt to know it).

Over the course of this book, you will see that some computer break-ins would have been impossible to execute without programming knowledge.

Using readymade programs written by other hackers, you can only become a cracker. To become a hacker, you must learn how to write your own programs.

Although I do not really like Visual Basic because of limitations including the fact that it is inconvenient to use and a slew of other shortcomings, I have seen some excellent programs written in this language. The authors of those programs deserve to be called Hackers — with a capital H — because of their superior and flawless work. Creating something magnificent from something mundane is exactly what the art of hacking is.

A hacker is a creator, a person who brings things into being. The things that are created are mostly programs, but nobody has said that they can't be graphics or music. Anything that requires a creative and inquiring mind belongs to the art of hacking. But, even if you use your computer to write music, learning programming will make you more proficient and productive. Writing your own programs is not as difficult today as it was in the past. Modern programming languages like Delphi let you create simple utilities in a very short time, using the same technology as is found in the most powerful programs. So make an effort to learn how to program.

❑ Do not hinder the progress. Hackers have always fought for freedom of information. If you want to be a hacker, you must promote this concept and help others who aspire to acquire knowledge. Some hackers do this by writing open-source programs. Others do it by simply sharing their knowledge.

Freedom of information does not mean that you cannot make any money of your knowledge. This has never been forbidden; after all, hackers are human too and they must also eat and support their families. But money should never be the main thing in your life. The main thing should be creativity, the process of bringing something new into being. This is another difference between hackers and crackers: Hackers create, while crackers destroy information. Writing a unique practical-joke program makes you a hacker. Writing a virus that destroys someone's hard drive while drawing smiles on the screen makes you a cracker and, in my opinion, a criminal.

Even breaking-in can be used as a weapon in the fight for freedom of information, but only if its purpose is not to destroy. You can break the protection for a program to learn how it works, but not to remove it. You must respect the labors of other programmers, because writing programs is how they earn their living. But if they do not protect their programs (it's the real world out there, after all), they will starve.

Consider stealing a television set. This would be considered a crime and punished accordingly. Many people who otherwise would not mind getting a television for nothing are deterred by the prospect of punishment. But why should crackers have no fear of the law and be permitted to break programs freely? What they do is also theft. I personally view breaking into a program in the same light as stealing a television set.

Nevertheless, you must have a right to look at what is inside the program. Take the same television set. You can open one that you have paid for and no one will persecute you for violating license agreements, as major software corporations do for cutting open their products. You are not forced to register merchandize you buy honestly, as is the practice now with software activation. I can understand software developers who are just trying to protect their labors, but they should not go to these extremes. Protection schemes only complicate the lives of law-abiding users while providing no effective protection from crackers. For any program there is a crack, which sometimes even becomes available before the program itself.

I am a programmer myself and sell my programs. But I never install complex protection for my programs, because it only makes things more difficult for lawful users and crackers will break it anyway. No matter what protection schemes major software corporations have devised to protect their products, most of them were compromised even before the product's official release. Other methods should be employed to combat software piracy; activation or key systems are as good as useless to stop this.

In a civilized world, a program should only have a simple field to enter the code confirming payment — and nothing else. There should not be any complex activation or registration procedures. But users also must be honest, because any labor must be paid for. And the mere fact that a product (a program) can be had for free does not mean that you should get it that way.

❑ Do not re-invent the wheel. Here is the hackers' creative function in action again. They must not stay in one place and must share their knowledge with others. For example, if you have written some great code, share it with others so that they will not have to spend their own time on it. You do not have to lay open all of your secrets, but you should help others.

By the same token, if you lay your hands on someone else's code, do not be shy to use it (with the author's permission, of course). Do not waste you time inventing something that has already been invented by others and has already had all of its bugs worked out by users. If everyone keeps on inventing the wheel anew, no cart, not to mention the automobile, will ever be created.

❏ Hackers are not just separate individuals, but a complete culture. This does not, however, mean that all hackers dress and look alike. Each of them is an individual. Do not copy others. Copying someone else's work will not make you a sophisticated hacker. Only your individuality can earn you a reputation.

For your work to be known in certain computer circles is considered to be a big honor. Hackers are the people who earn their fame by their knowledge and good deeds. So you should be able to recognize a hacker easily.

How can you tell if you are a hacker? It is simple: If you have a reputation as a hacker, then you are a hacker. There is a pitfall you have to watch for here, for most people think that crackers are hackers. So you might be tempted to break some site or crack a program to get talked about. But this is the wrong approach and you should not yield to this temptation. Try to stay within the boundaries described above and earn yourself a reputation by good deeds only. This is much more difficult than wreaking havoc, but what can you do... No one said being a hacker was easy.

❏ What is the difference between a programmer, a user, and a hacker? A programmer has a vision of what a program should be like and he writes it according to this vision. A user does not always know what the programmer had in mind and uses the program the way he or she thinks appropriate.

Because a programmer is not a user, he or she cannot foresee everything that users can do with the program. This often results in users selecting settings that crash the program simply because the programmer never imagined that this certain combination of settings would be of particular interest. This is a factor behind the instability of programs that have not been subjected to thorough testing prior to their retail release.

Hackers are just like the users who select the seemingly impossible settings but with the difference that they intentionally seek those settings or other loopholes to make the program work incorrectly or in a manner not intended. This requires a lively imagination and the ability to "think outside the box." You must feel the executable code and see in it what others cannot.

❏ If you discover a vulnerability, in a site's security, for example, you don't have to take advantage of it. This will not be a feather in your cap, but might bring you a pass to prison. You would be better off informing the site's administration about the weak spot. This is a more noble deed, but more importantly, it can earn you a reputation without exposing you to the danger of falling on the wrong side of the law.

As I mentioned above, getting your exploits publicized in trial proceedings is a faster way to acquire a hacker reputation because of all the media exposure.

But values are somewhat different in prison and a hacker reputation is not particularly esteemed in this milieu, to say the least. It's unlikely to do you much good in those circumstances. Moreover, this dubious fame very often makes it difficult to find a job after getting out. Not too many companies will want to hire a former criminal. What is worse, even after getting released from prison, you may be forbidden from using a computer for quite a long time. So it is much better to be famous and free (a hacker) than notorious and in prison (a cracker).

This gives rise to another question: Why does the author place computer jokes and writing prankish programs into the hacker art category? I will try to answer this question. First of all, hackers have always tried to prove their power and knowledge by writing amusing and whimsical programs. I do not place viruses into this category because of their destructive nature, although viruses with a sense of humor also sometimes occur sometimes. But simple and harmless jokes have always been appreciated among those in the know.

By writing these little jokes, a hacker not only shows deep knowledge of the intricacies of, for example, some operating system, but also makes people around him or her smile. It is no secret that many hackers have a sense of humor, so they look for ways to give reign to this humor. I recommend that your practical jokes be harmless ones.

One last thing: I already said that any hacker must know how to program in some programming language. Some people think that a hacker must know how to program in assembler. This is not the case. To know how to program in assembler is a desirable skill, but not a mandatory one. I personally like Delphi (but also use C++ and assembler) and find that I can do everything I want to in this language. Most importantly, I can do it rapidly and with quality.

For someone with a sharp mind, any programming language is a proper tool. But, despite my personal affection for Delphi, which is practical for writing almost any type of program, with the exception of games, C++ has always been and will always remain the uncontested master in this area. For network programming, in some situations C++ is more convenient, while in others Delphi gets the nod. But writing large applications in assembler is not only inefficient, it is simply stupid.

You must also make an intelligent judgment as to using various technologies. I am an economic manager by profession and went to school for six years to study in this field. Even before this, however, I knew that the customer is always right. For some incomprehensible reason, this maxim is not always followed in the computer and information technologies area. For example, Microsoft pressures programmers into writing certain types of programs without explaining what benefits the user derives from them. Many programmers blindly follow these recommendations without stopping to think twice whether what they are doing is really necessary.

Here is a supporting example. Now all programmers build XML support into their products without thinking whether this is really necessary. The truth is that not all users need this format and not all programs require it.

As a matter of fact, I recommend that you pay less attention to Microsoft, because I personally consider it a hindrance in the way of the progress. I can also prove this contention by an example. How many data access technologies has Microsoft invented? We can only but marvel: DAO, RDO, ODBC, ADO, ADO.NET, and this is not even the complete list. Microsoft regularly throws something new into the market while not using its own innovations itself. Every time a new technology appears on the market, every programmer rushes to retrofit his or her programs to the new standard, wasting huge resources on constant modifications as a result. Consequently, its competitors are held back while Microsoft is forging ahead, because it does not do not follow its own recommendations and does not modify any of its products. In my opinion, if a program was designed to use DAO, it is better left working this way and not modified to use ADO, because the user does not care how the program obtains its data from the database. Simply obtaining them is what counts.

The approach to using its interface that Microsoft has been following is another striking example of the way, in which they do not implement their own innovations. They constantly change the interface for MS Office, telling everyone in the process that the newer interface is the one the user wants. All other software developers rush to modify their programs to display new menus and toolbars, while Microsoft's Internet Explorer and other programs look the way they did 10 years ago. Their appearance practically doesn't change, meaning that Microsoft does not have to spend its time on it, while its competitors waste months rewriting huge volumes of code.

Yes, keeping up with the latest trend gives your programs some panache and other pluses, but following the leader unconditionally may see you lose much more than you gain. You must have your own individuality.

Despite all of this haranguing of Microsoft, I am not a Microsoft "hater"... I like their products — Windows or SQL server, for example — very much. What I object to is the way, in which they go after their competitors. I understand that software is a rough business, but there have to be limits.

Often programmers and hackers will try to impose their preferred programming language on the user as the only one suitable for the job. They are usually successful in this because the user frequently has very little understanding of programming. In fact, the user does not care what language you use to write the program he or she needs. The only thing the user cares about is a quality product, delivered on time. I can personally only deliver a quality product in minimal time when using Delphi. To provide the same quality working with VC++ will take me (and in fact any other programmer) significantly longer.

Only when a customer requires that a program be of a minimum size and work at maximum speed do I write it in assembler or C (the latter is not to be confused with C++). But this does not happen often, because nowadays removable information media can hold any practical amount of information and computers works millions of times faster than their predecessors. Consequently, program size and execution speed are of relatively little import, with product quality and development time coming to the forefront.

A Bit of Background

To understand the world of hackers better, you need to delve into history and look at the development of the computer and information technologies from the Internet's origins, the appearance of the first hacker programs, the first break-in, etc.

In 1962, the director of the Advance Research Projects Agency (ARPA) in the United States, J.C.R. Licklider, suggested using existing computer communications for military purposes. The goal was to create a distributed communications system based on the fundamental principle that it would continue to function even after a part of the system had been disabled. This suggestion resulted in computer networks becoming the main direction of the agency's research. This can be called the birth of the Advanced Research Projects Agency Network (ARPANET).

This failure is what gave rise to the development of the Internet. Why do I say failure? Because the system's fundamental principle was that it would continue functioning even if a part of it failed. The possibility of a failure was built into the system at its very inception. The main principle was system security, for it was developed for U.S. military needs. But security was exactly what no one paid attention to. This was the case because only professionals had access to computers, personal computers still being the stuff of science fiction. No one ever thought that a home computer could be used to connect to the military research network. It gets even worse later.

There is no general consensus as to the exact date of the birth of the network. Different sources give different dates, ranging from 1965 to 1970. Many single out 1969, the year ARPANET was created. This was also the year, in which the UNIX operating system was developed, which would form the backbone of the Internet for decades to follow.

At the beginning of the 1970s, ARPANET started to expand and connect various research universities. Its boundaries extended from one building to include the neighboring states. At first no one even imagined that the network would grow so rapidly and connect so many computers. Consequently, the original communications and data exchange technologies became obsolete in the first 10 years.

The phreaker decade started in 1970. Phreakers were also called hackers, even though they were not directly involved with computers. Their main field of activity was the telephone network. Telephone services were expensive, so teenagers (and quite often not even teenagers) tried to save some money on using this service.

The phreaker era begins from the moment Bell published the phone network control tone frequencies in Technical Assistance Program magazine. 1971 saw the appearance of the Blue Box, used to generate control signal tones. Over the following 10 years, many people used these boxes to save a pretty penny on long-distance calls while the phone companies suffered corresponding losses. Starting in 1980, this disease began to wane, because too many phreakers began getting caught and prosecuted, making this a dangerous endeavor.

Among phreakers were some well-known known individuals, including the founders of Apple Computers, for example. They sold students electronic kits, which included blue boxes.

In 1972, the first electronic mail application appeared, and a year later the network extended beyond U.S. borders, with computers in England becoming connected. The first propositions for and talks about the construction of an international network began in the same year.

But only in 1981 was the computer security center at the U.S. Defense Security Center established. This center was supposed to evaluate computer systems offered to the defense department with regard to their compliance with security requirements.

On Dec. 16, 1981, the trial started against Rosco, the most infamous of the phreakers. The notorious hacker Kevin Mitnick was also present at this trial, but this time only as a witness. Less than a year later he was not so lucky, was caught during one of his exploits, and was sentenced to a juvenile correction facility.

In 1982, the Transmission Control Protocol/Internet Protocol (TCP/IP) became the main Internet protocol. The number of hosts was increasing and their addresses were used to access network computers. With the appearance of TCP/IP, the development of the Domain Name System (DNS) began. This system allows computers to be addressed by names, taking care of converting names intelligible to humans into addresses understood by computers.

In 1983, Kevin Mitnick was set free. He did not, however, enjoy his liberty for long. Yielding instead to his hacker itch, he again reverted to breaking into computers and, again, was found out. He went underground on the run from the law, successfully evading the authorities until 1985.

In 1984, the DNS system was put into service. Four years later, the world learned about the worm threat. In 1988, one of the most extensive Internet worm infections took place. A young Digital worker and Cornell University graduate, Robert Morris, was developing a worm program that was supposed to travel over networks autonomously and infect the files of all compromised computers.

The worm used the password list to obtain logon passwords. The worm program had a list of the most commonly used passwords and looped through them to find those needed to obtain access to other computers. If the password could not be guessed by this method, the worm used the system dictionary to pick the necessary password. Over 7 percent of all Internet computers were infected using this simple method. This was quite a significant number, given the overall number of network computers. The worm was released accidentally and its code was not even finalized. It frightening to ponder what would have happened had Robert Morris finished the worm program.

This was not the end of it, however, for the year. 1988 was the most fruitful in terms of break-ins and resonant hacker trials. The law finally caught up with Kevin Mitnick during the year and, this time, he had to forget about computers for a much longer period.

In 1990, ARPANET ceased to exist, being simply absorbed by the Internet, which continues to swallow all separate networks.

In 1991, the world saw web pages, without which no one could imagine the worldwide web today, for the first time. The Internet community started seeing the Internet in a different light. In the same year, PGP, one of the most successful encryption systems, was introduced. It gradually became a standard in most areas, including E-Mail encryption.

In 1994, Internet users numbered in the millions. So as not to have people just wasting their time staring at monitors, the first attempts at full-fledged commercial activity were undertaken. The Internet was no longer just an information exchange conduit; it had become a vehicle for advertising and moving goods to the masses.

In 1995, domain registration became paid and the era of the domain wars began. Hackers tried to buy up all of the domain names the same as or similar to brand names, or simply to words that are easy to remember. Companies that wanted their domain names match their brand name had to spend big money to "buy back" domain names of this type.

This year was also notable for my buying a modem and joining the Internet community. Before this, I made only occasional and short forays into the net because it was a too expensive pleasure for me.

With this business announcement, I conclude the introduction and move on to the art-of-war practice, in which the main things are often stealth and victory with the use of minimal forces.

Chapter 1: Interesting Windows Settings

When I worked with Windows 95 for the first time, I fell in love with this operating system. Despite the fact that it was unstable, blue screens of death were common, and you had to reinstall it every couple of months or so, it offered a number of handy things for regular users and crusty hackers alike.

With the release of the following versions — Windows 98, 2000, and XP — my affection for this operating system has only grown stronger. With each new version, the system became more sophisticated and provided users with new and interesting ways for expressing their individuality. But, because of its instability and other difficulties, I was sometimes tempted to install Linux and work with it instead. With the appearance of the XP version, however, I understood that there was no longer a need for any operating system of the Red Hat variety. It's better to pay more and receive an excellent, practical, and stable system. The important thing is to take the proper approach and configure all of the settings properly — and there are plenty of settings to be adjusted, not only in order to improve its reliability, but also to enhance its outward appearance.

In this chapter, we will consider Internet Explorer settings that are hidden from the user and are accessible only through the registry. Because the number of parameters is very large, we will not describe them all, but those most interesting and useful to the hacker will be covered in sufficient detail.

Later in this book, a considerable amount of attention will be devoted to adjusting the outward appearance of Windows and, especially, of its latest version — XP — for it is with this version that the interface can be made more appealing and convenient with a minimal investment of time and effort.

1.1. Your Own Internet Explorer

The first thing I do when I tune up my operating system is to change Internet Explorer (IE). Some programmers write their own browsers based on the IE engine, but I see no point in this, as the program as is already provides the means for changing just about everything within it. We will now learn how to change the main browser window beyond recognition, after which you can tell your friends that you wrote the browser function yourself.

Today, there are special programs that allow you to adjust a number of settings automatically. In the past, however, everything had to be done manually. We will take this older path because doing the work manually will help us better understand how they work, won't limit what we can do, and, unlike programs written by others, is free.

Most of the adjustments we will make will be carried out in the registry, so you may have to reboot your computer for them to take effect. I myself have tested them on Internet Explorer 6.0, running under Windows XP, and did not, however, have to reboot the system even once.

1.1.1. Your Own IE Logo

Most Windows animations are created from simple BMP format bitmap images. For some reason, Microsoft very seldom uses animation formats like GIF or the AVI video format. The former can only be used on a commercial basis now, meaning that royalties have to be paid in order to use it. The AVI video format remains in the public domain, but its use is minimal.

So, what makes static pictures move? This is brought about in the same way as in the computer games in the 1990s. Fig. 1.1 shows several plane images, each at a different stage of the roll sequence. Each of the images is 180×90 pixels and they all are lined up vertically (like in IE, although the orientation is not important and can be horizontal). To create an animation, images from an array of this type are displayed sequentially, creating the illusion of movement.

Fig. 1.1. Animation of a plane roll sequence

In IE, images are also arranged in an array column. Their size does not really matter; the important thing is that they are square. To avoid potential problems, it is the best to prepare images of 26×26 pixels and to line them up vertically (we will later see what the potential problems are). The number of images is also not important, so you can prepare as many as you wish.

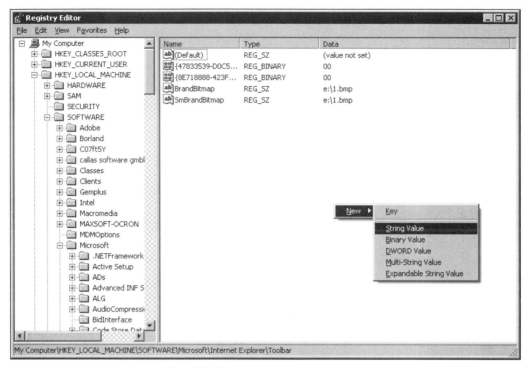

Fig. 1.2. The registry editor window

Save the prepared strip of images in a BMP file. I recommend that you save materials of this type in the Windows folder, in order to keep them from being mixed in with other images or being deleted accidentally.

Now the image has to be hooked up to Internet Explorer. To do this, we launch the regedit program (select **Run** from the **Start** menu, type regedit in the window that appears, and then press **OK**). The registry editor window will open (Fig. 1.2). Open the **HKEY_LOCAL_MACHINE\SOFTWARE\Microsoft\Internet Explorer\ Toolbar** key.

You will have to create two new registry keys in this section. This can be done by right clicking anywhere in the right panel and selecting **New/String Value** in the context menu that appears. A new string value will created that will have to be re-named **BrandBitmap**, and the path to the created BMP file entered as its value. Then create a **SmBrandBitmap** parameter in exactly the same way and specify the same path for it.

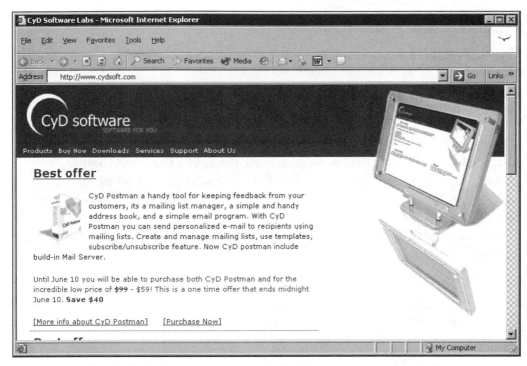

Fig. 1.3. An image too large will stretch the menu bar vertically

If you have done everything properly, the first image from your image array will be shown in the upper left corner when you launch IE. The animation will start when a site begins loading.

Now, let's take a look at a potential problem. If the images are made too large vertically, the menu bar can stretch visibly in that direction (Fig. 1.3). Some people might actually prefer this, but a menu that is too large isn't generally very attractive.

These modifications are both quite simple and impressive. They are worthwhile if for no other reason than the fact that, personally, I find the Microsoft flag and globe irritating.

You can find several images that I have prepared for use as substitutes for the IE logo on the companion CD, in the \Chapter1\IELogo folder.

NOTE

1.1.2. Coloring the Button Toolbar

The standard buttons toolbar for one of the earlier IE versions had a pleasing, washed-out look. This was achieved by using a corresponding image for its background. In subsequent versions, the background became gray and dull again. The possibility of setting a custom background, however, was retained.

Here is how this is done.

Prepare a BMP image of any size. Launch the registry editor, and go to the **HKEY_CURRENT_USER\Software\Microsoft\Internet Explorer\Toolbar** key. If your IE already has background installed, there should be the **BackBitmap** string value; otherwise, this will have to be created. Specify the image file path as its string data. Launch IE, and it will now have an entirely different appearance.

Fig. 1.4 shows IE with a background installed. Each change you apply makes the IE window look less and less like its parent.

NOTE

You can find several images that I have prepared to be used as toolbar area backgrounds on the companion CD in the \Chapter1\IEBackground directory.

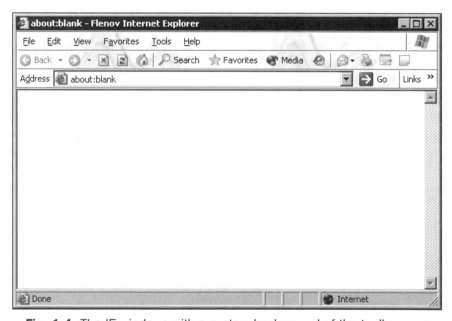

Fig. 1.4. The IE windows with a custom background of the toolbar area

1.1.3. Main Settings

Because we want the modified window to pass for our own design, it must have no references to Microsoft in the title bar. Let's insert our own title here. To do this, we go to the **HKEY_CURRENT_USER\Software\Microsoft\ Internet Explorer\Main** registry key and create a **Window Title** string value with our new title as its string data.

Starting with IE version 5.5, a context menu appears after the mouse pointer has been held over a picture for a certain time. I personally find this irritating and don't see the point, as the same context menu can be summoned by right clicking on the picture needed. To eliminate this source of irritation, we can create an **Enable_MyPics_Hoverbar** value in the same registry key with "**no**" as its string data.

1.1.4. Using Settings to Play Tricks

Let's leave cosmetic changes alone for a while and monkey around a little. One of the registry keys enables or disables the closing of the IE window by the user. When surfing the net, many sites generate pop-up windows, which, aside from being a source of great irritation in their own right, clutter up the screen. Disabling the window-closing parameter will cause them to multiply, while attempts to close them will produce a warning window like the one shown in Fig. 1.5.

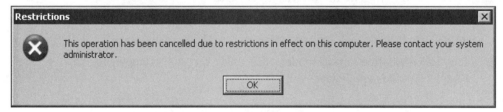

Fig. 1.5. A system warning window

To prevent the IE window from closing, go to the **HKEY_CURRENT_USER\ Software\Policies\Microsoft\Internet Explorer\Restrictions** registry key. This path may not exist on your machine, in which case you will have to create the missing intermediate keys yourself. This is done by right clicking on an existing key and selecting **New/Key** in the context menu that appears. For example, if your machine offers only the **HKEY_CURRENT_USER\Software\Policies\Microsoft** key, right-click on **Microsoft** and create the **Internet Explorer** key, then create the **Restriction** key here in the same way.

When you have all the necessary keys, create a **NoBrowserClose** value of the **DWORD** type, and set its data value to 1.

You can try all of this on a friend's computer, and then watch his or her reaction when your friend tries to close the window. I once played this trick on my co-workers. Their reactions varied, but the majority thought that their machines had been infected with a virus.

The problem is that making all of these changes requires some time, which you may not have when trying to do this on someone else's machine. Here is how it can be done quickly and inconspicuously.

1. Make the changes on your own machine.
2. Export the settings of the **HKEY_CURRENT_USER\Software\Policies\ Microsoft\Internet Explorer\Restrictions** key into a `.reg` file.
3. Save the resulting file on a diskette.

Then, go to and tell your prospective victim that you have something to show him or her. Insert the diskette into the drive and launch the file. All the necessary information will be added to the registry automatically. You don't have to do anything else, including asking him or her to launch IE. Simply say that you have obviously brought the wrong diskette, and leave. Wait until the user launches the browser and watch as he or she tries to close it.

You can find the ready-made REG file on the companion CD in the \Chapter1\NoClose.reg folder.

NOTE

1.1.5. Give Me Any Name You Like

I find titles like "My Computer" and "Recycle Bin" irritating and prefer to use titles that are more elegant and pleasing to the soul. That's exactly why, after re-installing Windows, I always dig into the registry to the following key:

HKEY_CURRENT_USER\Software\Microsoft\Windows\ShellNoRoam\MUICache

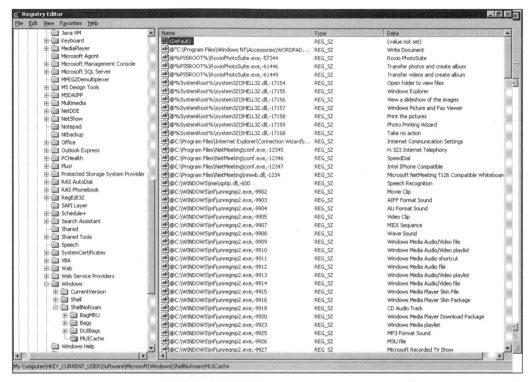

Fig. 1.6. Names of all variables

Because IE is the foundation of the entire operating system, the names that you find in Fig. 1.6 pertain to the desktop and the system in general. That's why I like this key and take special care in editing it.

1.2. How to Become a Microsoft OEM Partner

Sometime in 1999, I bought me a new computer with a preinstalled OEM (Original Equipment Manufacturer) version of Windows 98. When I started tweaking the operating system to suit my needs and opened the system properties window (**Start/Control Panel/System**), I saw the logo of the company, from which I bought the computer, on the **General** tab.

For the sake of experimentation, I installed the operating system on an old computer, which barely booted under it, but showed the same logo. Could it be that the computer manufacturer recompiled Windows source codes or redesigned the installation program? There were no signs of this, so the obvious answer was "No."

Everything became clear after I read the computer technical manual. As it turns out, Microsoft does not support OEM products, leaving this task to the computer manufacturers themselves instead. So that the user knows who the manufacturer is, the latter's logo, along with other information, is placed in the system properties window.

I spent a whole day looking for the loophole used to place them there before finally figuring it out. Fig. 1.7 shows what my current system properties window looks like.

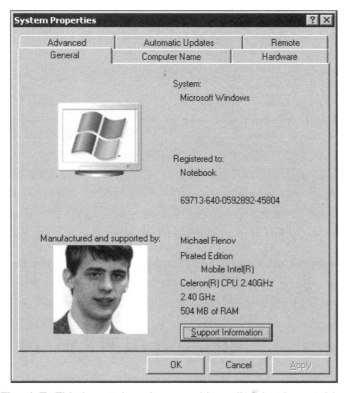

Fig. 1.7. This is not done in a graphics editor but by patching
a couple of the right files in the right places

This effect is relatively easy to achieve. A file named oeminfo.ini has to be created in the **Windows/System** (**Windows/System32** for 2000/XP/2003). Its contents are the following:

```
[general]
Manufacturer= Mikhail Flenov
```

```
Model = Pirated Edition

[OEMSpecific]
SerialNo = <12345>
OEM1 = <01.01.00>

[Support Information]
Line1 = I love Microsoft Windows XP
Line2 = You must love it too
Line3 = Just do it for me
Line4 = My lovely site is http://www.cydsoft.com
Line5 = Software For You
Line6 = Best regards
```

The first section — general — contains information that will be shown in the properties window. It has only two interesting parameters:

❑ Manufacturer   ❑ Model

If you take a look at Fig. 1.7, you will see that a new button — **Support Information** — has appeared at the bottom. It shows in the properties window if the oeminfo.ini file has the Support Information section. When this button is clicked, a window appears containing whatever support information was entered in that section of the file. An example of such a window is shown in Fig. 1.8.

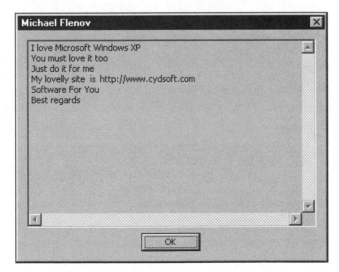

Fig. 1.8. A support information window

The **Support Information** section can contain several lines, which look like the following:

```
Line N = Text
```

where N is the line number.

It is best to number lines sequentially, without skipping any numbers; otherwise, the displayed text may not be justified properly. You can enter any text you want after the equal sign.

1.3. Install a Mouse Pad

Hackers are rather fun-loving people and like to play tricks on users constantly. There was a joke making the rounds way back in the days of Windows 95: When a computer would hang or the mouse pointer would not move, hackers immediately diagnosed the problem as an incorrectly installed mouse pad driver. Suckers would swallow the bait and begin looking for the driver. To assist users from this category in their task, I wrote a mouse pad driver.

Using Notepad, create a text file with the INF extension. Name it whatever you want to. Copy Listing 1.1 into this file.

Listing 1.1. Mouse Pad Driver Source Code

```
[VERSION]
SIGNATURE = "$CHICAGO$"
CLASS = SYSTEM
PROVIDER = %HORR%
SETUPCLASS = BASE

[CLASSINSTALL]
ADDREG = HORR
CLASSNAME = "MOUSE PAD"

[MANUFACTURER]
%HORR% = HORR

[HORR]
Standart_Mouse_Pad,,,,%CLASSNAME%

[STRINGS]
HORR = "Horrific Corporation"
```

Now go to the folder, in which you just saved the INF file, and right click on it. In the context menu that appears, select the **Install** item. Now, when you show the sucker the results, by opening the **System** icon in the **Control Panel**, he or she will see the MOUSE PAD driver among the rest of the system drivers.

This driver can also be installed using the **Add Hardware** option in the **Control Panel**. In this case, you have to decline automatic installation and choose installation from the specific location option, and then the **Have Disk** option. Then specify your INF file directly.

This trick works in Windows 9*x*, but in Win2000/XP no mouse pad driver will be shown among the system drivers. It appears that Microsoft has disallowed mouse pad drivers because of their incompatibility with newer mice or newer operating systems ☺.

You can find the file for the driver described above on the accompanying CD, in the \Chapter1 folder.

NOTE

1.4. Windows Controls

Personally, I have already grown tired of the built-in Windows XP styles. Most of all, the appearance of the **Start** button drives me mad. I had a sense of revulsion at this button with my very first look at XP's appearance, and it is precisely this button that got me started on battling with the styles.

As bad luck would have it, very few good styles can be found on the Internet those days. The only way to expand capabilities was to install the Microsoft Plus! package, which costs a tidy sum and, at the same time, includes a whole bunch of things that are useless to me. All I wanted to do was make my desktop more attractive and easier to work on.

In this chapter, you will learn how to expand the capabilities for changing the appearance of the XP shell and to consider in detail the workings of the styles. For now, we will stop at explaining how to do this using special programs, but you will later to find out all about XP's innards and their workings.

1.4.1. A Short Excursion into History

Before we start rearranging the desktop, we have to take a trip back down history lane and recall how the operating system and its appearance reached their present state.

From its inception, the Windows operating system was graphics based. At first it was just a graphics shell built on top of MS-DOS, but this shell eventually became a full-fledged operating system. To simplify and standardize the appearance of programs, Microsoft provided windows with several controls that made creating a user interface easier. This interface remained with us with practically no changes since the 1990s.

The controls turned out to be handy for everyone, including programmers. Now, all you had to do was write in your program that a button was needed in a certain place and the button appeared exactly there; it looked right and functioned according to the specified parameters. But writing code to describe how the button functioned was no longer necessary: Windows took care of this.

This is not, however, the main reason why most programs have similar interfaces and the same type of controls. For a program to be able to carry the "Designed for Windows" logo, it must comply with certain rules, including that its controls should not stand out too much, but should be standard Windows built-in controls. Moreover, the visual VC++, which is one of the most widely used development tools, supports only standard controls. Other controls only can be added as ActiveX elements or coded in. They can not be added using the available visual designer methods.

These, therefore, are the two reasons why we have been cursed with 16-color controls, rectangular buttons, and other user interface inconveniences for almost two decades.

1.4.2. Standard Controls

All standard controls are located in the ComCtl32.dll library, which is precisely the one, to which we owe this drab interface. Before Windows XP, we didn't even seem to notice that five new versions of the operating system had appeared, because the changes made were minimal and not obvious at a glance. Only with the sixth version did Microsoft change the library substantially, and the buttons lose their customary squarish look.

Everything would therefore be fine now, except for the fact that, unless they have a special manifest, old programs will continue to have a lackluster appearance under Windows XP when using the modern user interface. This is due to the fact that the library can work in two modes: the old and the new version. By default, the old controls from the User32.dll and from the fifth version of ComCtl32.dll libraries are used. Only a program containing a special manifest allowing it to use XP style will be allowed by Windows to work in the XP mode.

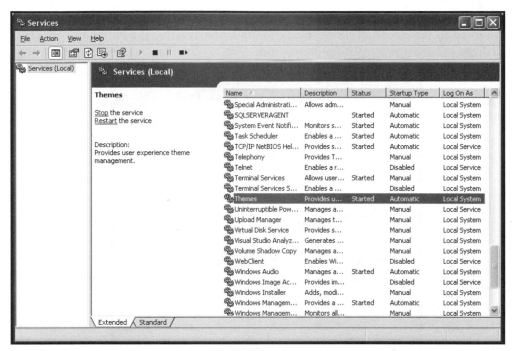

Fig. 1.9. The **Themes** service, which handles the XP styles

In contrast to all of the previous versions of the ComCtl32.dll library, the sixth version is tied to the operating system. Before, you could copy this library from Windows 98 to Windows 95 confidently and use those small modifications that Microsoft made to the library. This trick will not work now and, if the operating system does not have the sixth version library, there is no point in copying it: It won't work.

I tried to transfer the XP style to Windows 98 several times, but only with the release of Windows Server 2003 did I understand why my attempts had failed. When I installed this server for the first time I was surprised to discover that it looked like Windows 2000 and not like XP, even though the system contained the necessary styles. I tried switching styles, but to no avail. The problem was the **Services** component in the **Administrative Tools** (**Control Panel/Administrative Tools/Services**). One of its services is **Themes** (Fig. 1.9), which was disabled. I changed its **Startup** property to **Automatic** (Fig. 1.10), and everything started working like clockwork.

This led me to the realization that, in order for themes to work, the **Themes** service must be available in addition to the library. This service simply will not work with Windows 9*x*/ME, and all attempts simply to copy the library are, at best, doomed to failure or, at worst, likely to crash the system. It's better to use a specialized program (e.g., WinBinds) for this.

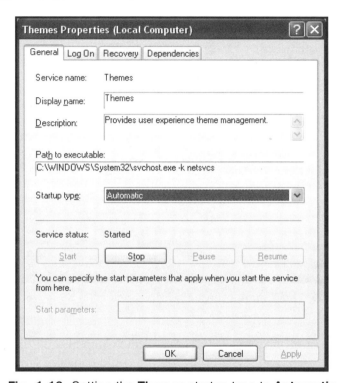

Fig. 1.10. Setting the **Themes** startup type to **Automatic**

If you run into the same problem launching themes, open the **Services** component of the **Administrative Tools** and double click the **Themes** item. In the window that appears, set the **Startup** type field to **Automatic**. This will make this service start up automatically when the operating system is loaded.

1.4.3. How Version 6 Controls Function

The selected system style is, by default, only used for controls of the non-client area of the window. These are the window border, the title bar, and the system scrolling bars. The rest of the controls (buttons, lists, etc.) will only have the selected style if their program contains the necessary manifest. An example of such a manifest is provided in Listing 1.2.

Listing 1.2. A manifest file generated in Visual Studio for a C++ program

```xml
<?xml version="1.0" encoding="UTF-8" standalone="yes"?>
<assembly xmlns="urn:schemas-microsoft-com:asm.v1" manifestVersion="1.0">
<assemblyIdentity
    version="1.0.0.0"
    processorArchitecture="X86"
    name="Microsoft.Windows.ProgramName"
    type="win32"
/>
<description>Your app description here</description>
<dependency>
    <dependentAssembly>
        <assemblyIdentity
            type="win32"
            name="Microsoft.Windows.Common-Controls"
            version="6.0.0.0"
            processorArchitecture="X86"
            publicKeyToken="6595b64144ccf1df"
            language="*"
        />
    </dependentAssembly>
</dependency>
</assembly>
```

A manifest is created in XML format and must have the MANIFEST expansion, for example MyApp.manifest. The first section of the XML file — assemblyIdentity — must contain the following attributes:

❏ version: the manifest's version.
❏ processorArchitecture: the processor type, for which the program was written, for example x86. If your program is optimized for the 64-bit architecture, this parameter has to be IA64.
❏ name: includes the manufacturer, product, and application names.
❏ type: application type, for example, win32.

Additionally, the manifest may contain a description of the program (in the `description` section) and a dependency section, with the following fields:

- ❏ `type`: the type of the dependent components, for example, win32
- ❏ `name`: the name of the component set
- ❏ `version`: the components' version
- ❏ `processorArchitecture`: the architecture of the processor, for which the components were created
- ❏ `publicKeyToken` — the key symbol used for the components
- ❏ `language`

This file may be built into the resources of the startup file or saved as a separate file. The important thing is that it can be seen by programs and used as intended. Some experts place the manifest into one DLL file and then use it and all its utilities from there.

The program itself needs to be modified slightly to connect the manifest file to it, but this is a separate subject concerning programming and individual programming languages. Connecting XML in individual programming languages requires a special discussion that is beyond the scope of this book.

You can give any old program, however, the XP appearance without even resorting to programming. All you need to do is find its startup flag. Let's suppose that you want provide the new look to the Program.exe program located in the c:\ProgramFiles\CyD\ folder. For this, you just go to the program's folder and create a file named Program.exe.manifest there. Then, copy Listing 1.1 into this file and save it. You can now launch the program and all of the controls will have the XP look.

NOTE

You can find the universal.manifest file on the accompanying CD-ROM in the \Chapter1 folder. All you have to do is to replace "universal" with your program's name, and then place this file into the folder for the program.

1.5. Windows XP/2003 Themes

Using the ComCtl32.dll library, you can only obtain access to the new capabilities and make the buttons oval. This library has no control over program appearance. A little bit later, you will learn how themes are constructed and how they work at the operating system level. For the time being, let's just learn how to change and edit themes using special programs.

The first question is: Where can you find a ready-made set of themes? My advice is to add the address **http://www.themexp.org** to your browser favorites or, better yet, carve it into your monitor. This site (Fig. 1.11) will provide you not only with themes, but also wallpapers, system shells, and many other things that will be interesting and useful in your everyday life.

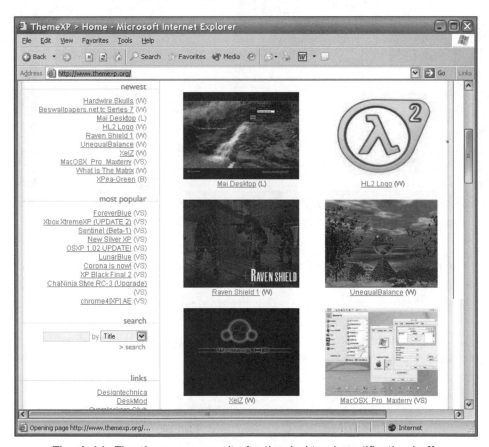

Fig. 1.11. The **themexp.org** site for the desktop beautification buffs

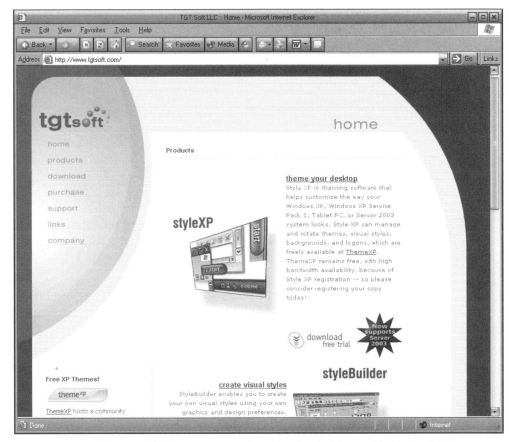

Fig. 1.12. The styleXP program can be downloaded from this TGTsoft site

Most add-ons downloaded from the Internet require that you have TGTsoft's styleXP program, which can be downloaded from the following address: **http://www.tgtsoft.com** (Fig. 1.12). This program will allow you to work with various themes, but the pleasure will cost you $19.95.

During your visit to on this site, I recommend that you download the **StyleBuilder** program, which you will use later to edit themes. For the present, we will content ourselves with installing ready XP themes and performing various adjustments.

After installing the program and rebooting the computer, a new icon with some bubbles on it will be placed in the system tray. Double clicking on this icon will open the program's theme control console (Fig. 1.13).

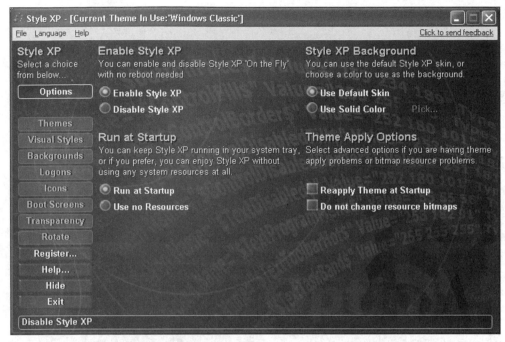

Fig. 1.13. The theme control console of **StyleXP**

At the time of writing, the third beta of the program's second version was available on the site. Compared to the first version, support for a large number of languages catches your attention right away, as do several interesting settings. There are some problems with the localization of certain languages though: Not all of the messages and control labels for the new capabilities have been translated. This shortcoming was reportedly supposed to be fixed in the final version, so there was a bit of a wait ahead.

The settings sections are controlled by buttons located on the left side of the main window. Let's take a look at what the program has to offer.

1.5.1. Options

The settings for the program itself are located in the **Options** section. Here you can enable (**Enable Style XP**) or disable (**Disable Style XP**) the XP style at any moment.

The **Run at Startup** option can be selected if you want the program to show in the system area. This option lets you access theme settings faster, but eats up some system resources (e.g., memory, operating system loading time). This option is useful in the early stages, when you are still experimenting with themes and have yet to settle on your preferences. When you have made up your mind regarding the theme, you can select the **Use no resources** option to save system resources.

If you run into problems setting a theme, you can try to enable the **Reapply Theme at Startup** or **Do not change resource bitmaps** options. The purpose of the first option is self-explanatory, while the nature of the bitmaps, to which the second option refers, will be discussed in *Chapter 2*.

1.5.2. Themes

In the **Theme** section, you can rapidly switch, add, and delete themes. A theme consists of a visual style, icons, wallpaper, sounds, cursors, and screensavers.

Fig. 1.14 shows the custom theme setting window. To the left are buttons with the names of the themes installed in the system. When a theme button is pressed, the theme is previewed in the **Preview** window. When you click the **Background** button, the **Preview** window shows the wallpaper that will be installed with the theme; clicking the **Sound** button will provide descriptions of the system sounds.

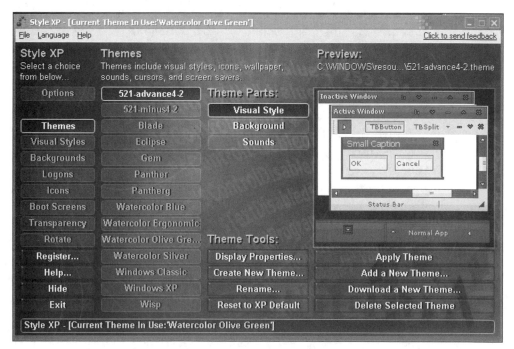

Fig. 1.14. Customizing themes

Clicking the **Apply Theme** button will apply the selected theme. A new theme is added by clicking the **Add a New Theme** button. Themes are deleted by clicking the **Delete Selected Theme** button.

1.5.3. Visual Styles and Wallpapers

In the **Visual Style** section, you can only set a style. You cannot change icons, wallpapers, and other system resources. In the **Visual Style** section, you can select window appearance and the style of buttons and standard Windows controls. Here you can also pick a color scheme, as one style can have a number of color schemes.

In the **Background** section the desktop wallpaper can be selected. Style XP doesn't do anything new in this respect. The program designers added this section simply so that the program would have all of the necessary controls for customizing Windows appearance.

1.5.4. Logon Schemes

The appearance of the window, in which you select a user and enter the password to enter the system, can be customized in the **Logons** section. Fig. 1.15 shows the section's window. The standard program has no additional system logon screens, so you will have to download these from the Internet before installing them with Style XP.

The information displayed during Windows loading can be customized in the **Boot Screen** section. When you enter this section for the first time, the program will warn you that fiddling with boot screens may be dangerous for your system's health and ask you to make a reserve copy of the boot.ini file. Assent to this request and the program will create a boot.bkk file on disk C:. If, as a result of your experiments, you run into problems loading Windows, you can always restore the system to its original state by simply replacing the corrupted file with the backup copy.

You will now see a prompt to change the load line. Once again, agree with the suggested modifications. The program will add a new, line similar to the following, to the boot.ini file:

```
multi(0)disk(0)rdisk(0)partition(1)\WINDOWS="Windows XP (bootscreen)"
/fastdetect /KERNEL=kernel1.exe
```

Now, when you start the computer, you will have an additional menu item to select: loading with or without your custom boot screen. This is necessary because,

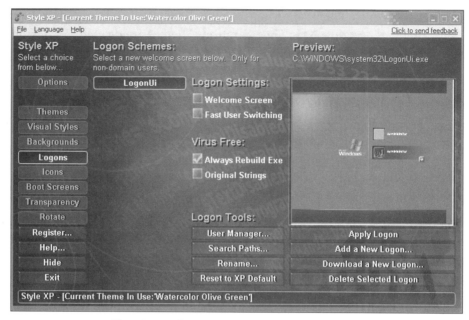

Fig. 1.15. Customizing **Logon Schemes**

Fig. 1.16. Customizing the boot screen

without Service Pack 1 (SP1) installed, Windows XP uses a different format file to describe the boot screen than with SP1. If an improper file is installed, the computer might not boot.

If the changes you make create problems with starting the operating system, you can start the computer without the boot screen and delete the offending changes. This is done by clicking the **Reset Boot.ini file** button.

Boot screens suited to your style can be downloaded from the Internet (e.g., from **http://www.themexp.org**). To install a screen, select the **Add a New Boot Screen** button (Fig. 1.16) and select a theme file. When it is installed in Style XP, select it, and then click on the **Apply Boot Screen** button.

I have tried to provide screen shots using various themes to show you how windows can be customized. But remember that this is not the limit. There are many unexplored nooks and crannies on the Internet, from which interesting and beautiful things, even if at first glance they appear to be absolutely useless, can be obtained.

Only people not compatible with IBM PC tend to consider PC decorations as useless. It pains me to recall the days when the windows on every computer looked the same, with different wallpapers providing the only variety. But where only a few years ago a small number of users decorated their machines, now anyone can do it — including you. So, rise to the occasion and turn your machine into a masterpiece.

I personally think that it is high time to organize a competition to select the best desktop (including best wallpaper and window appearance) at demos parties, as this type of activity is becoming an art form. If such a competition is going to be held, you should be ready and armed.

1.5.5. Is StyleXP Really Necessary?

Why do we need to use StyleXP when ready-made themes can be downloaded from the Internet and installed using standard Windows XP functions? In principle, it is not necessary to install the entire program. It consists of a handy shell, which you can use to change themes, and the uxtheme.dll file. If you do not want to clutter up your system tray with another icon, you can simply update the uxtheme.dll system file for your version of XP. The file for XP with the SP1 is different from the file for XP without SP1, so you have to be careful, lest you render the system inoperable.

From the **Download** section on the same TGTsoft site, download the UxTheme Util utility. It will patch the uxtheme.dll file and allow you to work with any theme downloaded from the Internet, without resorting to StyleXP.

If you run into problems modifying the system file (e.g., you are denied access), try one of the following remedies:

❑ Boot in safe mode: Press <F8> at startup, and then select Safe Mode from the menu.

❑ Boot into another operating system (if you have a multiboot system) and modify the uxtheme.dll file from there. If your other operating system is of the 9x series, while the XP is installed on NTFS (New Technology File System), you will need a special utility to allow the 9x to see the advanced NTFS. A utility of this type can be found on the following site: **www.ntfs.com/**.

❑ If the XP is installed on FAT32, you can boot from a diskette and change the file under DOS.

❑ Launch XP installation, but select console instead of installation at reboot, thus obtaining access to the main DOS commands, including those for copying.

After the uxtheme.dll file has been patched, Windows might report that some system files have been corrupted and, in order to restore them, request that you insert the installation CD. Under no conditions should you do this, as it will restore the file that you have just patched to its original form. All requests for restoring system files must be answered politely but firmly with "Cancel" and "Thanks, but no, thanks." For this exact reason, the Windows XP installation CD must not be in the drive when doing the patch. Otherwise, Windows will restore everything to its initial form in a heartbeat.

Why does this file have to be patched? Are themes found on the Internet that different from the original? Does the patched file provide us with some new capabilities? To be honest, the themes found on the Internet are not different in any way, nor have I been able to identify any new capabilities in the patched library file. The only thing I found was something akin to a protection mechanism in the standard uxtheme.dll file that prevents the use of non-Microsoft themes. I may be wrong, but all of my diggings points only to this conclusion. This protection is removed in the patched library. Perhaps there is something here besides the protection, but all of my searches and the resources of the worldwide web have not provided anything specific in this respect.

If your XP has SP1 installed, the regular version of the patched library may not install. Although it did install without any problems on my system, this has not always been the case on other systems. In such an eventuality, I recommend that you download a special patch from: **http://download.lightstar1.com/install/PatchXP-SP1.zip**.

1.6. Creating Own Themes

To create your own themes, you can use StyleBuilder utility from TGTsoft that was mentioned above. It can be downloaded along with StyleXP from the following site: **http://www.tgtsoft.com/**. If you have not done this yet, it is a good idea to do it now. It took me a whole week to download the newest version of this program, as either the download would not complete or the file would not open. When I finally did manage to download it without errors, I discovered that it did not differ in any significant way from the previous version. Nothing is worth the tortures I underwent in downloading the new version. So, if you run into similar problems, download the old version. You won't be missing much and will do your nerves a great service.

The program installs on Windows XP without any problems. However, in Windows Server 2003 the installer will not even launch and you will get a message to the effect that StyleBuilder works only in Windows XP. Do not believe it, because the developers either simply didn't take into account or didn't know that Windows 2003 supports themes. Open the **Compatibility** tab in the file properties window and select the compatibility for Windows XP mode (see Fig. 1.17). After this, the installer will launch and the program will never suspect that yours is not an XP system, but something more powerful.

Now start the program. You will be greeted with a prompt to use the **Apply** button to apply the changes, as the automatic update does not always work. After the modifications have been accepted, you can test the created theme by pressing the **Test** button.

Start by creating a new project. A panel with images for various control sets is located on left of the program's main window. When a control set is selected, **Parts Tree**, with a list of controls and their graphic representations, will appear in the main window. Controls can either be selected from the tree or from the graphic representations, although the latter method is probably easier and more convenient.

When a component is selected, a frame with three tabs — **Properties**, **Zoom**, and **Colorize** — appears in the lower right part of the main window. The **Colorize** tab is used to change colors and brightness. You simply move the sliders and the result will be visible instantly. I recommend that you clear the checks from **Lock Brightness**, **Source Brightness**, and **Gamma Brightness**, allowing each of the sliders to be moved individually. To save the color adjustments you have made, click on the **Apply Colorization** button.

A graphics element is selected for editing by right clicking on it and selecting **Edit** or **Edit With** in the menu that appears in order to select the raster graphics editor you want to use. This allows you not only to change colors, but also to draw additional effects.

If you already have a ready style, but want to change something within to improve it, you can edit it in StyleBuilder (Fig. 1.18). Select the menu sequence **File/Import .msstyles file** and open the theme you want.

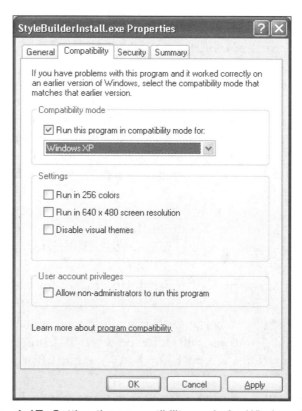

Fig. 1.17. Setting the compatibility mode for Windows XP

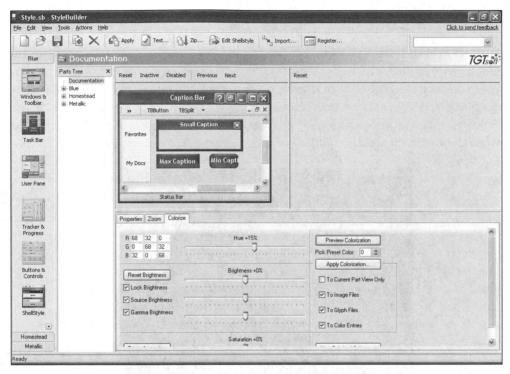

Fig. 1.18. The main window of StyleBuilder

To check your work, select the **Test System Style** item from the **Tools** menu. When your style is ready, select the **Compile** item from the **Actions** menu. If you want to install the new style right away, you can select the **Compile and Apply** menu item.

The program has a built-in zip archiver, which is handy if you want to share your creation with friends over the Internet. This relieves you of the tedious job of selecting needed files through the computer file system: They can be archived directly from StyleBuilder. To archive, select item **Zip** from the **File** menu and enter the style's name into the dialog window that appears.

If you have some experience working with graphics editors and were not shorted by nature with regard to basic artist skills, you will have no problem creating a beautiful and striking theme that you will be able to brag of to your friends.

1.7. XP Style Loader

I am often asked how my Windows XP Pirated Edition (Fig. 1.19) differs from the Home or Professional editions. My simple answer is that this is my own operating system, which assembled from the source codes stolen from Microsoft. Quite often, people believe this, as the boot screen looks quite smart. But those in the know understand that the stolen codes aren't even enough to compile even the kernel, let alone the entire operating system.

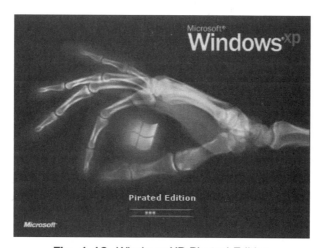

Fig. 1.19. Windows XP Pirated Edition

I could, of course, continue with the story that I myself broke into some computer system and stole some code, but this story won't fly with anyone who knows me, because they know that I would have never broken into anything on the Internet. Moreover, my Internet connection is a plain dial-up modem and, in order to steal all of the necessary source codes, I would have to work around the clock for about two weeks, without sleep or smoke breaks!

Nevertheless, it strokes your ego when the neophytes believe your stories! The most difficult thing is not to keep from bursting out laughing as I spin my tale.

If you are tired not only of the Windows interface, but also of the visuals that accompany the computer boot — that stupid Windows XP logo in particular — you can easily change your life for the better. You can do this with the Boot Editor program (Fig. 1.20), which can be found at the following address: **http://members.rogers.com/userxp/**.

You do not have to install this program. It is, however, a good idea to unpack the downloaded archive in a separate folder, as the program creates a whole slew of files in its installation folder on the first run. Thus, if you run it from the desktop or the **My Documents** folder, these areas will not become a complete mess as a result.

Having unpacked the archive, execute the following command from the command line in this folder:

```
regsvr32.exe AxImage.ocx
```

This is necessary in order to register the program's ActiveX component. Without this, all you will see when starting the program will be a ton of error messages, or a few beeps accompanied by nothing else.

Just in case, I recommend that you reboot the computer. Otherwise, there is a good chance that the program will not start successfully. This appears to have something to do with the problems registering the component. You can now launch the BootEditor.exe file and take a coffee break, because it will take this file about two minutes to load. It would not load at all on my notebook, while it took a long time to start on my desktop computer, although it did finally start without any further problems. This was the case despite the fact that the same operating system versions are installed on both machines and their settings are the same.

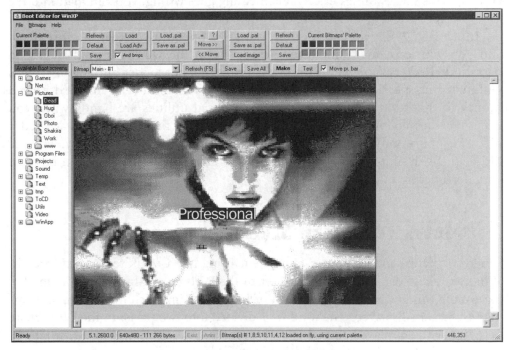

Fig. 1.20. The boot editor window

How does the program work? There is a file named ntoskrnl.exe in the Windows system folder (\Windows\System32\). This file controls the boot screen's appearance. Using Boot Editor, open this file and you will see a window with the boot image. It is actually a graphic image and can be edited just like any other graphic image. The program's capabilities, however, are rather limited, so you would be better off using a more advanced graphics editor. Boot Editor can only be used to load a ready image into the ntoskrnl.exe file, but not to edit the images themselves.

Before starting working with the program, I recommend that you make a backup copy of the \windows\system32\ntosrnl.exe, just in case, because I can't guarantee that this program will always work as intended. Only then should you open the ntoskrnl.exe file in Boot Editor and edit it.

While editing, you must keep in mind that the palette is limited to 256 colors during operating system boot, so don't even try to introduce a high-quality photograph here. I also do not recommend changing the image size. If you have only one operating system installed on your machine, you will have to be careful using the editor, because it will be difficult to restore the initial file (this will only be possible through the recovery console in Windows installation). The presence of two operating systems makes things easier. If something goes wrong, you can load into the other operating system and restore the original file.

In *Chapter 2*, we will consider the Windows operating system in more detail and you will learn many interesting things from the world of bootstraps and password checkers. You will learn how to edit the boot loader and logon screens without using special utilities, so don't be in rush to hand over your hard-earned money to the extortionists who sell these. Special utilities are handy when you need to create a boot loader screen in a hurry but, for fine tuning, you are better off using more universal techniques. We will look into these shortly. For the moment, I will simply show you some of the interesting things that can be done with perfunctory tuning.

1.8. Windows 9x in WEB Style

When inspecting the computer file system using **My Computer** or **Explorer** in Windows 9x, folder windows can be set to the Web mode. In this mode, the left part of the window is taken up by an auxiliary panel, in which the tips, main commands, etc. are displayed. The window is divided into two parts: In the left part, an HTML page is displayed (a real HTML page, like those on web sites), while the right side displays the contents of the current folder or disk.

How do HTML pages get into the **Explorer** window? There is a hidden folder named Web in the Windows system folder. The files in this folder are also hidden. To make this folder and its files visible, the corresponding system settings must be enabled. In the **My Computer** window, select the **Tools/Folder Options** menu sequence. Then, in the **View** tab, select **Show hidden files and folders** in the **Advanced settings** list.

When you can see the contents of this folder, the thing that I recommend you look at first is the wvleft.bmp file: It contains the HTML page background. This file can be edited easily in any graphics editor. Next, you can move on to editing HTT files. Any text editor, including the standard Notepad, can be used for this purpose.

If you are on a first-name basis with HTML, you will know how to handle the contents of the HTT files in the Web folder and will be able to customize web appearance to your liking. If your knowledge of HTML is limited, change only those things, about which you feel certain.

Don't be afraid to experiment with the HTT files, as they have no effect on system integrity and, regardless of what you do to them, will not do any harm to Windows. All the same, I recommend that you make backup copies of these files — just in case you decide you want everything to look like it did before — and only then start your experiments.

1.9. MP3 Coding

By default, Windows Media Player can encode music only in the Windows Media Audio (WMA) file format. But not all devices and programs understand this format and, currently, the most commonly used format is still MP3. So what are we to do now, buy another program for MP3 encoding? Don't rush to spend your money, because Windows Media Player can be made to encode audio in MP3 format.

Here is how this is done: Launch the registry editor and go to the **HKEY_LOCAL_MACHINE\SOFTWARE\Microsoft\MediaPlayer\Settings\MP3Encoding** key. The last two keys may not exist on your machine, so you will have to create them (right click on the previous key folder and select **New/Key** in the context menu that appears). In the MP3 key, create the following four values:

❏ HighRate — DWORD type, with its value equal to 2EE00h or 192000
❏ MediumHighRate — DWORD type, with its value equal to 1F400h or 128000
❏ MediumRate — DWORD type, with its value equal to FA00h or 64000
❏ LowRate — DWORD type, with its value equal to DAC0h or 56000

Do these figures remind you of anything? To me, they look like the bit rate — the quality of digitized sound. With these settings, the best recording quality will be 192,000 bps. Changing `HighRate` to 256000 will increase the recording quality.

To start encoding music in MP3, you start Media Player and select **Copy Music** tab in the **Tools/Options** menu sequence. Here, you will see settings for copying (Fig. 1.21). In the drop out **Format** list, select MP3, and move the **Audio Quality** slider to the best audio quality.

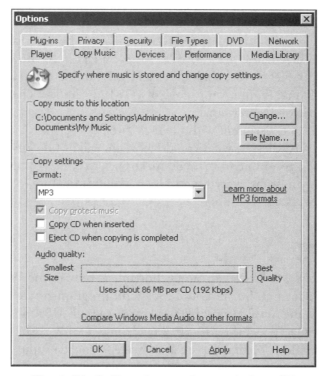

Fig. 1.21. Settings for copying music from CD

You can find a file named mp3.reg on the CD in the \Chapter1\ folder. To save yourself a bit of trouble creating the previously described values manually, simply launch mp3.reg and import the settings from it.

Chapter 2: The Inside World of Windows

If in *Chapter 1* we examined Windows at a rather skin-deep level, in this chapter we will learn about more detailed settings, tunings, and decorations. You will learn what programs consist of and how they can be changed. The knowledge you will acquire will allow you to change practically any software to your liking.

In this chapter, you will also learn how to configure certain settings without the aid of the special programs that we used for the same purpose in the last chapter. This knowledge will provide you with a better understanding of and comprehensive control over your computer world.

You will also learn how to work with a wonderful program called Restorator. You will use it to edit the resources of executable files and dynamic libraries. To provide practice, you will edit Windows XP boot loaders and logon programs using Restorator and without resorting to special programs.

The resource-editing techniques that will be considered in this chapter can be used for any version of Windows. Boot loaders, which will be discussed a little later, have a simple construction for Windows 9*x*. Moreover, there is a wealth of information about these available on the Internet. Consequently, there is no reason to consider how they operate here, so I will limit myself to the description of Windows 2000/XP boot loaders, as they have a new format with many more settings of interest to hackers.

2.1. Windows Resources

Before starting any serious system modification, you must learn at least some theory. The main subject of this subsection is working with program resources, so we will start with the theory behind them.

Executable Windows files bear the EXE extension. They generally consist of three parts:

❏ Header   ❏ Executable code   ❏ Resources

The header contains the auxiliary information that the operating system uses when launching the file. One example is the program entry point, which is a very important piece of information for any program. Another example is information about where the program's resources begin. They are usually located immediately following the executable code, but sometimes there are exceptions.

You will not modify the executable code because this is quite difficult, requiring strong familiarity with assembler and sophisticated debugging programs. Resources, however, will be examined with a fair degree of detail, as they contain many things of interest for the true hacker.

All resources are divided into the following sections:

❏ **Bitmap**: contains simple images used in dialog windows.
❏ **Menu**: a menu is a menu.
❏ **DIALOG**: the location of various dialog windows.
❏ **STRINGTABLE**: contains messages appearing in status lines and dialog windows.
❏ **ACCELERATORS**: contains command hotkeys.
❏ **CURSORS**: a cursor is a cursor.
❏ **ICON**: self-explanatory.
❏ **VERSIONINFO**: also self-explanatory. This section does not contain anything of interest to us and we will not use it in our resource explorations.

All resources are stored in plain form and can be modified. Resources can be stored not only in executable files, but also in dynamic link libraries (DLL), screensavers (SCR), separate resource files (RES), and a number of other file types.

Resources cannot be modified using the standard operating system tools, but there are a large number of programs that have been written for this purpose.

Practically any programming language has a utility or a built-in module for editing resources.

❑ Borland Resource Workshop is supplied with some Borland development tools.
❑ Microsoft Visual C++ can open an executable file for editing resources.

It should be noted that programs written in different programming languages may have different types of resources. Visual C++ compiler, for example, creates programs, in which all visually created dialog window resources are stored in a standard format. Borland Delphi, on the other hand, has more powerful visual capabilities and uses a proprietary format. So it would be a good idea to learn to determine, in which language the program is written.

2.2. Restorator

The most effective utility for editing resources would be one that works equally well with programs written in any language. Personally, I prefer the Restorator utility, which can be downloaded from the following site: **http://www.bome.com/Restorator/**. Restorator allows you to edit boot loader files and has significantly more to offer in the way of capabilities than any other program I have had the pleasure to use. As a result, this is the program we will consider here.

Before proceeding to the following material, I recommend that you install this program on your computer so that it will always be handy, allowing your to check into the described operations as they are covered. This book is not a help file for this program, so we will only consider those basic elements that are relevant to breaking programs and providing them with a more pleasant appearance.

You can see Restorator's main window in Fig. 2.1. The main window has three parts:

❑ **Resource tree**: Here you can view the resources of the open file according to categories organized in a tree structure.
❑ **Resource view**: view of the selected resource.
❑ **File browser**: An Explorer-style browser for viewing computer resources. The organization of the window allows for very convenient resource viewing.

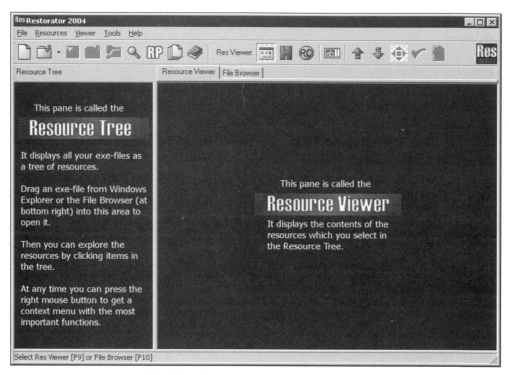

Fig. 2.1. The **Restorator** main window

Let's open a program to use as a guinea pig to help us learn how to alter resources. The dialer.exe program, which is installed with Windows, will fit this purpose as well as any other. This file can be found in the Windows folder, so, if your operating system is installed on the C: drive, the path to the file will be the following: C:\Windows\dialer.exe.

To open the file in Restorator, select the **File/Open** menu sequence. You will see the standard file open dialog window. Navigate to the dialer.exe file and open it. The program will load the resource names into the **Resource tree** window. To open the entire resource tree, select the file name in the **Resource Tree** window (it should be at the root of the resource tree) and press the asterisk key on the number keypad. The result should be that as shown in Fig. 2.2.

I picked this program with a purpose, as it contains practically every type of resource, so it is a handy example in learning how they may be edited.

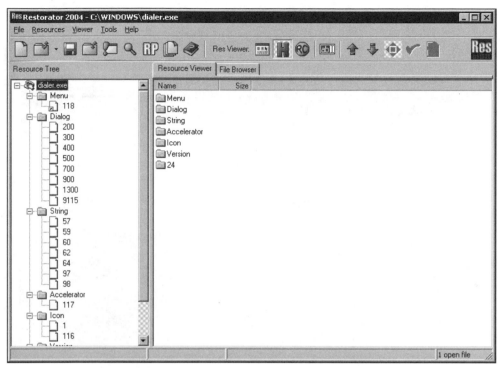

Fig. 2.2. The **Restorator** window with an open file

2.2.1. Editing Menus

After opening the **Menu** section in the resource tree, you will see only one item, numbered 118. Select this, and the menu's source code will be shown in the **Resource Viewer** window. To edit the source code, select the **Viewer/Edit mode** menu sequence. This will display the resource as source code in the **Resource Viewer** window and cause a window for previewing the editing changes to appear (Fig. 2.3).

Listing 2.1 shows the complete source text of the Dialer menu coded in resource instructions. These instructions are easy to understand and we will examine their function here. After this, you should have no problems with creating any kind of menu of your own.

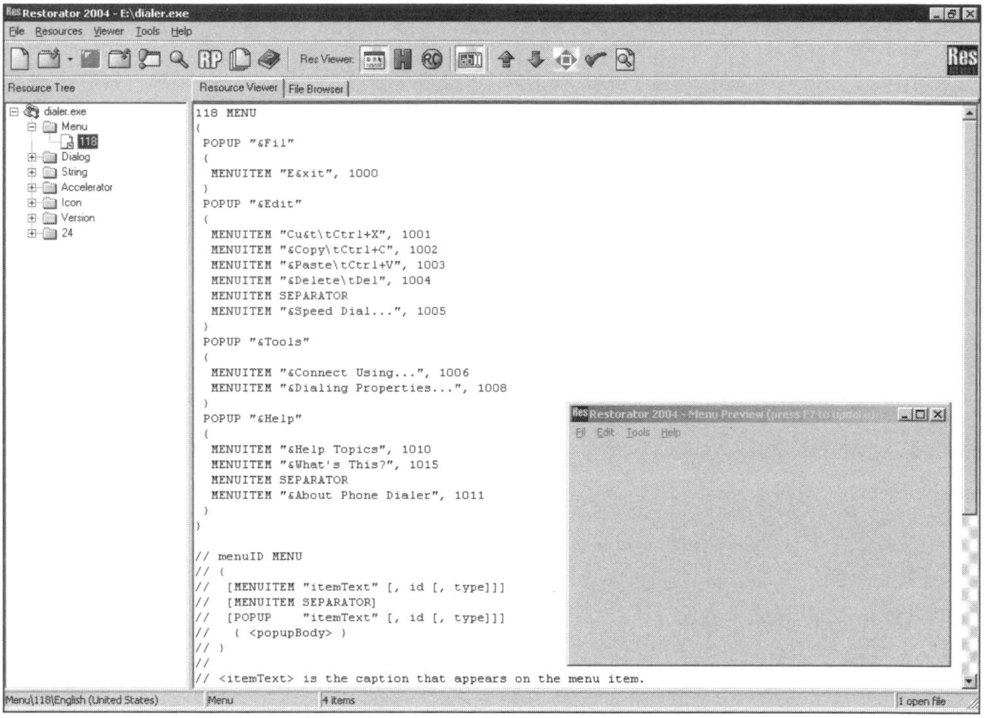

Fig. 2.3. The menu source code and the preview window

Listing 2.1. Menu source code

```
118 MENU
{
 POPUP "&File"
 {
  MENUITEM "E&xit", 1000
 }
 POPUP "&Edit"
 {
  MENUITEM "Cu&t\tCtrl+X", 1001
  MENUITEM "&Copy\tCtrl+C", 1002
  MENUITEM "&Paste\tCtrl+V", 1003
  MENUITEM "&Delete\tDel", 1004
  MENUITEM SEPARATOR
  MENUITEM "&Speed Dial...", 1005
```

```
}
POPUP "&Tools"
{
 MENUITEM "&Connect Using...", 1006
 MENUITEM "&Dialing Properties...", 1008
}
POPUP "&Help"
{
 MENUITEM "&Help Topics", 1010
 MENUITEM "&What's This?", 1015
 MENUITEM SEPARATOR
 MENUITEM "&About Phone Dialer", 1011
}
}
```

Prior to examining the source code in Listing 2.1, you need to know a few things about comments. Comments are optional text that has no effect on the resource, but allows you to add your own explanations or notes. When the resource compiler encounters a double slash, it treats the text that follows in that line as a comment. Consequently, I will insert explanations to the code under consideration and you can use comments to mark the changes that you make.

Menu source code begins with a number, which defines the name of the resource. It is followed by the keyword MENU. In this case, the resource's name is 118, so the menu source code starts with this number. The beginning and end of the menu are delimited by braces {}:

```
118 MENU
{
 // Menu description goes in here
}
```

If you have some experience in programming in C/C++, this description will be familiar to you.

Popup menus and their elements are defined between the braces delimiting the main menu. The definition of a popup menu begins with the keyword POPUP, followed by the name, in double quotes, that will be shown in the main menu. The ampersand (&) character can be placed anywhere in a menu's name. The letter following this character will be the menu's hotkey; that is, pressing this letter along with the <Alt> key will make the popup menu appear. In the popup menu's name, the hotkey letter will be underlined.

The popup menu `File` can be defined like follows:

```
POPUP "&File"
{
}
```

A popup menu definition is again followed by braces, in which elements of the popup menu are defined. The definition of the elements is done as follows:

```
MENUITEM "Name", Code
```

The same rules apply to the names of the popup menu elements as to the menu itself, i.e., the use of the ampersand character to designate hotkeys. Moreover, hotkeys can be designated by writing their combination after the `\t` character sequence; for example, `\tCtrl+X` designates the combination of the <Ctrl> and <X> keys as a hotkey.

A pull-down menu item code is an identifier used by the program to determine the requested action and respond to it properly. Consequently, changing menu items' names will not affect the operation of the program. Changing their code, however, will.

Resource editors can be used to switch the places of identifiers. For example, the following are some items in the **Edit** menu and their correct codes:

```
MENUITEM "Cu&t\tCtrl+X", 1001
MENUITEM "&Copy\tCtrl+C", 1002
MENUITEM "&Paste\tCtrl+V", 1003
```

Suppose that you change the codes as follows:

```
MENUITEM "Cu&t\tCtrl+X", 1002
MENUITEM "&Copy\tCtrl+C", 1003
MENUITEM "&Paste\tCtrl+V", 1001
```

Now, when you try to execute the `Cut` command, data will be copied onto the clipboard. The `Paste` operation will be performed when you attempt to copy, while cutting will be the result of trying to paste. This type of editing, of course, belongs to the practical joke category, which is another story altogether.

All you can do is change the places of menu item code. Changing the codes themselves is useless, as nothing will work.

A separator between menu items is inserted with the following code:

```
MENUITEM SEPARATOR
```

The modified menu can be previewed in the preview window that opened when you entered the edit mode. To see the changes that have been made, however, you must update the information by pressing the <F7> key.

2.2.2. Editing Dialog Windows

Editing dialog windows is somewhat more complicated than editing menus. Many commands are used for this purpose, making it simply impossible to describe them all here. Instead, we will focus on the most important examples. Open the **Dialog** section in the resource tree and select resource number 200. You should see the dialog window form in the Resource Viewer window (Fig. 2.4.)

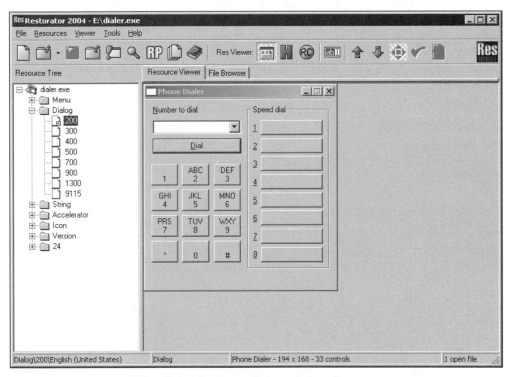

Fig. 2.4. Viewing a dialog window form

You can switch into editing mode by selecting the **Viewer/Edit Mode** menu sequence. The source code of the dialog window number 200 is shown in Listing 2.2.

Listing 2.2. Dialog window source code

```
200 DIALOG 50, 50, 194, 168
STYLE DS_SETFONT | DS_3DLOOK | WS_MINIMIZEBOX | WS_CAPTION | WS_SYSMENU
MENU 118
CAPTION "Phone Dialer"
FONT 8, "MS Shell Dlg"
{
 CONTROL "", 224, "STATIC", SS_ETCHEDHORZ | WS_DISABLED, 0, 0, 194, 1
 LTEXT "&Number to dial:", 223, 7, 7, 90, 10
 COMBOBOX 201, 7, 21, 90, 104, CBS_DROPDOWN | CBS_AUTOHSCROLL | CBS_SORT
 | WS_VSCROLL | WS_GROUP
 DEFPUSHBUTTON "&Dial", 1, 7, 38, 90, 14, WS_DISABLED | WS_GROUP
 PUSHBUTTON "\n1", 202, 6, 62, 27, 20, BS_CENTER | BS_MULTILINE | NOT
WS_TABSTOP
 PUSHBUTTON "ABC\n2", 203, 37, 62, 27, 20, BS_CENTER | BS_MULTILINE | NOT
WS_TABSTOP
 PUSHBUTTON "DEF\n3", 204, 69, 62, 27, 20, BS_MULTILINE | NOT WS_TABSTOP
 PUSHBUTTON "GHI\n4", 205, 6, 86, 27, 20, BS_CENTER | BS_MULTILINE | NOT
WS_TABSTOP
 PUSHBUTTON "JKL\n5", 206, 37, 86, 27, 20, BS_CENTER | BS_MULTILINE | NOT
WS_TABSTOP
 PUSHBUTTON "MNO\n6", 207, 69, 86, 27, 20, BS_CENTER | BS_MULTILINE | NOT
WS_TABSTOP
 PUSHBUTTON "PRS\n7", 208, 6, 110, 27, 20, BS_CENTER | BS_MULTILINE | NOT
WS_TABSTOP
 PUSHBUTTON "TUV\n8", 209, 37, 110, 27, 20, BS_CENTER | BS_MULTILINE |
NOT WS_TABSTOP
 PUSHBUTTON "WXY\n9", 210, 69, 110, 27, 20, BS_CENTER | BS_MULTILINE |
NOT WS_TABSTOP
 PUSHBUTTON "\n*", 212, 6, 134, 27, 20, BS_CENTER | BS_MULTILINE | NOT
WS_TABSTOP
 PUSHBUTTON "\n0", 211, 37, 134, 27, 20, BS_CENTER | BS_MULTILINE | NOT
WS_TABSTOP
 PUSHBUTTON "\n#", 213, 69, 134, 27, 20, BS_CENTER | BS_MULTILINE | NOT
WS_TABSTOP
 GROUPBOX "Speed dial", 222, 103, 7, 84, 154
 LTEXT "&1", 225, 109, 24, 7, 10
 PUSHBUTTON "", 214, 117, 21, 63, 14, BS_LEFT | WS_GROUP
 LTEXT "&2", 226, 109, 41, 7, 10
 PUSHBUTTON "", 215, 117, 38, 63, 14, BS_LEFT | WS_GROUP
 LTEXT "&3", 227, 109, 58, 7, 10
 PUSHBUTTON "", 216, 117, 55, 63, 14, BS_LEFT | WS_GROUP
```

```
LTEXT "&4", 228, 109, 75, 7, 10
PUSHBUTTON "", 217, 117, 72, 63, 14, BS_LEFT | WS_GROUP
LTEXT "&5", 229, 109, 92, 7, 10
PUSHBUTTON "", 218, 117, 89, 63, 14, BS_LEFT | WS_GROUP
LTEXT "&6", 230, 109, 109, 7, 10
PUSHBUTTON "", 219, 117, 106, 63, 14, BS_LEFT | WS_GROUP
LTEXT "&7", 231, 109, 126, 7, 10
PUSHBUTTON "", 220, 117, 123, 63, 14, BS_LEFT | WS_GROUP
LTEXT "&8", 232, 109, 143, 7, 10
PUSHBUTTON "", 221, 117, 140, 63, 14, BS_LEFT | WS_GROUP
}
```

A dialog window is defined as follows:

```
n DIALOG x, y, w, h
STYLE Style flags
MENU Menu number
CAPTION "Caption"
FONT size, "Font name"
{
// A description of the window's elements goes in here
}
```

where:

     n — resource number
     x — window's left position
     y — window's top position
     w — window's width
     h — window's height

The window styles are defined in the next line. If a window has a menu, it is indicated in the following line by the MENU Number command. The window's caption is defined by the CAPTION "Caption text" command.

This is followed by the font description (size and name) and by a pair of braces, inside of which the window's elements are defined. Let's examine how some main elements are defined in the window's source code.

Beginning with version 3, it became possible to edit windows in visual mode. To do this, first select the default resource view mode (menu sequence **Viewer/Default view** mode), and then switch into the edit mode (menu sequence

Viewer/Edit mode). A property panel for the selected window element will appear in the resource view window and you will be able to use the mouse to move any element, change its size, and review changes in the property panel.

The only shortcoming of the visual editor is the inconvenient method for adding components. This is done by writing code manually, which is not particularly convenient if you only need to add one image. It is better to add new using the Resource Workshop program, which we will discuss later.

Icons

Icons allow you to add graphic images to dialog windows. Although this does not make them more effective, they do look more appealing. Icons are added with the following command:

```
ICON n, i, x, y, w, h
```

where:

- ❏ n is the icon number in the resource file. The number can only refer to an existing icon. For example, there are two icons in the Dialer program, numbered 1 and 116; either of these numbers can be used. You can add new icons, assign them numbers yourself, and then use them in dialog windows.
- ❏ i is the index used by the program to access the icon. Do not change this index when editing an existing icon, as the program will then not be able to find the icon. When adding a new icon, its index can be given any number (preferably not one that conflicts with the indices of the window's other elements): The program will not be aware of the new icon and will not access it.
- ❏ x is the icon's left position.
- ❏ y is the icon's top position.
- ❏ w is the icon's width.
- ❏ h is the icon's height.

Labels

Labels are used to write explanations to controls. They are defined as follows:

```
LTEXT "Text", i, x, y, w, h
```

where:

- ❏ "Text" is label text in quotation marks.
- ❏ i is the index used by the program to access the label. Do not change this index when editing an existing label, as the program will then not be able to find it. When adding a new label, its index can be given any number (preferably not

one that conflicts with the indices of another window's elements): The program will not be aware of the new label and will not access it.

- ☐ x is the label's left position.
- ☐ y is the label's top position.
- ☐ w is the label's width.
- ☐ h is the label's height.

Buttons

Buttons are buttons everywhere. They are defined as follows:

```
PUSHBUTTON "Text", i, x, y, w, h, flags
```

where:

- ☐ "Text" is button text in quotation marks.
- ☐ i is the index used by the program to access the button. Do not change this index when editing an existing button, as the program will then not be able to find the button. When adding a new button, its index can be given any number (preferably not one conflicting with the indices of other window elements): The program will not be aware of the new button and will not access it.
- ☐ x is the button's left position.
- ☐ y is the button's top position.
- ☐ w is the button's width.
- ☐ h is the button's height.

Flags describe the button's properties. There can be several flags divided with | character. The main flags and their functions are the following:

- ☐ BS_CENTER: The button text is centered.
- ☐ BS_LEFT: The button text is left-aligned.
- ☐ BS_RIGHT: The button text is right-aligned.
- ☐ BS_MULTILINE: The button has a multiline text.
- ☐ WS_DISABLED: The button is disabled.
- ☐ WS_GROUP: The button is grouped with other window buttons.

Decoration

Now, let's apply your newly-acquired theoretical knowledge in practice and give the dialer dialog window some cosmetic treatment. First, widen it to 225 pixels.

This is done by changing the third numerical parameter in the first line to 225, as follows:

```
200 DIALOG 50, 50, 225, 168
```

Then change the third line, the title: CAPTION "Horrific Dialer".

After this change, the window's title will read *Horrific Dialer*. Next, add an icon and a label. This is done by inserting the following two lines after the opening brace:

```
FONT 8, "MS Shell Dlg"
{
 ICON 1, 0, 195, 5, 18, 20
 LTEXT "Copyright: Horrific", 223, 40, 1, 90, 10

 // The rest remains unchanged
}
```

Press the <F7> key. Here, the program may say that there is an error in the following line: CLASS DialerClass. If this happens, simply delete this entire line. If there is the CLASS command in the window definition, saving modifications often produces errors. In most cases, deleting this line will not affect the program's operation.

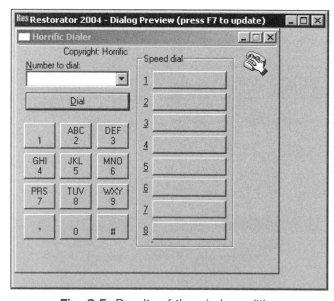

Fig. 2.5. Results of the window editing

If you are satisfied with the result (Fig. 2.5), press <F8> to perform a final save of the resource, and then press <Ctrl>+<S> to save the entire file.

2.2.3. Editing Strings and Accelerators

The **String** section is for the storage of... strings! These can be various messages, names, or simply string lines used by a program. Select any resource in this section and switch into the editing mode (menu sequence **Viewer/Edit Mode**). Use resource 57 as an example to examine source code that can be edited:

```
STRINGTABLE
{
 901, "Dialer"
 902, "Phone Dialer"
}
```

The string resource code starts with the keyword STRINGTABLE. It is followed by a pair of braces, inside of which strings are defined as follows:

```
Number, "String"
```

Number is the numerical identifier used by the particular program to find a certain string. This number is better left alone, as changing it may have undesirable effects on the program's operation. The string follows the comma and is enclosed in quotation marks; it can be modified in any way you wish without any problems.

Accelerators are hotkeys that are used to access corresponding program functions. If you do not like a particular hotkey combination, you can easily change it to something more convenient, even if the program being dissected does not provide the means for reassigning hotkeys.

The Dialer program has only one set of accelerators, which is given the number 117. Selecting it will produce the following code in the editing window:

```
214: "Alt+1"
215: "Alt+2"
216: "Alt+3"
...
...
1003: "Shift+Ins"
1001: "Ctrl+X"
```

Accelerators are defined in a similar manner as strings. First the accelerator code is given, which is used by the program to find the necessary key combination. Then comes a colon, followed by the accelerator keys in quotation marks.

2.2.4. Editing Images

Resources can contain two types of images: icons (stored in the **Icon** section) and bitmaps (stored in the **Bitmap** section). Both formats are edited in the same way. Therefore, their editing will be treated together here.

The Restorator program has no built-in graphics editor, so an external graphics editor has to be used for this purpose. The process starts by saving the image resource to be edited into a graphics file. This is done by right-clicking on the graphics resource and selecting the **Extract/Extract as "File name"** menu sequence in the context menu that appears. "File name" is the resource's actual name. Next, switch the view window to **File Browser**, and navigate to the created file.

The file can be edited and then reconnected to the resource. This is done by right-clicking on the resource and selecting **Assign/Assign to** menu sequence in the context menu that appears. A standard file open dialog window will open, in which you will have to navigate to and open the edited version of the graphic file.

Bitmap images can be edited by any graphics editor, including Windows' own Paint. Windows offers no tools for editing icons, so here you can do one of the following:

❒ Find a good icon editing program.
❒ Simply replace the program's icons with your own.

I personally opt for the latter, as I cannot draw and am unable to create anything remotely attractive with even the best icon editor. Fortunately for me and others who share my affliction in this area, many quality, ready-made professional icons can be found on the Internet. You will have to pay for some of these, but good enough free icons can also be found.

2.3. Visual Resource Editing

Editing resources by editing their source code is not that difficult, but there is an even better way. I have already mentioned Borland Resource Workshop (BRW), which is included in some programming language packages from Borland, Borland C++, or Borland Pascal, for example.

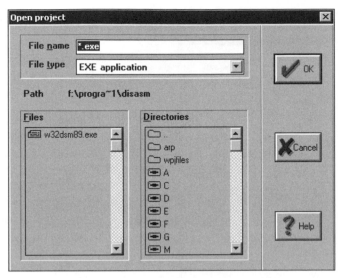

Fig. 2.6. The file-open dialog window

Even though the company no longer supports the program and no updates have been offered for a long time, the program is still useful. BRW can be used to edit practically any standard Window format files containing resources. This means that it cannot be used to edit programs written in Borland Delphi.

The program's only shortcoming is that it is distributed only as a part of Delphi and other development environments. It is not sold as a separate component, nor can it be downloaded from the developer's site.

After launching the program, you will see a plain window, containing only an empty work area and a menu. A file is opened by selecting the **File/Open project** menu sequence. This will open the **Open project** dialog window (Fig. 2.6). The window is not quite standard, as it does not support long Windows file names, but it is not difficult to get used to. When opening a file, the type must be selected in the **File type** dropdown list. Otherwise, it will not show in the file list.

Once a file is open, the program opens a two-part window (Fig. 2.7). Its left panel shows the program resource tree, while the right panel is used to preview selected resources.

Double clicking a resource will open its resource editing window. Let's consider how various resources are edited using the same Dialer program as the guinea pig.

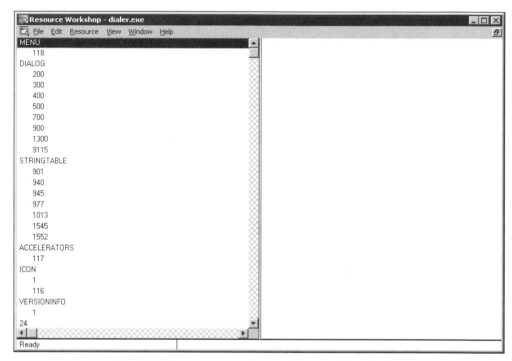

Fig. 2.7. The resource tree and the preview window

2.3.1. Editing Menu

Double clicking the only menu resource numbered 118 will open the menu editor window (Fig. 2.8).

The resource editor structure and functions are as follows:

☐ The menu's visual representation is located in the upper right part.

☐ The menu's source code is located in the lower right part. The code shown here is identical to the code examined when studying Restorator.

☐ The left panel shows the properties of the selected menu item.

An element can be selected for editing either in the visual view or in the code view of the menu to be edited. Simply select the necessary item and then change its properties.

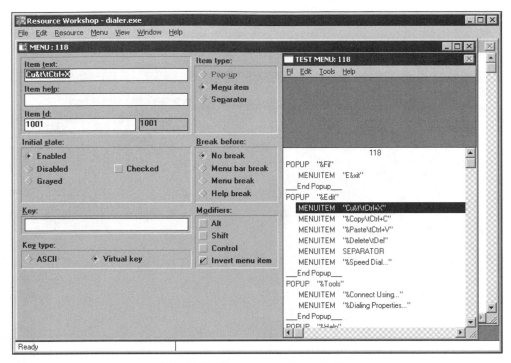

Fig. 2.8. The menu editor window

Which properties can be modified? You can start with the **Item text** field. This is the text that will be shown in the menu item name. You can also edit the **Item help** field. This is the help text that is displayed in the status line. Under no circumstances should the **Item id** field be changed, since this is the identifier, by which the program accesses menu items.

2.3.2. Editing Dialog Windows

Double-clicking on any dialog resource will open the visual dialog window editor (Fig. 2.9). All visual programming languages have this type of editor, which is how programmers work. Resources are no longer created manually (i.e., by coding); all work is now done visually.

New elements, like images and text to decorate your favorite program, can be added in the visual editor. Components that can be added to dialog windows are shown in the small **Tools** window in the upper right corner. Deleting anything from dialog windows is not recommended, because, in accordance with Murphy's Law, the deleted elements always seem to turn out to be those that are vital to the program's normal functioning.

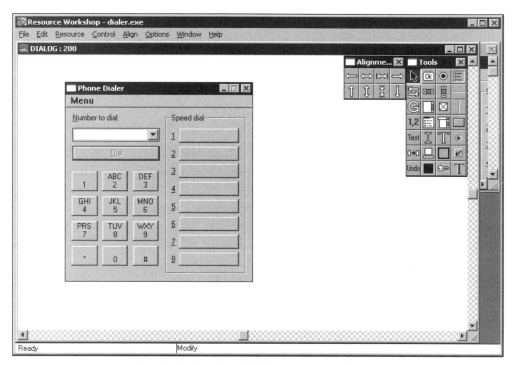

Fig. 2.9. The visual dialog window editor

To edit existing text, double click it, and the text property editor window will open (Fig. 2.10). Text is edited in the **Caption** window. As I have already mentioned, I like to provide new names according to my current mood. Sometimes all of the names I choose are slangy, while sometimes I prefer to use army jargon.

In the **Control type** section of the text editor window you will see many settings. I will not describe them, as you can discover the effect associated with each of them by experimenting with these settings.

Sometimes, you will see mysterious characters in the text, such as asterisks, underlines, and similar things that may appear to be simply garbage. Don't be in a hurry to delete these, especially if they do not show up when the program is running. Some more "creative" programmers, when lacking the brains to do something properly, stick a hodgepodge of characters into their program that, during execution, change into something else. If this coding is deleted, the program might not even launch.

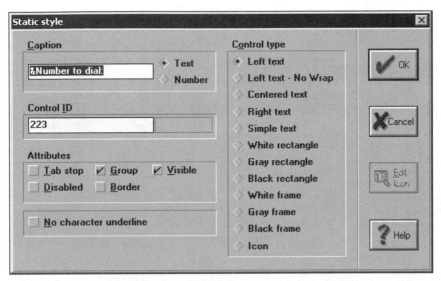

Fig. 2.10. The visual dialog window text editor

2.3.3. Editing Strings and Images

The **STRINGTABLE** section contains sets of strings that are shown in the **String** section in Restorator. Double-clicking on any line in the **STRINGTABLE** section will open the editor. It contains a table with the following three columns:

❏ ID Source   ❏ ID Value   ❏ String

The first two columns are message numbers and must not be modified. We are mostly interested in the third column, in which the message text is stored. Simply click on the line you want to edit and enter your own text.

Editing resources from the ICON and BITMAP sections, i.e., images, is the easiest. For example, double clicking on icon number 1 in the ICON section will open the icon selection window. There are two different sized icons in the resources: 32×32 and 16×16. Double-clicking on any of them will take you into a simple graphics editor (Fig. 2.11).

Do not change the image size when editing it. In some cases, there will be no effect on the program's functioning, but sometimes you don't get quite this lucky. Therefore, if you want to replace an image, the new image must be the same size.

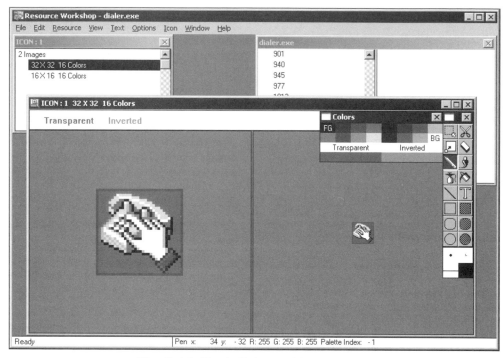

Fig. 2.11. The built-in graphics editor

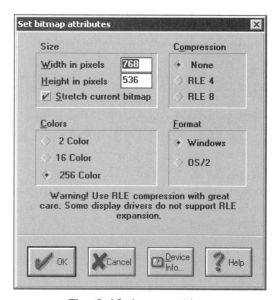

Fig. 2.12. Image settings

Further, the resource image color depth can not be greater than 8 bits. This means that you won't be able to give complete rein to your color fantasies here, as the color palette is limited to 256 colors. In most cases, changing the number of colors will not affect the program's operation. Therefore, if you are unhappy with the image quality with regard to the number of colors is concerned, you can change it. Select the **Bitmap/Size and attributes** menu sequence. This will open the image attribute setting window (Fig. 2.12).

Other than the number of colors, do not change anything here. As I have already mentioned, many programs are sensitive to image size changes (especially in the case of making images larger, which may result in the program being unable to allocate enough memory to load the image). The Compression and Format properties are better left alone altogether.

2.4. XP Themes

In *Chapter 1*, you were introduced to Windows XP themes and learned how to edit them using special programs. In such a case, however, we are limited by the capabilities of the utility being used (the graphics capabilities of StyleBuilder, in particular, are minimal) and can only create very simple themes. Moreover, the StyleXP program needs to be installed or the system file replaced. It is much better to create a totally XP-compatible theme manually.

Themes are stored in the Drive:\WINDOWS\Resources\Themes folder. Open this folder and inspect its contents. At first, the folder may look the same as in the old Windows 9*x* — the same useless files with the theme extension and a bunch of useless folders.

The Luna folder contains all of the files necessary for the standard XP theme. Let's take a look at this. Whoa, what is this strange thing: *luna.msstyles*?! I don't remember seeing this extension in the old Windows. Let's take a closer look at it. The first thing I did the first time I saw this file was to examine its contents in Windows Commander (pressing the <F3> key). The immediate thing that catches your eye is that the first two bytes of this file are MZ. This tells me that this file likely contains byte code like that in executable files. Looking further, we can see the magic message: "This program cannot be run in DOS mode." This means that the luna.msstyles file not only contains byte code, but is also executable, or, at least, that its structure is very similar to the executable file structure.

You already know that any executable or DLL file can contain resources, and you also know how to edit those resources. I was hoping that this file would also hold some resources, so I tried to open it with Borland Resource Workshop. I was deeply disappointed, because BRW simply issued a system error message, and terminated. The program's age does have some undesirable effects.

An attempt to open the file with Restorator will be successful. You will have to select **All files** in the dropdown list in the **Files of type** field, however. The program is simply not recognize the MSSTYLES extension and will not show the necessary file, so you have to instruct it to show all files.

I was right. This file indeed abounds in resources. Look at Fig. 2.13, which shows the luna.msstyles file structure. The tree structure headings by themselves tell us that this is just what we were looking for. Open the **Bitmap** branch and inspect its contents. Fig. 2.14 shows one of the items in this branch, containing images used to show the **CheckBox** control.

For practice, let's consider the same **CheckBox** control. For this, you will need the BLUE_CHECKBOX13.bmp, BLUE_CHECKBOX16.bmp, and BLUE_CHECKBOX25.bmp files in the **Bitmap** section. They contain different size images of this control.

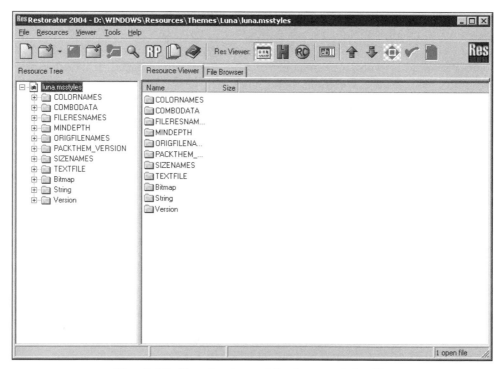

Fig. 2.13. The structure of the luna.msstyles file

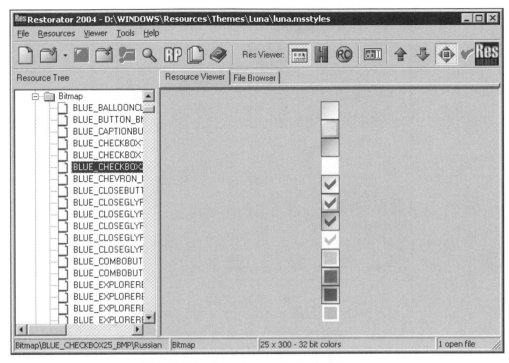

Fig. 2.14. CheckBox actual components

Right-click on each of these items, and select **Extract/Extract as BLUE_CHECKBOX13.bmp** in the context menu that appears. Next, find these files in the **File Browser** window, and edit them in any graphics editor. Just for practice, draw a simple vertical line across the entire image. To load the edited file, right-click on the corresponding resource, and select the **Assign to BLUE_CHECKBOX13.bmp** item.

As soon as you finish editing, save the file under a new name (using the **File/Save as** menu sequence), and copy the new file into the Drive:\Windows\Resources\Themes folder. To install this file in the system, launch the luna.msstyles file like any other program, and apply the new theme. If you experience any problems launching the edited file, open the display property window and select the **Browse** item in the **Themes** dropdown list on the **Themes** tab. This will open the standard file open dialog window. Navigate to the edited file and open it.

Fig. 2.15 shows the Windows Commander property window. It has many checkbox controls and you can see that all of them have a line drawn across them.

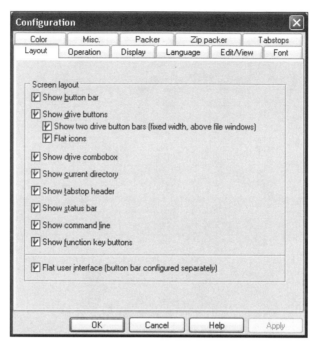

Fig. 2.15. The Windows Commander property window
with lines across the checkbox controls

Consequently, a brand new theme can be created based on an old one, and then installed in the system without any problems.

Creating a new theme using a resource editor is both difficult and a bit inconvenient. Each image has to be saved and then edited in a graphics editor individually. But this process allows you to create extraordinary themes that can be installed without resorting to special programs like StyleXP. All you have to do is simply copy your luna.msstyles to another computer, and the theme is ready to use. By the way, the file name can be changed, which I recommend that you do in order to avoid any potential problems. Name it something like X.msstyles. This is how you can create an entirely new theme on your computer.

2.5. The Right Way To Enter

In this section, you will learn how to modify the system logon program. We will limit our discussion to Windows XP, because it uses a separate, kind of cute, logon program that can be changed. The system logon rights are too simple in Windows 9*x* and do not require separate programs, while in Windows NT/200 a simple dialog window is used and can be summoned by pressing <Ctrl>+<Alt>+<Del>.

The system logon screen (used to select a user and enter a password) that you see after the operating system has already loaded is produced by the Windows\ System\logonui.exe program. Personally, I am sick and tired of the way this logon screen looks. If you feel the same way, you can change its appearance to your liking. This should be easy for you, as it is done by modifying the resources, which you already know how to do.

Before modifying anything, do not forget to make a back-up copy. An even better idea is to leave the original file intact and modify the backup file. A little bit later, you will learn how to configure the system to accept your file instead of the original logonui.exe.

Open the program in Restorator and take stock of what you have here (Fig. 2.16).

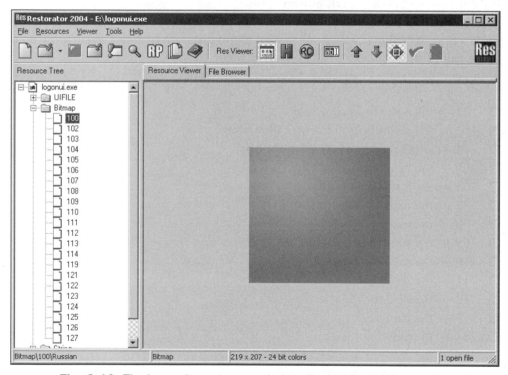

Fig. 2.16. The logonui.exe program being dissected in Restorator

All images of interest to us are in the **Bitmap** section. The one numbered 100 stores the screen background. Looking at this image, it is difficult, because of its

219×207 size, to understand that this is the background. To cover the entire screen, this image is stretched. The stretching is done using smooth color gradations, so it looks pleasant enough, even when scaled up significantly. Nevertheless, it is not as nice as you might want it to be.

To correct matters, take any BMP image. The optimum situation is where the size of the image is the same as the screen resolution, so as not to make the system scale it and waste system resources when loading the logon program. The resolution on my monitor is set to 1024×768, so that's exactly the size of the image I prepared.

Because of the large size of the image, the size of the logonui.exe file will increase, growing to as much as 2 or 3 MB. This is a normal reaction to the resource increase, as they are not compressed.

Next, select resource number 100, right-click on it, and select the **Assign/Assign to** menu sequence. This will open the standard file open dialog window. Select your BMP image, and click the **OK** button.

The editing process could basically be concluded at this stage, but there are quite a few more things within the system logon program that can be customized to make things more pleasant and convenient. For starters, there are a large number of images that can be changed. Let's consider the function of the rest of the images:

- ❏ 102 — the password input field
- ❏ 103 — the arrow button to enter the system
- ❏ 104 — another copy of the arrow button
- ❏ 105 — the help button
- ❏ 106 — the active help button
- ❏ 107 — the turn off button
- ❏ 108 — up arrow
- ❏ 109 — the scroll down button
- ❏ 110 — the scroll up button
- ❏ 111 — the scroll bar
- ❏ 112 — the field for the selected user
- ❏ 113 — the icon field
- ❏ 114 — the default user icon
- ❏ 119 — the selected user icon field
- ❏ 121 — the turn off button
- ❏ 122 — the up arrow
- ❏ 123 — not used
- ❏ 124 — the vertical divider line

❏ 125 — the line at the top of the screen
❏ 126 — the line at the bottom of the screen
❏ 127, 128 — the horizontal dividers

The numbers of some of the bitmaps can be changed, that is, the scripts referencing these bitmaps can be changed to use the new numbers. But I recommend that you leave the bitmap numbers alone and add new images that can be used later. You will learn how to do this later, when examining scripts. First, though, let's take a look at the strings.

The **String** section has five sets of strings. They hold the messages that are displayed when logging onto the system. We have already considered string editing, so there is no sense in going over it again. What you write here depends on your own preferences and the general impression you are trying to achieve with your theme. For example, if you selected the movie Terminator as your logon theme, it would make sense to change the "Turn off computer" string into "I'll be back". This is done by changing lines 11 and 13 in string resource 1.

2.5.1. Script

Now you are ready to explore the script file. It is located in the **UIFILE** section. There is only one resource, number 1000, in this section. When we were learning resource types, we did not consider the UIFILE type, because it is not a system type. This can be a user type that can contain anything you want. In this case, this is simply a text file with a script in the XML format. The script describes font styles, colors, and the locations of controls (resource images) on the screen.

For a standard Windows XP theme, this resource may be empty, with the system using default element locations and styles. If it happens not to be empty, I recommend that you pay no attention to it, as we will now consider a general script of my design. This is a universal script suitable for any needs. The script's source code is given in Appendix 1 and on the accompanying CD-ROM in the /Chapter 2/ uifile.txt file.

If you have any experience working with HTML or XML files, you will not have many difficulties with the script file. The UIFILE uses the same tag principle as these markup languages. For example, consider the first block:

```
<style resid = framess>
    element
    {
```

```
        background: argb(0, 0, 0, 0);
    }
    element [id = atom(contentcontainer)]
    {
        background: rcbmp(100, 6, #FF00FF, 0, 0, 1, 0);
    }
    button
    {
        background: rcbmp(112, 6, #FF00FF, 0, 0, 1, 0);
        borderthickness: rect(8, 8, 0, 8);
    }
</style>
```

Let's examine the first line: `<style resid = framess>`

Tags are enclosed in triangular brackets. The first word is the tag name, `style` in this case. This is followed by tag parameters. In this case, there is only one parameter: `resid` (resource identifier), which is given the value `framess`.

So, the first line opens a new style that has the identifier `framess`. In this case, `framess` means that a description of the main working area parameters will follow. Later, we will consider styles with other identifiers and find out what they are used for.

A tag is closed in the following way: `</Name>`. In our case, the opening tag was `<style>`, so the closing tag will be `</style>`. Descriptions and parameters are enclosed between the opening and closing tags.

This information should provide you with a sufficient understanding of script basics and allow you to edit the main parameters. Each style has many parameters. The following list provides the main parameters you will need to adjust and customize the appearance of the logon screen:

❐ `Background`: defines the background color. This parameter is specified as follows — `background: argb (0, 0, 0, 0);` Colors in the Alpha RGB format are specified in the parentheses. Consider the following examples:

`background: argb(0, 255, 0, 0)`: defines red background color
`background: argb(0, 0, 255, 0)`: defines green background color
`background: argb(0, 0, 0, 255)`: defines blue background color
`background: argb(0, 255, 255, 0)`: defines yellow background color

How are the specific Alpha RGB values determined? The first number inside the parentheses is the transparency and will always be set to 0. The three colors are also determined quite easily. Start the MS Paint program. Select the **Colors/Edit colors** menu sequence, and in the dialog window that appears, click the **Define custom colors** button. The resulting dialog window is shown in Fig. 2.17. Select the color you need, remember its red, green, and blue constituents, and put these values inside the parentheses.

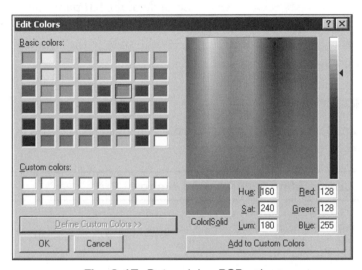

Fig. 2.17. Determining RGB values

☐ Foreground: the definition of the foreground (text) color. Set it the same as the background color.

☐ Bordercolor: If the element has a border, its color can be changed in the same way as the Background color.

☐ Fontstyle: the font style. For example, underlined font is set as follows — fontstyle: underline.

☐ Fontweight: the font weight. Bold font is set as such — fontweight: bold.

☐ Cursor: the cursor type. A hand-shaped cursor is denoted as follows —🖐 .

There are many parameters of this type, but I recommend that you limit yourself to using those described above and be judicious with the changes that you make. A mistake in the script may cause problems with loading Windows. In the script located on the accompanying CD-ROM, I tried to use as many parameters as possible, so it is better not to add any new parameters and stick to modifying the values of the existing ones.

Let's take a look at the styles the script has:

- ❏ `<style resid = framess>`: the main background, which was discussed earlier
- ❏ `<style resid = toppanelss>`: the elements located at the top of the window
- ❏ `<style resid = toppanelss>`: the elements located at the bottom of the window
- ❏ `<style resid = leftpanelss>`: the style of the left panel elements
- ❏ `<style resid = rightpanelss>`: the style of the right panel elements
- ❏ `<style resid = hotaccountlistss>`: the style of the window, in which active user accounts are shown

2.5.2. Constructor

After styles are defined, the window based on these styles is constructed. The corresponding code is shown in Listing 2.3.

Listing 2.3. Constructing a style-based window

```
<logonframe resid=main id=atom(frame) sheet=styleref(framess)
layout=borderlayout() layoutpos=client>
<element id=atom(contentcontainer) layout=borderlayout()
layoutpos=client>


 <element id=atom(toppanel) sheet=styleref(toppanelss)
layout=borderlayout() layoutpos=top height=80rp>
   <element id=atom(logoarea) layout=verticalflowlayout(0,3,3,2)>
    <element id=atom(product) contentalign=topright
padding=rect(10rp,0rp,20rp,20rp)/>
    <element id=atom(help) contentalign=wrapright width=1rp
padding=rect(0rp,0rp,40rp,0rp)/>
   </element>
   <element id=atom(msgarea) layout=verticalflowlayout(0,0,0,2) >
    <element layout=filllayout() width=384rp>
     <element id=atom(welcomeshadow) content=rcstr(7)/>
     <element id=atom(welcome) content=rcstr(7)/>
    </element>
   </element>
  <element id=atom(divider) layoutpos=bottom height=2rp/>
 </element>
```

```
<element id=atom(bottompanel) sheet=styleref(bottompanelss)
layout=borderlayout() layoutpos=bottom>
  <element id=atom(divider) layoutpos=top height=2rp/>
  <element id=atom(options) layout=borderlayout() layoutpos=client>

  // The following line defines the turn-off button alignment
   <element layout=borderlayout() layoutpos=left>
    <button id=atom(power) layout=borderlayout() layoutpos=top
accessible=true accRole=43 accName=rcstr(11)>
     <element layoutpos=left content=rcbmp(107,3,-1,26rp,26rp,0,0) />
     <element id=atom(label) layoutpos=client margin=rect(2rp,0,0,0)/>
    </button>
    <button id=atom(undock) layout=borderlayout() layoutpos=top
margin=rect(0,2rp,0,0) accessible=true accRole=43 accName=rcstr(14)>
     <element layoutpos=left content=rcbmp(108,3,-1,26rp,26rp,0,0)/>
     <element id=atom(label) layoutpos=client margin=rect(2rp,0,0,0)/>
    </button>
   </element>
   <element id=atom(instruct) layoutpos=right content=rcstr(25)
width=325rp/>
  </element>
 </element>


 <element id=atom(contentcontainer0) layout=flowlayout(1,3,2,3)
layoutpos=client content=argb(0,0,0,0)>
  <element id=atom(leftpanel) sheet=styleref(leftpanelss)
layoutpos=client>
  </element>


 <element id=atom(rightpanel) sheet=styleref(rightpanelss)
layout=borderlayout() layoutpos=left width=920rp>
   <element id=atom(divider) layoutpos=left width=1rp/>
    <scrollviewer id=atom(scroller) sheet=styleref(scroller)
layoutpos=client xscrollable=false margin=rect(0rp,0rp,0rp,0rp)>
     <selector id=atom(accountlist) sheet=styleref(accountlistss)
layout=verticalflowlayout(0,3,3,2)/>
```

```
        </scrollviewer>
      </element>
    </element>
  </element>
</logonframe>


<logonaccount resid=accountitem id=atom(accountitem) layout=filllayout()
accessible=true accRole=43>
 <element id=atom(userpanelayer) layout=borderlayout() height=80rp>
    <element id=atom(userpane) layout=borderlayout() layoutpos=top>
     <element id=atom(pictureframe) layout=flowlayout(0,2,2)
layoutpos=left width=58rp height=58rp>
      <element id=atom(picture) />
     </element>
     <element id=atom(username) layoutpos=top/>
     <button id=atom(status0) class="status" layoutpos=none/>
     <button id=atom(status1) class="status" layoutpos=none/>
    </element>
  </element>
</logonaccount>


<element resid=passwordpanel id=atom(passwordpanelayer)
sheet=styleref(passwordpaness) layout=borderlayout() height=80rp>
 <element layout=borderlayout() layoutpos=bottom>
    <edit id=atom(password) layoutpos=left width=163rp/>
    <element id=atom(keyboard) layoutpos=left/>
     <button id=atom(go) layoutpos=left accessible=true accRole=43
accName=rcstr(100)/>
     <button id=atom(info) layoutpos=left accessible=true accRole=43
accName=rcstr(13)/>
  </element>
 <element id=atom(instruct) layoutpos=bottom content=rcstr(6)/>
</element>
```

The listing has many `rcstr(XX)` type references, where `XX` is a numerical value. What does this mean? `rcstr` is a command that takes line number XX from the resources and outputs it to the screen. Accordingly, the numbers of string resources can be changed, with the important thing being to correct all references to this resource in the script.

There are also many commands to load images. The command format is `rcbmp (parameters)`. There are many various parameters and we will not be considering them all. The parameter we are interested in is the first: the number of the image from the **Bitmap** resource section that needs to be loaded.

The `layoutpos` parameter also appears in a large number of instances in this script. This specifies the alignment. For example, the following block of code sets the turn-off button alignment:

```
// The following line defines the turn-off button alignment
<element layout=borderlayout() layoutpos=left>
```

The same block is indicated by the corresponding comment in Listing 2.3 to make it easier for you to find it there. There, this parameter is assigned the value `left` (`layoutpos=left`). Changing it to `right` will make the button shift to the right.

This parameter can be changed in any line without creating any problems; the choice is not that big, though: `left` can be changed only to `right` and `top` only to `bottom` (or vice versa). Changing `left` to `bottom` may create a mess on the screen. The operating system will not, however, suffer from erroneous alignment changes like these and will load regardless. But the logon program may not be so easygoing, and may issue a number of error messages when running.

2.6. X-Style Loader

In *Chapter 1*, you learned how to create boot loader screens using special programs. But why pay for these special programs when the Restorator program can do the same things? This will not take much time and will require no extra expense in the future.

The boot loader is contained in ntoskrnl.exe in the \Windows\System32 folder. You will not actually be able to change this file directly, because it is blocked. Although this protection can be disabled by booting into the safe mode (by pressing the <F8> key during the boot until the boot type selection menu appears), I strongly urge you not to do this.

There is a better way to skin this cat. Simple make a copy of this file with a different name, for example, kernel1.exe, and use this copy for your experiments. If something goes wrong, you can always use the original file to boot the system.

So, open a copy of the ntoskrnl.exe file (named kernel1.exe for our work) in Restorator. Once again, you can see a large number of resources. The resource we are interested in is number 1 in the **Bitmap** section. Selecting it will not produce anything other than a "Bitmap image is not valid" message in the preview window. No worry, this is just a slight program shortcoming: there actually is an image there. Right-click on the resource, and select the **Extract/Extract as "1.bmp"** menu sequence in the context menu that appears.

Now, if you open the image file you just saved using any graphics editor, the only thing you will see will be a black rectangle. This is just what is seems to be: It has to be edited in a more sophisticated graphics editor.

Photoshop if not the most sophisticated example, is quite sophisticated, so open the image file in it. Again, you see a black rectangle. Don't despair. Select the **Image/Mode/Color Table** menu sequence. This will open the color table dialog window. In the dropdown list, select any item other than **Custom**, and look at the image again. The black rectangle has turned into something more acceptable and the real boot loader screen image can be seen. Fig. 2.18 shows the image displayed using the **System (Windows)** color table. Of course, the image is distorted because of incorrect color assignments, but at least it is visible. So this is where the problem was! Microsoft's developers tried to hide what rightfully belongs to the people! As it turns out, all that you need to do is to use the correct color table.

Advanced graphics programs know how to work with color tables (palettes) and use the PAL format to load images. Adobe Photoshop uses another format: ACT. You can find files boot.pal and boot.act on the accompanying CD-ROM in the Chapter 2 folder. These files can be used to load the correct color table and display the undistorted image.

To load the table, select the **Image/Mode/Color Table** menu sequence and, in the color table dialog window that appears, click the **Load** button. This will open the standard file open dialog window. On the CD-ROM, find and open the boot.act file. Now you can edit the image in any way you desire.

After editing, the image is loaded back into resource 1 and the boot loader screen image is ready.

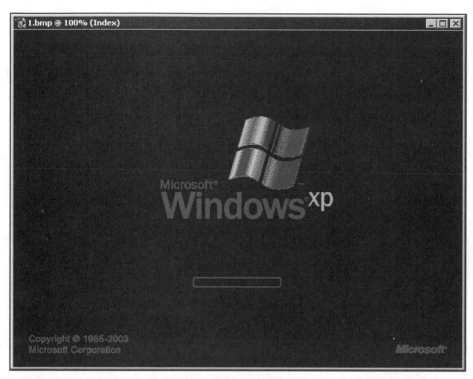

Fig. 2.18. The boot loader screen image displayed using System (Windows) color table

What other resources can be edited? Well, just about all of them. Some of the images will be displayed correctly, while others have to be opened with a special palette. Consider the other images that are stored in the **Bitmap** section:

❏ 2: the message displayed when the computer is switched into hibernation mode (used very often in notebooks)
❏ 3: the "Now it is safe to turn the computer off" message
❏ 4: the slider that runs while the computer is loading
❏ 5: the logo displayed when the computer is turned on or switches into hibernation mode
❏ 6: the logo displayed during Windows installation
❏ 7: the gradient color stripe displayed during Windows installation
❏ 8 and 9: used for the operating system loading indicator
❏ 10: the "Professional" text image

❏ 11: the "Home Edition" text image
❏ 12: the "Embedded" text image
❏ 13: the central logo
❏ 14 and 15: the logo and the gradient color stripe used when loading in safe mode
❏ 17: the "Tablet PC Edition" text image
❏ 18: the "Freestyle" text image

It is best not to change image sizes in the process of editing them, as this may cause damage to the file. I advise that you do not change the color spectrum either, because, during the boot, the monitor is limited to 256 colors whose values are defined by the system.

Now let's see how to install this file and use it during the boot. Copy the edited file into the Windows/System32 folder and then open the boot.ini file in the disk C: root folder. This file may be invisible and read only. Both of these attributes need to be cleared. To save yourself the trouble of fiddling with the attributes, I recommend that you do the following:

1. Right-click on **My Computer** and select the **Properties** item in the context menu that appears. This will open the **System Properties** dialog window.
2. Select the **Advanced** tab, and click the **Settings** button in the **Startup and Recovery** section.
3. At the very bottom of the **System startup** section, find the "To edit the startup options file manually" label, and click the **Edit** button to the left of it.

This will open a Notepad file containing approximately the following:

```
[boot loader]
timeout=0
default=multi(0)disk(0)rdisk(0)partition(1)\WINDOWS
[operating systems]
multi(0)disk(0)rdisk(0)partition(1)\WINDOWS="Windows Server 2003,
Enterprise" /fastdetect
```

If you have more than one operating system installed on your computer, there will be more than one line after the [operating system] line. Each line starts with a command telling the boot loader where to look for the operating system. The text in quotation marks after the equal sign is what you will see when there are multiple operating system menu choices. Find the line that corresponds to the operating system with the boot loader screen you want to change. Make a copy of this line and change the text in the quotation marks to contain two options for loading this operating system. At the end of this line, add a space and the following text:

```
/KERNEL=kernel1.exe key.
```

Here, kernel1.exe is the name of the file you have modified. Consequently, selecting the old menu item will start the old boot loader, while selecting the other menu item will start the modified boot loader.

Now, you can go to the line that begins with the word Timeout (in most cases, this is the second line) and change the number after the equal sign to 30. This is the time, in seconds, during which the operating system selection menu will be displayed. When this time expires, the default operating system will load. The menu will not show at all if Timeout is set to 0.

Save the changes and reboot the computer. Enjoy the completely new look of your boot loader screen. It looks more hackish and more individual.

Windows 2000 also has a ntoskrnl.exe file, which has a structure similar to the Windows XP version structure. This means that it can also be modified in the same way.

2.7. The Mysterious Shell Style

Let's return again to the themes that are stored in the \Windows\Resources\Themes folder. We have studied this folder quite thoroughly, but there is still one interesting file that can routinely be found in different folders: shellstyle.dll. A reasonable question would be: What is this for? The easiest way to answer this question is to open this file in any resource viewer (e.g., Restorator).

I examined all shellstyle.dll files that I could find on my machines, and they all had the same resource structure. The most interesting things in them are kept in the **Bitmap** and **Html** sections. In the first section are located bitmaps used by Media Player; in the second section is the CSS file used to format HTML information displayed in the player.

The file is amenable to editing and can be installed on another computer, along with the corresponding MSSTYLES file.

I have not been able to figure out the connection between the MSSTYLES and shellstyle.dll files. Here is what little I have been able to dig up:

❐ The shellstyle.dll file is located in a subfolder with a name related to MSSTYLES. The names of folders match the color spectrums of the particular theme.
❐ There is an interesting item, THEMES-INI, in the **TEXTFILE** section of the MSSTYLES files. In Restorator, right-click on it and, in the context menu that appears, select **Extract/Extract as "THEMES_INI.raw."**
❐ Now, examine the THEMES_INI.raw file in Notepad. Personally, I only found references to the folders with the color schemes, but no mention of the shellstyle.dll file.

It looks like each color scheme folder must have this file, but that the name cannot be changed.

There is actually nothing particularly interesting in the shellstyle.dll file. You can decorate Media Player a little, but I could not figure out how to perform any global modifications. However, some pictures from the **Bitmap** section are worth a second look, to make, for example, Media Player look much better. You already know how to edit images in resources, so there is no need to go into it again here.

2.8. Desktop under the Hacker's Knife

The foundation of the Windows desktop is explorer.exe. This program is responsible for the desktop's appearance, icons, menus, and main messages. Let's take a look how all this looks in the file. Open the file (it is located in \WINDOWS folder) in Restorator.

Opening the **Bitmap** section, you will see many images there. Of special interest are images numbered 157 through 169. They are different versions of the image that you can see along the left edge of the main menu after pressing the **Start** button. Look at your image. Don't feel like changing it? I have changed mine and now my menu looks as shown in Fig. 2.19.

So which image to edit? There are many of them in the resources, numbered from 157 to 169. This is because the explore.exe file is universal and, depending on the Windows version (Home Edition, Professional, or Server), a corresponding picture is selected.

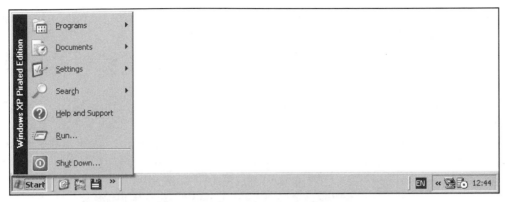

Fig. 2.19. A customized Windows main menu

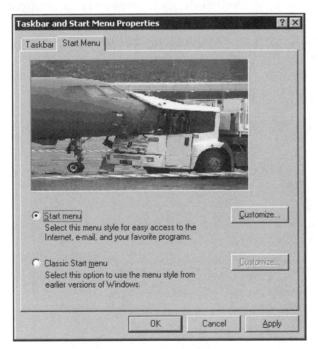

Fig. 2.20. A customized main menu properties window

In Windows XP, resources 170 and 171 store the preview images of the main menu style. Right-click on the **Start** button and select the **Properties** item in the context menu that appears. On the **Start Menu** tab in the properties window that appears you will see these pictures. To tell the truth, they aren't that pretty and can definitely be improved upon. I, for example, inserted a comical picture, which is shown in Fig. 2.20.

Resources numbered 145 through 153 are also preview images for the various states of the taskbar. In addition, there are pictures of various logos, which must also be drastically customized.

The **Menu** section of resources contains various context menus that appear in response to right-clicking on different areas of the taskbar (the **Start** button, system area, a program button, etc.). You can change the menu names and make them more fitting to your style. For example, the text for the menu item "Hide all" can be changed into "*Get outta here!*", "*Scram!*", etc. Change only the text, and not the numbers of the menu items. The command sequence can also be changed by switching places for the lines.

The **Dialogs** section hides all of the dialog windows for configuring the taskbar and the start button. You can add your own icons to these windows, hide those you do not like, or rearrange them to your liking. For example, resource 205 is the dialog window shown in Fig. 2.20. Now look at Fig. 2.21 and see what can be done to this window in only five minutes. All I did was add one button and the copyright text and rearrange all of the controls.

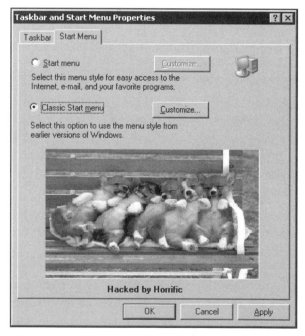

Fig. 2.21. The main menu properties window after I got through with it

The **String** section holds the texts of various window headers and system messages. These cannot be left unchanged either. You can make them sterner or funnier — it all depends on your tastes. I personally like funny messages. For example, the message "Windows is operating in safe mode now" can be changed into "Windows is in safe hands now" or "Klutz free zone." The type of messages you can create is limited only by your imagination.

The **Accelerators** section holds hotkeys for rapid command execution (e.g., for switching windows or calling up the object properties window). If you find a key combination inconvenient, you can change it to something more to your liking.

The **Icon** section stores the system's main icons, which you trip over wherever you go. The icons for **Recycle Bin**, **My Computer**, printers, documents, etc. are some of its tenants.

NOTE

Do not be in a hurry to close Restorator after saving your changes. Wait a second until the system message warning about a system file having been changed is displayed. If no message appears, try to change something in Restorator. When the message does appear, asking you to restore the explorer.exe file, refuse the request. Otherwise, your changes will not be applied.

After saving the file, save a copy in a separate folder. In some cases, the operating system can restore system files from their backup copies, which can happen to the customized explorer.exe. If this happens, you will not have to edit the file again, but can simply use the reserve copy.

The explorer.exe file is a very important system file and we see its resources everyday, which is why editing it can change the interface significantly. In *Chapter 3*, you will learn some practical jokes that can be played on your friends by editing the explorer.exe file.

NOTE

The changes take effect only after rebooting or after logging off and logging on again.

2.9. The XP Shell

The next file we are going to edit is shell32.dll. This is the shell file, which contains even more interesting resources that the user sees every day. The shell32.dll file is located in the \\Windows\System folder (\\Windows\System32 for NT systems). Open this file in Restorator, and you will immediately see many sections. Let's consider each section individually and see what interesting things it has to offer.

2.9.1. AVI

This section contains AVI format video files. These files provide animation that you can see when searching for files, computers in the network neighborhood, deleting or copying files, etc. Files can be edited using a special graphics program. There are many programs that can be used for this purpose, but they all are quite expensive. I personally prefer the much more affordable CyD Animation Studio or GIF Studio Pro editors (available at **www.cydsoft.com**). You can find both programs on the accompanying CD-ROM in the Soft folder. The programs are intended for working with GIF files, but they can also read and save AVI files. This means that you can convert any GIF animation into AVI.

The only shortcoming with regard to these programs is that they do not save the transparency information, which may lead to the appearance of an undesirable background. But the background can be easily changed and made more attractive and suitable for any window. For example, each frame can be given an attractive border.

If you use another program to edit video files, you should never use compression when saving them. The reason files should not be compressed lies in the fact that the system works only with non-compressed files and does not use codecs for playback. (As a last resort, you can try installing Microsoft RLE).

2.9.2. Images

The **Bitmap** section contains numerous images. It contains images for the buttons on the task bars of **My Computer** and **Explorer** windows (resources 204–228), as well as the browser logo animation image (resources 240–247), which we learned to modify using the registry resources in *Chapter 1*. There also are numerous images used as the background for various system windows. I direct your attention to image 14351, which contains the background of the window you see when Windows XP terminates operation.

Not all Windows versions use all of the pictures. For example, Windows 2000 has no resource 14351 and uses a simple window, without a background image, for shutting down the system.

2.9.3. Menu

The **Menu** section contains various dropdown menus. For example, resource 197 is the pop-up menu for the right-button dragging operation. It contains the following four items:

❐ **Copy Here.** This item could be changed to "*Clone.*"
❐ **Move Here.** You could change this item to "*Get here on the double!*"
❐ **Create Shortcuts Here.** This could be changed to "*Remember the link.*"
❐ **Cancel.** And here you could say "*I've changed my mind*" or "*Just forget* it."

In this way, all the main Explorer menus can be modified.

2.9.4. Dialog

This section contains all of the **Explorer** dialog windows. For example, resource 1003 contains the window that appears when the **Start/Run** menu item is selected. There are dialog windows galore, so you have plenty or room to let your imagination fly.

Different controls very often use special character strings instead of plain text. They start with character %, followed by a letter, most often *s*. During operation, these strings are replaced with meaningful strings. For example, in the "&Current User(%s) string," character % and letter *s* specify the key that will be replaced with the user name in the window.

2.9.5. String Table

As usual, the **String Table** section contains many strings and I am going to show you, which way to go to improve them. Open string resource 5. Message 65 here says the following: *Are you sure you want to delete it*? It sounds like a baby talk, doesn't it? Don't you think it could be changed to something like "The Disintegrator is ready. Shall the annihilation process be initiated?"

All messages contained in this section are used in **Explorer** for various operations: copying, deleting, moving, etc. If you do not use a file manager (e.g., Windows Commander) but simply make do with Windows tools, you see these messages every day and might as well make them more agreeable to behold.

2.9.6. Icon Group

The name of the section makes it clear that it contains icons. These are the icons used by **Explorer**, **Control Panel**, **My Computer**, and other components. These icons are pretty nice-looking in Windows XP, but if you have installed a Mac or Linux theme, it would be logical to make it so that all of the icons appear in the same style. The system will then look and feel more genuine.

I personally prefer the Apple style, so I have made Windows look like Mac OS X. I also know people whose first love is Linux and, when forced to work in Windows, they change everything they can to try to feel more at home.

As you can see, the system can be tuned up completely by simply editing the resources of the main system files manually.

2.10. Conclusion

Resource editors can be used for purposes other than simply embellishing programs. Some hackers use them to localize programs in various languages and, as rumor has it, make good money in the process. This is not the old-fashioned way of making an honest buck but, instead, just another variety of software piracy. The user, of course, is happy, but the software developer suffers profit losses.

I personally edit resources only for personal use. I never distribute my work on the Internet and have no intention of doing so in the future.

Remember, when you change resources, you change the executable file. Even minor changes can sometimes have negative effects on the program's functioning. This is why it is strongly recommended that you always make a backup copy of the file, with which you want to experiment. The Restorator program considered in this chapter makes backup copies automatically. But don't rely on the computer, and make your own backup copy every time you edit a file.

Also don't forget that changing an executable file may violate the license agreement, an eventuality that is fraught with the danger of losing developer support for the software you have altered. In some countries, violating the license agreement can lead to even graver consequences (just how grave depends on the seriousness of the violation). But nobody gets put in jail simply for repainting their car. The same should apply here: It is not a crime to make a program look better, more convenient to use, and more individual.

Software developers cannot take into account the needs of all users, so they often aim at satisfying the common denominator of our wants. But we don't have to settle for this. We can solve some usability problems by editing the resources of our favorite programs on our own.

Chapter 3: Friendly Pranks

Practical jokes are one of the ways you can express yourself. They can be used not only to put one over on someone, but also simply to unwind or make your colleagues laugh. Personally, I'm fond of a good computer joke and enjoy playing them on my friends.

Right from the start, I want to make clear what I mean when I talk about jokes here: slowing down a computer's operations, creating temporary boot problems, forcing constant reboots, and other relatively harmless things. At the same time, there is a line that I don't believe should be crossed: destroying information and/or damaging the computer and its components. This is simply nasty and mean and is not funny at all. Practical jokes should make people laugh.

The best pranks are those that do not interfere with the computer's functions, make people laugh, and can even be played on advanced users. Playing jokes on inexperienced and computer illiterate users is not particularly ethical.

Some jokes can potentially be harmful to computer hardware and are described only for educational purposes. Unless you have enough experience and know what you are doing, do not try those jokes yourself.

Please pay careful heed to the following warning! You must turn off the computer when attempting to play a joke that involves opening the physical body of the computer. Computer work on the basis of electrical current and touching the innards of a plugged in computer can be hazardous to your life, let alone your health.

3.1. Mouse Jokes

Let's start off with a classic and one of my favorite practical jokes. Without disconnecting the mouse, hide it somewhere. If the system block is set up on a desk, the mouse and its wire can be hidden behind it.

Now, put another, dummy mouse, on the desk and throw its wire behind the desk to create the impression that it is connected to the computer. The most important thing is that the substitute mouse should look like the one that you have hidden. When your victim starts working, he or she will grab the sham mouse and quickly decide that it isn't working. It will be difficult for them to determine the root, as the computer won't issue any error messages (the computer knows that a mouse is connected — it's not its fault that no one is trying to use it) and a cursory inspection of the back panel confirms that the mouse is plugged in properly.

The same trick can be played with the keyboard, but a keyboard is more difficult to hide. If you hide it behind the computer, a cursory search will reveal it and putting two and two together will be relatively simple.

Another mouse-related trick is to simply remove the ball inside. This will render the mouse inoperative. It takes a while for novice users to figure out that the ball is no longer present. Those with more experience will notice right away that the mouse is significantly lighter (some balls account for as much as half of the mouse's weight) and will not be taken in. You should also try to play this one in the near future, as mice are rapidly going optical.

But this does not necessarily mean that the future will be bland, as optics form the basis of new vulnerabilities. Turn an optical mouse upside down and you will discover a lens in the hollow in its middle. It is simple enough is to cover this lens with something thin and opaque. Non-transparent scotch tape will do well for this purpose. The mouse stops working and, from what I've seen, the lens is about the last thing that the perplexed user checks.

The mouse can also be taped to the mouse pad or the desk with two-sided tape. The problem here is, of course, figured out pretty quickly, but this does not make it any less effective. Colleagues and friends with a good sense of humor should appreciate the joke for what it's worth.

ATX cases with a PS/2 mouse and keyboard connectors are very common nowadays. These connectors are identical, so it is a snap to swap the plug places. In this case, while seemingly connected, neither the keyboard nor the mouse will work.

There's no danger to the system itself if you swap the places for the plugs while the computer is turned off, so nothing will burn out. Moreover, on computers with

good motherboards, the mouse and keyboard plugs can be switched with the computer on. I experimented with hot swapping on motherboards from Asus, Abit,
and Gigabyte without any adverse results. The only problem in this respect is that,
when the plugs are returned to their correct connections, the mouse may refuse to
work without rebooting. The keyboard is more compliant and works without rebooting. But this depends not only on the motherboard, but also on the type and
version of the operating system.

Another trick is to switch the left and right buttons. This is done by selecting
the **Start/Control Panel** menu sequence and then opening the **Mouse** item. This
will open the mouse configuration dialog window (Fig. 3.1). Put a check in the
Switch primary and secondary buttons box. This will assign the left button function to the right button and vice versa. This is a rather simple joke that will generally only have at least a medium-term effect on novice users.

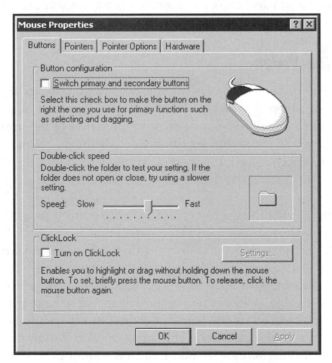

Fig. 3.1. Configuring mouse settings

In the same mouse properties window, the mouse double click speed can be
set to the maximum possible (**Fast**). Now, in order to double-click, the user has

to develop a Speedy Gonzalez index finger. When I set the **Double-click speed** to **Fast** on my computer, I couldn't pull off a double-click operation, no matter how hard I tried.

3.2. Hardware Jokes

These jokes require delving into the computer's hardware and opening up the system unit case (remember that the unit must be unplugged, due to the extreme hazard of electrical shock). For these jokes, it is best to have unobstructed access to a computer, for which the case can be opened easily.

Because these jokes require having access to the computer's insides, they can obviously only be carried out when the intended victim is not around. You can try it while the intended victim is out of the room, but coming to work before everyone is an even better way to ensure the necessary privacy. Of course, you also need to be sufficiently familiar with computer hardware.

3.2.1. Death of the Video

To pull this one off, first open the system unit case. Next, unscrew the screw holding the video card and pull the video card out of its connector slightly. The card only has to be pulled out a little — one or two millimeters of the upper connector part showing above the connector on either side is enough. Now, close the case again. A cursory inspection will not reveal anything wrong, but the computer will not boot. All the victim will get during attempts to boot the system will be a bit of beeping.

If you are unsure, which expansion card the video card is in, you can find this out easily by tracing the monitor cord to the system unit.

What makes this joke difficult to solve is that only someone who knows the beep codes of the particular motherboard can pin down the problem. Others will search for the cause of the problem for a long time, as a small gap in the contacts won't be easily noticeable, so everything inside will appear to be in place.

To make the task of sorting out what is wrong difficult even for a professional, the PC speaker can be disconnected. This small speaker inside the computer is often fixed to the bottom of the system unit or to the lower part of the front panel. I personally always disconnect this speaker in my computer to keep its shrieks and wailing from getting on my nerves. This does not affect the audio obtained from the sound card and its speakers. It simply provides even fewer clues for your victim, as system error beep messages are not routed through the audio card.

3.2.2. Forgetful Memory

Some motherboards have three memory connectors. The third of these memory slots may not work with two-sided memory modules. If this is the case, and the computer has only one memory module (which is often the case in older models), this memory module can be installed in this third memory slot. It is doubtful that the owner will know about this peculiarity, let alone be aware which slot is the first and which the third.

Modern motherboards may have four memory slots, into which an even number of memory modules is installed (two or four). If there are only two memory modules, they often have to be installed into the first two slots. In this case, they can be switched from the first two slots to the last two.

This will not damage the computer, but it won't work when configured in this way. The important thing for our purposes is that the cause will not be discovered easily.

3.2.3. No ATX System Case Is a Stronghold

I am in an ongoing state of computer joke war against my boss and his assistant, because they both have a good sense of humor. They also both have ATX system cases with special loop tabs, through which you can put a lock for their computers. One day my boss used a screw with a nut instead of lock (no lock happened to be handy at the time) and stripped the thread off the screw end. But he did not realize that, very often, ATX cases have an upper lid or the front panel that can be removed easily and that cannot be locked. I took off the top, one side wall (the other was locked with the screw), and then the front panel. This particular computer had three 5-inch bays. The upper one had a CD-ROM installed in it, but the other two were empty. I stuck my hand through the opening made by these two vacant bays and, by feeling my way around, disconnected the power from the 3.5" floppy drive. Afterwards, I fished a whole stack of perfect diskettes out of the trash can that my boss thought were defective when, in fact, the problem was with the floppy drive. In addition, I received the respect of my coworkers for my inventiveness and was deprived of bonus pay by the boss for my brazenness.

3.2.4. Disconnections

The motherboard battery can be taken out. The computer will work on the whole, but its settings will reset after each power down. The user affected will make full use of a special vocabulary (I don't mean technical), and even possibly invent new words, until it dawns upon him or her to check the battery, which may take a couple of days — or even longer.

Moving on to the next trick, you can pull the monitor plug out of the video card connector just a little bit. The computer will work, but there will be no sign of this on the monitor. Actually, there are a number of things that can be disconnected. Printer power plugs are especially well suited for this purpose. Their female connector is deep, so it is easy to insert the male plug without making actual connection. Everything looks normal, but the printer doesn't work.

I just advise you not to get carried away with jokes involving connectors that have power-carrying contacts. Should the contacts arc, both the computer and the device you are trying to play the joke with (e.g., the monitor) will burn out.

If you have complete access to the innards of your victim's computer, the jokes move to an entirely new plane. On the motherboard, you can switch the places of the wires connected to the **Reset** and **Power** buttons. Here, even a sharp victim will take a while to figure out why the computer refuses to respond to the **Power** button.

Anything can be disconnected, from the hard disk and CD-ROM drives to the processor cooler. I personally like the latter trick the best because, if it is an Intel processor on the motherboard, it simply turns off a short time after the computer is turned on — when it overheats. This makes the computer appear to hang, or to turn off altogether.

However, if you are not sure now how the victim's hardware will react, I advise you not to monkey around with processor cooling, lest you burn out the processor (some earlier AMD processors do not turn off when overheated, with all of the natural consequences). In such an event, the recognition you receive for your ingenuity may be in the form of a black eye or a concussion.

3.2.5. Monitors

On some monitors, the brightness can be turned all the way down to the point that the screen is simply black. My beloved LG FLATRON 795FT is such a monitor. Turning the brightness all the way down leaves all of the vital signs on, but no information is displayed on the screen. This is the only joke that has been played on me that took me a long time to figure out. I was dancing around the computer, attempting all kinds of conjuring, checking all of the cables, but all in vain: All indications were that the monitor was working but, an image simply refused to appear. The only thing displayed was the monitor menu, but it never occurred to me to check the brightness and contrast settings. Finally, the trickster could no longer suppress his laughter, and revealed the root of the problem. I spent the days following this moment of infamy viciously trying to pay my tormentor back for the humiliation I had suffered. No one had ever been able to pull one over on me like this before.

Another little trick is to place a magnet somewhere out of sight behind the monitor. This will create significant interference on the monitor, which will cause the user a bit of eye strain. The victim will badmouth the manufacturer, but will most likely never discover the cause on his or her own. None of the guinea pigs I have tested ever has. You should keep in mind, however, that not every magnet creates interference and not every monitor is susceptible to it. My understanding of electronics, unfortunately, is not strong enough to explain why this is the case.

If the victim does not discover the magnet on his or her own, you should remove it yourself after a short time. Otherwise, you could end up doing some real damage to the person's eyes, which is not a joking matter. Somebody's health is not something to joke with. Moreover, doing it periodically for short periods is much more effective.

Despite all of these health warnings, this joke is quite harmless when played with care. For the interference created by the magnet to damage the user's eyesight, the user must work at his computer eight hours a day without smoke or lunch breaks for a long time. For example, a large air conditioner (about two meters long, but I don't know how much power it consumes) is constantly on in the summer at the place where I work. The interference it creates on my monitor makes the image jerk like no magnet does. I have had to work like this for two years. Summers around here are quite hellish without an air conditioner, but it is a hell of a different kind whenever it is switched on. Still, after two summers of this annoyance, I have not gone blind or experienced any other eye problems.

All the same, just to be safe, do not keep the magnet in place for more than a half an hour. If the victim does not notice the flicker in this time, there's no sense to the prank anyway. Even if the victim does notice the flicker and starts worrying, fretting and entertaining coworkers with searches for its source, it is not advisable to let the joke go on for more than an hour.

3.2.7. A Turbo Cooler

How irritating a loud cooler fan can be for some! Perhaps it is simply because these people have not met me. Cooler jokes are my favorite now. Not long ago, I received a fresh idea by e-mail that filled me with excitement.

Find a plastic ruler and chip a few small pieces off it. Next, throw them into the power supply fan casing and wait for the victim to turn on the computer. When the machine is switched on, the rattle these chips will create will make his of her eyes pop out. But if there is no rattle, turn the computer off at once. It may be the case the fan has become jammed, in which case the power supply might burn out — not exactly the effect, for which we are striving. So don't overdo it with the chips in the fan, for you may discover that there is a fine line between being funny and being a complete and total idiot.

When I tried this joke on a friend, he first became frightened, but then had a good, long laugh. It got him so excited that he attached some toilet paper and chocolate bar wrapper foil strips to the cooler grill. Now the cooler blows air over all this stuff, which makes a terrible racket behind the system block, while my friend gets a hell of a kick out of it. It's as if he hears some kind of melody in that cacophony. I have to wonder whether the melody is of the loony tune variety, and whether my friend might be wise to get some professional help before he is too far gone.

As a matter of fact, toilet paper and foil can also be used for a joke. When a user hears noise from the power supply fan without knowing that it is harmless toilet paper and foil making it, it can cause some serious concerns.

3.2.7. Super Scotch

At my old job, I wrote a program that printed barcodes and other information about merchandise on self-adhesive labels, which clerks then pasted on the product boxes.

Where am I going with this? To the fact that a self-adhesive label is very difficult to peel off something once it's stuck. At first, we used them to seal desk drawers shut in such a way that the labels remained unseen. From here, we moved on to electrical outlets and, finally, to computers. Here, the first victim at our hands was the computer's power button, which we pasted over with a double, or even triple, layer of labels. Next came all floppy and CD-ROM drives and connectors on the back of the system unit (USB, LPT, etc.).

Scotch tape is even better for this purpose. One time I used it to tape over the entire system unit of one of the users at work. This necessitated sacrificing a whole roll of scotch tape, but what a show it was watching him taking it all off! Seeing a system unit liberated from a roll of scotch type was worth all the trouble that went onto the exercise. This prank is particularly entertaining when there are no scissors or other cutting tools at hand to liberate the system.

My favorite, however, remains using clear scotch tape to tape over floppy disk drives. If the job is done neatly and cannot be seen, it will be difficult to figure out at once what is preventing the diskette from going in.

3.2.8. A Double-Breasted System Unit

My computer has three **Power** and four **Reset** buttons. Why are there so many of them and how did they get there? It is all very simple. Only one of the buttons is real, while the others are simply pictures. I myself know, which of the buttons are real, while other people start panicking or pressing all of the buttons indiscriminately when trying to turn the computer on.

With this joke, the important thing is that the button pictures are of good quality. Picture buttons may differ from the real McCoy, and you can have several different types of buttons on your computer.

After this got a little old, I went a step further. On my computer at work, I moved the actual power switch from under the button to the side. Now, anyone who is unaware of the alteration gets very frustrated when repeated pressing of the power button produces absolutely no result. This takes the form not only of a little joke, but also of a bit of protection for myself, as it will be tough for a stranger to figure out how to turn my computer on without me around. This is only right: Strangers have no business nosing about in my private files.

3.3. Network Jokes

The office of my assistant manager was located in another building, and he called me regularly to discuss Visual C++ programming problems. The telephone was on another employee's desk and I had to get up constantly to answer it. I soon got tired of this, and showed the assistant manager how to use the `net send` command to send messages over the network. Messages are sent in the following format:

```
Net send Address Message text
```

Execute this command from the command line and a message window will pop up on the addressee's monitor screen. This command works only in NT systems (Windows NT/2000/XP/2003). However, this is not a much of a restriction in most modern networks today, as majority run under these systems.

Well, it took less than a week for the manager to get on my nerves with these messages as well. You can't imagine how nuts it makes me when, just when I am locked in mortal combat with the next monster, a message window pups up and the game window folds! Without much thinking necessary, I wrote a short Delphi program to rid myself of this pestilence. All that was involved was one button, the pressing of which executed the following code:

```
var
  i:Integer;
```

```
begin
 for i:=0 to 10 do
  begin
   WinExec("NET SEND 192.168.1.121 You will suffer every day",
           SW_SHOW);
   Sleep(100);
  end;
end;
```

The following is the same program in C++:

```
for (int i=0; i<10; i++)
{
 WinExec("NET SEND 192.168.1.121 I will make you cry.", SW_SHOW);
 Sleep(1000);
}
```

What this does is launch a 10-iteration loop sending a message to address 192.168.1.121 every 100 milliseconds. Removing the delay line will bombard the poor victim's screen with messages making it impossible for him or her to work. If you have a sadistic streak in you, you can make the loop altogether endless, which can only be stopped by ending its process. This will flood the user with messages.

A program playing a similar trick can be written in any programming language in a short time. You can even do this with a batch file. Everything depends on your knowledge and skills.

If you are being bombarded with messages, the first thing I advise you to do is disconnect the network cable. Then, select the **Start/Settings/Control Panel/ Administrative Tools/Services** menu sequence. This will open the services configuration window (Fig. 3.2). Double clicking on the **Messenger** service will open its properties window (Fig. 3.3). Press the **Stop** button to stop the service, and then select **Disabled** from the **Startup type** drop-down list to prevent the service from launching when the system is started.

Connect the network cable back and continue your work. Now your computer will simply refuse to accept any messages that your assailant's computer tries to throw at you. This will not only protect you from unwanted messages but will also backfire on the smart alec, as the message flood will only slow his or her computer.

The conclusion that can be drawn from this prank is that the Microsoft **Messenger** service is, as always, not protected from flood messaging and swallows everything that comes its way. Not even Windows 2003 has the type of protection that is sorely needed. Should you come under such an attack, the only way out is to shut down the service and deprive yourself of a convenient communication tool.

If there are printers connected to your network computers and the system administrator is finding his shoes too large to fill, you can play some good printer jokes. By default, any local printer becomes networked when a computer is connected to a network. This makes it a good target for jokes. Trough the network, get onto the victim's computer and double-click its printer. It will install on your system and you will be able to use it as your own.

Just don't send pictures or text, because this will give away the network origin of the document. The user can open the print manager and see, from which computer the document originated. A blank page sent to the victim's printer every fifteen minutes or so is a much better choice: It will print out quickly, thus not providing enough time for the victim to trace it. Seeing empty pages in the receiving

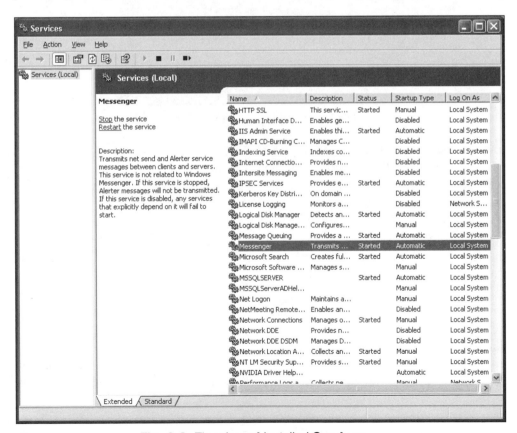

Fig. 3.2. The view of installed **Services**

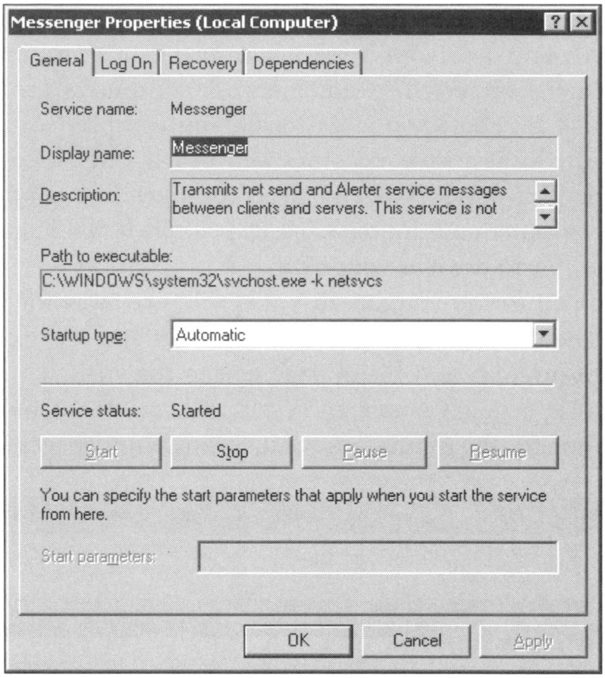

Fig. 3.3. The **Messenger** service property window

tray will likely lead the poor user to believe that the printer is faulty or that there is a bug in the driver. Repeat this operation until you get tired of laughing at the poor schmuck, or until you get found out. In the latter case, it will not hurt to have your escape route planned in advance.

As you can see, the obvious things are not always the funniest. Sometimes, it is better to think a little and do something really original without giving yourself away in the process. Your victim can and, of course, has every right to pay you back and start a joke assault on your computer.

One of the classic network jokes is to send a message in someone else's name. For example, if the NET SEND command is used extensively to send messages in your network, you can send author notes bearing the names of other users. Suppose that you work in a small office and want to send a message to a colleague that is, supposedly, from the boss. This requires that the boss' computer either be turned off or, at least, not be on the network. This can be achieved in the following three ways:

❏ Temporarily pull the network cable out of the boss' computer. Beware, however, for if the boss decides to use the network at this moment and subsequently finds out who was the culprit behind his or her network problems, you might have problems with your next bonus.

❏ Wait for the moment when the boss reboots or turns his or her computer off. For this, you can use the CyD Careful Observer program (**www.cydsoft.com**), which monitors network computers and informs you when a connection is lost.

❏ The most dangerous method is to change the IP address of your computer to the same one that is used by your boss' computer. This will create an addressing conflict and both computers might be taken off the network. Wait a short time. The boss will most likely reboot his computer to resolve the conflict. As soon as he does this, change your IP address to the one used by your boss.

If you manage to get your boss off of the network, you need to change the name of your computer to the one used by the boss. Right-click the **My Computer** icon, and select the **Properties** item in the context menu. Select the **Computer Name** tab, and click the **Change** button. In the **Computer Name Changes** dialog window, change the computer name, and click the **OK** button.

Now, while your boss is rebooting and is off the network, you can send messages bearing his name. Messages like "I want to see you in my office at once." or "You are fired." can be sent. The victim will think that they are coming from the boss and will at least be spooked.

Remember, however, that you do not have that much time at your disposal. It takes about three minutes, maybe a little longer, for Windows to reboot. As soon as you send your message, rename the computer and change its IP address back to what it is supposed to be. After the reboot, the boss' computer may issue an error message again, because of the conflicting IP addresses and computer names, which will likely trigger an investigation by the network administrator, which will more than likely lead to you.

The task is made easier if e-mail is used on the network. In *Section 5.5*, we will consider how to send anonymous e-mail messages in someone else's name. You can even send orders to your colleagues, as if they were from the boss. They will almost certainly take them for the real thing. What to say in the messages depends on each specific situation.

Remember, of course, to play message jokes only on people with good sense of humor. This will reduce the likelihood of getting in trouble or, in extreme cases, suffering some physical injury.

3.4. Jokes on Windows

In this section, you will learn some pranks that can be played using Windows operating system. They are some of the easiest to put into practice, but the effect they produce is as interesting as any of the tricks considered previously.

3.4.1. A Sham System Crash

Using the **Print Scrn** button, make a copy of the entire desktop, but without any programs running. Open any graphics editor, paste in the desktop picture, and save it as a BMP file. Now, remove all of the icons from the desktop and hide the taskbar and the **Start** button. Then install the image of the desktop as the wallpaper. Even professionals have been taken in by this sham-desktop trick. It is quite amusing to watch the victim trying to click a wallpaper icon or the **Start** button without getting any reaction.

3.4.2. Shortcuts

I am very fond of assigning shortcuts to programs altogether different from those they are supposed to launch. This is done by right-clicking the shortcut and selecting the **Properties** item in the context menu that appears. Next, go to the **Shortcut** tab and change the **Target** field path to whatever program you want. The best option is to swap programs for two shortcuts.

The important thing here is to be careful that the shortcut's icon does not change to the one used by the newly-assigned program, which it may try to do automatically. If this happens, open the shortcut's property window again and click the **Change Icon** button, which will open a file open dialog window. Navigate to the executable file of the original program and select it. The operating system will assign the old icon back to the shortcut.

In this way, the calculator or the notepad can be launched via the Microsoft Word icon. Users most often simply become baffled, and it may take them a few unsuccessful tries to launch the program to realize that they have been had.

3.4.3. Desktop Trash

My boss keeps all of his shortcuts to documents, files, and programs on the desktop. When it becomes so cluttered that there is not enough room for another shortcut, he reinstalls Windows. It seems that the desktop becoming totally cluttered is his own personal reinstall indicator. It's a good one, huh? I could never have thought up something like that myself.

The cluttered-desktop-Windows-reinstall indicator is not the only sign of my boss' ingenuity. He uses a very original password for everything: 11. Indeed, why use something more complex that is difficult to remember, easy to forget, and, most important, will be made a short work of by hackers anyway? Recently, however, he gathered up enough courage to strain his intellectual abilities and make the job more difficult for hackers: He changed his password to 1111.

Knowing the administrator's password gives you access to his computer, where you can do whatever your heart desires. Way back in the days of Windows 98, my boss would often leave his C: drive shared, so we had a real good time all over the network. If the C: drive of the computer, to which you have the administrator password, does not show in the network environment, this is easy to fix. Type the following address in the network environment address field:

```
\\Computer\c$
```

Here, instead of `Computer`, type the name or IP address of the victim's computer. If you do not have access rights to this drive at this moment, you might get a dialog window asking to enter the user name and password. Enter the administrator's name and password and you will obtain unlimited access to the C: drive.

Having made our way onto the boss' computer, the first thing we did was send a pile of small files, shortcuts, and documents over the network into his desktop folder (C:\Windows\Desktop in Windows 9x or C:\Documents and Settings\All Users\Desktop for Windows 2000/XP). Try to do to someone something like this yourself. You will discover how much fun it is to watch someone's reactions while their desktop fills up with all kinds of trash right before their eyes.

If you have no network access to the victim's computer, but can manage to get some time at its keyboard (during a lunch break or when the owner is away from the machine for some other reason), you can do the following:

On the desktop, create a batch file and give it some kind of intriguing name. Enter the following code in this file:

```
md hi
md format
md c
md delete
//and so on
```

Hide the file among the icons or, better yet, place it in some folder. Next, create a shortcut for this file on the desktop, assign it an attractive icon, place it in a prominent place on the desktop, and lurk around waiting for the victim to fall prey to his curiosity. If you have given a truly intriguing name and icon to the shortcut, he or she will launch this file, which will create a plethora of new folders on the desktop. The important thing, however, is that their names will be **format, c, delete**: words that will make any system administrator's heart sink.

3.4.4. Windows 9x Death

A year ago, I changed to a new job as a system administrator. I had simply grown tired of working as a programmer and wanted a job where I would have the free time to write programs for myself and work on new articles and books. In the new job, I was responsible for taking care of a network of 40 computers and two servers. The previous administrator had left the system in a real shambles. Only two of the computers were running under Windows XP, while there was one other running Windows 2000 Professional. The rest were running under Windows 98. I was shocked, but they explained that no one had wanted to interrupt his or her work to install a new system. Some computers actually had Pentium III processors, but had only 32 MB of RAM installed! This when 512 MB of RAM can be had for pittance! I wish I could have man-to-man talk with the administrator who cobbled the systems together. I would be tempted to knock on his processor a bit, and then clean up his RAM.

Fortunately, a short time before I took the job, I was provided with an excellent idea on how to kill Windows 98 so that it won't start. All it takes to prevent Windows 98 from starting on its own is to create an empty file named win.com in the root folder of the C: drive. The only way around this is to write C:\Windows\win.com path in the command line or to delete the sham file.

So, one at a time, I wrote this file into the computers running the ancient operating system and then, when the users in the office complained that their computers had crashed, took them away for "repairs" and installed either Windows 2000 or XP, depending on the processor's rating and the amount of memory on the particular system. Unfortunately, my plan backfired, as I was let go because computers had begun to breaking down too often after I took over. All I wanted to do was enhance the reliability and security of the network. Now I know what they mean when they say that the road to hell is paved with good intentions.

It is a good idea to make the sham win.com file invisible, so that some genius wouldn't notice and delete it.

3.4.5. Windows Dressing

There is an IE.exe program in the \Chapter 2 folder on the accompanying CD-ROM. Go ahead and start it. It looks like the real thing, doesn't it? In fact, it took me all of five seconds to write this program. Nothing will work in this program, because it is nothing but a picture. Drop this file into your next victim's computer and change the Internet Explorer shortcut properties to launch this file instead.

As soon as the victim tries to start the program, the term "asshead" (most likely in another, harsher form) will likely be the kinder he or she will come up with in the stream of epithets that is sure to follow.

If you are comfortable with programming, you can pull this trick with any program yourself. This is done as follows:

1. Choose a program that the intended victim uses often.
2. Make a screenshot of this program's window.
3. Create a simple application in any Windows programming language. Delete the header with the cross from the form and make the screenshot the form's background. In Delphi, this is done by setting the BorderStyle property to bsNone, placing the TImage component on the form, and loading the screenshot of the program's window into the form.

The mockup is ready to be passed along to your unsuspecting friends.

NOTE

The Delphi source code for the Internet Explorer joke can be found on the accompanying CD-ROM in the \Chapter2\IEDelphiSource folder.

3.4.6. Schedule This

Windows contains a handy thing called task scheduler. You can start it by executing the following menu sequence: **Start/Programs/Accessories/System Tools/ Scheduled Tasks**. The resulting dialog window is shown in Fig. 3.4.

Double-clicking the **Add Scheduled Task** icon will open the **Scheduled Task Wizard** window. During the first step, it simply presents you with some information. After you have familiarized yourself with this, click the **Next** button. Here, in the second step, a list of the programs that are installed in the system will appear.

Select the program that you want to launch, press the **Next** button again, and select daily execution of this task. The last step consists of setting the time, at which the selected program is to be launched. Choose a time when the intended victim is most likely to be working at the computer.

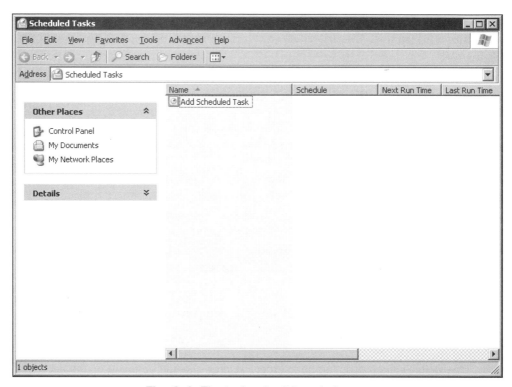

Fig. 3.4. The task scheduler window

Now close the wizard. The selected program will, subsequently, be launched automatically at the specified time. When this happens, the person working on the computer will be taken aback. This will give rise to speculation about viruses or gremlins in the system unit, among other conjectures.

3.4.7. Internet Explorer Death

In *Chapter 1*, you learned how to change the Internet Explorer logo. This modification can easily be turned into a joke. All you need to do is place a logo that is larger than the screen's resolution, which is guaranteed to generate shock. The logo will take up all of the screen area, meaning that there will be no place left for menus, toolbars or the browser's work window. All the victim will see is the Internet Explorer window frame and your picture over the entire screen.

3.5. Resources

We have spent quite a bit of time studying resources. This knowledge can be used not only to configure system settings, but also to play practical jokes. Resource pranks are best suited for use on novices or those who may have been at it longer but have still managed to avoid learning anything too useful about their system. Members of both of these groups generally read and trust all of the labels they see. Experienced users know the programs they work with thoroughly and do not bother reading menu labels, using toolbars and hotkeys instead.

More advanced users, who have been working with computer for quite a while, will know most of the labels by heart. But any event that is even slightly out of ordinary may leave them stumped. More than once I have seen relatively knowledgeable people begin to invent outlandish theories to explain some out-of-the-ordinary trifle. Some of these clever folks will attribute the fact that the program is hanging to faulty chips, some kind of ghost in the motherboard, or something of the like, when the problem is actually the result of program error.

3.5.1. Windows (a.k.a. Total) Commander

This is one of the most popular file managers. The labels for its menu items are stored in the WCMD_ENG.MNU file, which can be opened using any text editor. They look like the following:

```
POPUP "&File"
  MENUITEM "&Change Attributes...", cm_SetAttrib
  MENUITEM "&Pack...\tALT+F5", cm_PackFiles
  MENUITEM "&Unpack...\tALT+F5", cm_PackFiles
  ...
  ...
END_POPUP
```

As you can see, the menu items are described here in exactly the same way as they are in the resources. The executable file stores English-language resources, while resources in other languages are stored in the text files. Instead of editing the executable file in a resource editor, you can use a text editor to modify any language resources in the text files, and then apply the changes in the program's configuration options. At a minimum, you can make the menu items sound more interesting or exotic, but this will simply be decoration. Our task is to play a practical joke on the user, so it would be more entertaining to mix up the hotkeys. This will not affect the program's operations, but the ensuing confusion will be significant. In the menu, the user will see hotkeys that are entirely different from the ones actually used to call the corresponding operations.

To achieve complete bliss, switch the names of the menu items around. The majority of the even most-experienced users will not remember all of the hotkeys and far from all menu items have corresponding buttons on the toolbar. Moreover, nobody memorizes the hotkeys for infrequently used commands, so these will have to be called up from the menu, where all of the names have been switched around and issue commands entirely different from those expected. If some dummy happens to launch your program with the modified menu, he or she will be in for an interesting ride. May Redmond Bill help him not to delete all his files! Try to arrange the menu in as interesting a fashion as possible and switch around everything you can click a mouse on.

The users' first reaction to the modified program's performance will likely be to fall into a bit of a stupor, after which he or she will begin to invent elaborate virus and Trojan horse theories.

Next, you need to modify the string messages. These are the text messages issued by Windows Commander while it works. These are stored within the program resources and can be edited with Restorator or any other resource editor. You can also let your fantasies run free here by switching message places or simply by replacing them with your own to help the poor victim on the road to losing his or her sanity. Here are some suggestions:

- ❏ *"File cannot be copied into itself!"* can be changed to *"Copying successful."*
- ❏ *"Copy file(s) %i to:"* can be changed to *"Rename file(s) %i to:"*
- ❏ Packing can be changed to unpacking, moving to copying, and so on. Do your best to modify everything you can.

Having completed this heavy labor, take another look around. Perhaps another, even wilder, idea will come to your mind. While I have long experience at playing jokes, a fresh mind is almost always able to come up with something original.

3.5.2. Windows Themes

In *Chapter 2*, you learned how to edit Windows themes. Hopefully you studied the material presented in that chapter carefully. If not, now would be a good idea to read it over again, just in case you missed something.

One of the things that you learned in *Chapter 2* is that all controls are just images. So what is to prevent you from changing these images and making Radio Buttons from Check Boxes, like shown in Fig. 3.5, or something along these lines?

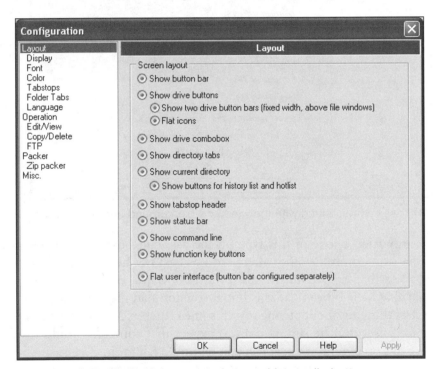

Fig. 3.5. All check box controls turned into radio buttons

This is done as follows:

1. Using a resource editor, open the theme file.
2. Select the resource with the **CheckBox** picture (BLUE_CHECKBOX), and save it to a file.
3. Find the **RadioButton** resource (BLUE_RADIOBUTTON), and also save it to a file.
4. Load the **CheckBox** image, instead of the **RadioButton**, and vice versa.

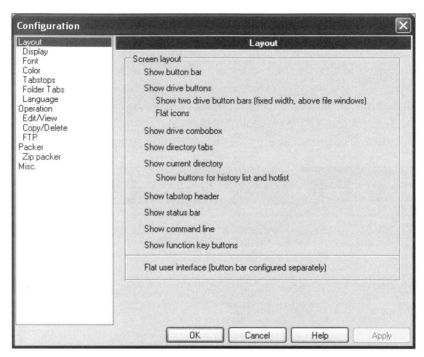

Fig. 3.6. All controls blend with the window's background and, thus, disappear

I recently tried a joke of this type on the assistant boss. The stream of comments emanating from his office afterward was best not heard by the sensitive and revealed a less-than-respectful attitude toward Bill Gates. What was worse, when he found out that he had been had, his initial reaction had me worrying that I might have to start thinking about buying myself some crutches. My assistant boss is quite an advanced user, but he simply did not expect that someone would try to play a joke like this on him or, even worse, that he would fall for it.

A couple of days later I made all of the resource components the same color as the dialog window background, which, naturally, made them all invisible. Take a look at Fig. 3.6. It shows a Windows Commander property window, in which only labels can be seen and with all controls simply gone. The same is the case in all windows. Had I made the controls white in the themes' resources, they would have shown up as white patches in windows.

There are a number of interesting things to be found in the Windows themes resources that will keep inquisitive minds and skilful hands busy. I have merely provided you with some food for thought. How you use it is up to you. The important thing is to turn on your imagination and steer it in the right direction.

3.5.3. Dialog Windows

The controls can be rearranged and the places of the labels for the **OK** and **Cancel** buttons changed for all of the windows found in resources. The user will wear his index finger off pressing the OK button, all to no avail.

For modal windows (these windows block their programs until closed), I would recommend that you remove their headers, so that the **Minimize**, **Restore**, and **Close** buttons will be inaccessible. While busy at making buttons disappear, the same can be done with the **Yes** and **Cancel** buttons. In this case, the program will wait for the user to press the **OK** button — which is simply not there. The program can only be closed by ending its process. I don't recommend removing the buttons altogether, however, because this may make it so that program will not launch. Setting their `Visible` property to `false`, however, will be quite effective. In fact, absolutely everything can be hidden in windows, leaving the user with nothing from which to choose.

Launch Restorator, or any other resource editor, and get down to work on editing everything you can get your hands on. Most programs written in Visual C++ have lots of interesting stuff within their resources that can be edited with ease. I can't give any specific advice in this respect, as this is a creative process and each case calls for an individual approach.

Just don't forget to make a backup copy of the file you intend to edit, in case some of your creative efforts render the program inoperable, which will come across as a lot more stupid than funny. If deleting files is your goal, simply do it the conventional way and leave the resources alone.

3.5.4. The System

In *Section 2.8*, you learned how to change some of the system settings, namely, how to edit the explorer.exe file. The resources of this file contain the main labels, pictures, and dialog windows that we see every day. Changing these will have a very strong effect on the user. For example, these resources contain the **Recycle Bin** and **My Computer** icons. Swapping their places will create quite an interesting effect, as most users usually don't read icon labels, but simply make their way around by the images. Of course, the labels can also be changed.

Edit all of the images and give them whatever labels you may fancy. I, however, recommend keeping your creative instincts within the bounds of decency, as a lack of sensitivity in this area could end up offending. For example, change labels to read something like *"Attention! Virus!"* or *"The Martians are coming!"* instead of something obscene. This will me more interesting and will better demonstrate your sense of humor and intelligence.

I like to edit the explorer.exe file, because I can do it on my machine and then slip the file into the victim's computer. Placing this file in the root folder of the C: drive will make the system use this file instead of its own. For the joke to work, the file infiltrated into the victim's computer must be from the same version of Windows that is installed on his/her machine. Explorer.exe from Windows XP will not work with Windows 9x and Windows 2000.

3.5.5. Summary

Editing labels, removing or switching messages, and rearranging control elements all work well on users of all types. Even experienced users are often stupefied when they encounter something unexpected, while someone with less of an idea can lapse into a prolonged coma altogether.

Your task in playing pranks with resources is to prepare the necessary files on your computer and then slip them onto the victim's computer.

In conclusion, I want to thank Bill Gates and his people for providing us with an operating system that makes playing jokes on our fellow man so such fun. Without question, this operating system provides a real hacker with more room to show off than any other.

3.6. Total Control

Suppose you know the administrator's login and password for another computer or for a network domain. In this case, even more elaborate and effective jokes can be played. First, create a mail account on your system with the same settings as the boss's. This is done in the following manner:

1. Right-click **My Computer** and select the **Manage** item in the context menu that appears. This will open the Computer Management window (Fig. 3.7). Its left panel contains a tree structure for computer components that can be managed.
2. In this tree, open the **Computer Management/System Tools/Local Users and Groups/Users** node. A list of all computer uses will open in the window's right panel.
3. Right-click on the free area in the right panel and select the **New User** item in the context menu that appears. A **New User** dialog window will open, in which you need to create a new user with the same user name and password as the administrator for the computer that you want to control. You also need to remove the check mark from the **User must change password at next logon** box.
4. Save the changes. Reboot the computer and enter the system under the login and password you have just created.

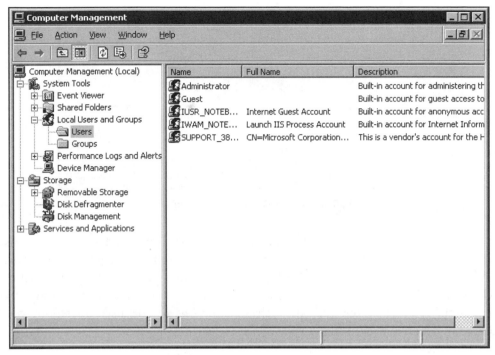

Fig. 3.7. The **Computer Management** window

Right-click **My computer** again, and select the **Manage** item in the context menu that appears. Right-click **Computer Management**, and select the **Connect to another computer** item. This will open a **Select Computer** dialog window (Fig. 3.8). Select the computer that you want to manage, and click the **OK** button.

The **Computer Management** window should not change much. Only the name of the computer being managed will change. The nodes in the tree in the left panel will be practically the same, but will refer to the other computer. Now you are all set to play a multitude of practical jokes.

One of the best tricks is ejecting the CD-ROM tray. The effect is truly wonderful when the unsuspecting user suddenly sees the CD-ROM tray open. Selecting the **Computer Management/Storage/Removable Storage/Libraries** node will show all of the CD-ROM drives in the right panel. Right-click any of them, and select the **Inject** item in the context menu that appears. This will open the **Media Inject Wizard** dialog window. At this point, all that it offers is some information. Pressing the **Next** button opens the CD-ROM tray. Pressing the Next button again will close the tray.

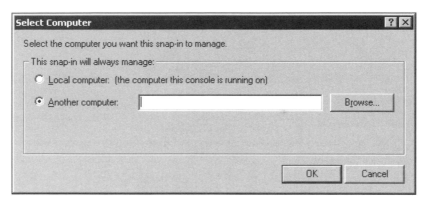

Fig. 3.8. The **Select Computer** dialog window

You can also start disk defragmentation on the controlled computer. This will make the hard drive of the remote computer toil at optimizing its contents. The computer will work slower during the optimization but, in the end, the victim will likely come out a winner. Because the files become optimized, the computer may actually work faster after the defragmentation, so the user on whom you played this joke may even thank you.

3.7. Software Jokes

The most effective jokes are those played using software. I have been developing software for a long time and sometimes like to create a little something entertaining. If you want to learn how to create such programs yourself, I recommend that you read my book *Hackish C++ Pranks & Tricks* published in 2004 by A-LIST. If you are not inclined toward writing your own software, you can take advantage of ready-made solutions, plenty of which can be found on the Internet.

I consider RJL Software (**www.rjlsoftware.com**) to be one of the most entertaining software development companies. Their site offers a plethora of joke utilities that can bring a smile to the face of even the dourest character.

These can be downloaded from the following page: **http://www.rjlsoftware.com/ software/entertainment**. The programs offered do not even have to be installed: They are simply launched for execution. When launched, the programs do not show on the task bar and cannot be closed conventionally. To close one of these programs, you have to terminate its process by way of the **Task Manager**, which is called by pressing the <Ctrl>+<Alt>+<Del> key combination. If your operating system is Windows 2000/2003, this will open a window with buttons to select the desired action. Select **Task Manager** to launch **Windows Task Manager** (Fig. 3.9). (In Windows XP, the three-finger combination opens **Windows Task Manager** window right away.) Open the **Processes** tab in this window, and find the program that you need to terminate in the process list. Select it, and click the **End Process** button.

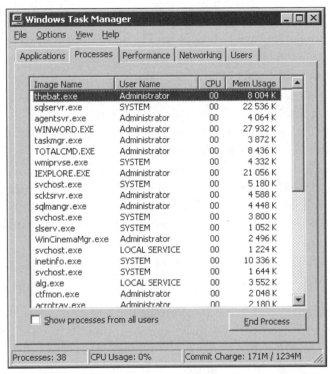

Fig. 3.9. The **Windows Task Manager** dialog window

Another way to close a gag program from RJL is to move the mouse cursor into the upper left corner of your screen, which will make the **About** window of the program appear. Closing the window will close the program.

I think the funniest RJL programs are the following:

❒ *AVoid.* Having started it, you will not be able to click the **Start** button: It will run away from you by moving along the taskbar.

❒ *Click Start.* This program clicks the **Start** button every 45 seconds.

❑ *Cursor Fun.* Makes the cursor move randomly around the screen, confusing the user.

❑ *Clippy.* This simulation of the same name MS Office assistant pops up about every minute in the lower right corner, offering asinine advice.

❑ *Fake Format.* Simulates formatting the specified hard drive. Uses an authentic-looking Windows format window to scare the unsuspecting user to death.

❑ *Fake Delete.* This program simulates deleting in a folder. If you have already tried Fake Format on someone, try Fake Delete on him or her as well. If the user is still alive after Fake Format, Fake Delete will finish the job.

❑ *Fake Start Menu.* This program replaces the standard Windows taskbar with a clone that does not react to any user actions.

❑ *Headache.* Makes the screen flash black and white. To close, press any key or click the mouse.

❑ *Open/Close CD.* Just as the name suggests, this opens and closes CD-ROM tray. A simple but effective way to confuse any user.

❑ *Rotate.* This little software gem flips the desktop into all sorts of positions. Of course, it does this not with the real desktop, but with a picture of it that it uses as the wallpaper. The program is closed by pressing <Alt>+<F4>.

❑ *Show – Hide Desktop.* The program periodically hides and displays the desktop icons.

❑ *Time Traveler.* This masterpiece changes the computer clock to a random value every 30 seconds.

I personally consider *Floppy Madness* to be the best of the RJL prank programs. The program tries to access the A: drive every minute. But, when the user inserts a diskette into the drive, he or she gets a message that "The diskette cannot be read." This message can be customized, making the joke even more entertaining. To change the message, specify `setup` parameter (FLOPPY.EXE setup) when launching the program. Here are some suggested messages:

❑ Finally, I was beginning to think you would never feed me.
❑ Thanks for the sandwich.
❑ This diskette stinks. Don't you have anything fresher?
❑ Format you say? No problem.
❑ Is the diskette really empty or I am just seeing things?
❑ You read this diskette, I've had enough already.

One of the advantages of RJL software is the small size of the programs, which makes it easy to slip them into someone's computer. Program files can be sent by e-mail or placed on the desktop for a curious user to launch them himself.

But RJL Software does not hold the monopoly on writing gag software. There is also Dewa Soft, with its Key Panic. You give the program a word, any word, and it will generate an executable file, about 70 KB in size. When this file is launched, it will replace every word entered from the keyboard with the given word. So, if your word is mum (or whatever it may be), that is what the content of the victim's document will be. The program can be downloaded from the following site: **http://dewasoft.com/Software/KeyPanic/KeyPanic.html**. The only drawback is that it is shareware and, unless you pay the authors $10, it will inform the user of its presence. Paying up guarantees the stealth required for it to be effective.

You can find many various prank programs on the Internet, but creating one on your own is much more fun. If you want to learn how to write joke programs, or just to learn programming, I again recommend that you read *Hackish C++ Pranks & Tricks*. You will find many ready solutions there that will allow you create something on your own, even if your abilities aren't on par with those of a professional programmer.

3.8. Conclusion

Perfection has no limits other than your own imagination. If you share my penchant for playing jokes on your friends, coworkers, and acquaintances, and have a good joke, share it with me by sending it to me to the following e-mail address: horrific@vr-online.ru. I collect good computer jokes and will definitely try your joke on the assistant boss. I'll get back to you with his reaction.

Just remember one thing: A good joke must not destroy data or hardware. Things like a temporary shut down or hanging the operating system are acceptable, but mangling data or burning up hardware are not. This is unethical, if not outright criminal. Besides, if this is the effect you are after, it is easier to simply smash a monitor with a hammer. This will be more interesting and easier than thinking up some sophisticated joke. Also, before playing a joke on someone, make sure that the victim has a sense of humor and will take your joke the right way. Some people may take your attempts to lighten things up a little too personally.

And don't forget to share your ideas with me. If you have something original, spread a good thing around and let the people know about it. Play a joke on your neighbor before he or she revels in the opportunity to get you first ☺.

Chapter 4: Hacker Advice

In this chapter, you will learn some hacker secrets. This will allow you to squeeze the most out of your computer and to increase your efficiency working with your system. We will consider not only how to work with the computer, but also with the Windows operating system and the Internet.

Personally, I spend almost all of my waking hours online, and emerge from this state only to eat and sleep. Therefore, being able to get the most out of my computer and the Internet is very important for me. During my many years of work, I have acquired many methods for increasing the efficiency of my work on the computer. I want to share these with you here.

In this chapter, I will teach you how to optimize your computer's operations to make it work faster by overclocking the processor in various ways. But, first, we need to take a look at some security issues.

4.1. How to Avoid Virus Infection

This is a major sore point for many Internet users. Many people think that installing a good antivirus program will make their computer safe from being penetrated by malicious programs. To a great extent this is true, but no virus defense is more than 10-percent effective. Why is this so? It is very simple. Most antivirus programs cannot detect a new virus, even when they use heuristic analyses.

New viruses spread very rapidly and infect all computers that get in their way. The chances are nine out of 10 that, unless you have proper virus defenses installed, your computer will be infected by any new virus strain that hits it. Some time after the outbreak, Internet users update their antiviral bases and remove the virus from their computers. The chances of being infected by the same virus again become much lower, as the new databases will likely detect it.

As it turns out, antivirus programs deal with infections, whereas we need a means to prevent infection occurring in the first place. A new virus may turn out to be especially malicious and destroy information before you have a chance to update your databases and neutralize it. In such a case, it will be too late to treat the infected computer.

In all of the time that I have been working with computers, no virus has been able to carry out its dirty work on one of my computers. They may get into my computer by way of e-mail or the Internet, but they are immediately rounded up, in most cases without even the assistance of any antivirus utilities. I do, of course, have an antivirus program installed, and I update the databases regularly. In order to economize on computer resources, I do not, however, keep it running at all times. What I do is run periodic sweeps of the system. This reduces the chances of infection but, unfortunately, does not eliminate them completely.

Information about current virus activity can be found on the site of one of the largest antivirus software developers: Kaspersky Laboratories (**www.kaspersky.com**) (Fig. 4.1). The green virus alert code means that activity is low. This code is displayed only when old viruses, for which there are "vaccines," are roaming the Net, or new variants created on the basis of older examples are making the rounds.

When a new virus comes out and starts infecting systems, the virus alert code is raised. This, however, does not make things much easier for us. Having been warned about a new virus, all you can do to protect yourself from it is turn off your computer and wait for your antivirus utility developer to update its databases. You can then download them and continue surfing the Net carefree until next alert.

But there are more effective and less painful defense methods than this. However, to learn them, you have to learn about the nature of your enemy first — to find out how it is built and what methods it uses to penetrate computers uses. Only then can the problem be solved effectively.

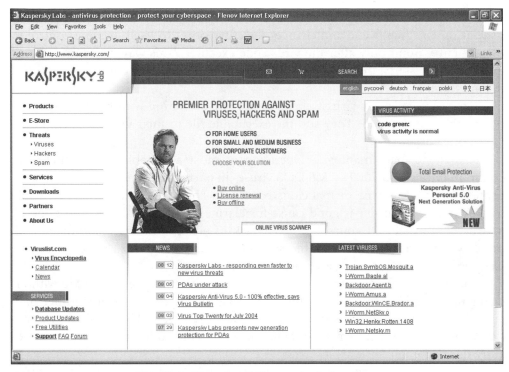

Fig. 4.1. The site of Kaspersky Laboratory

Most of the following materials will help you to protect your computer not only from viruses, but also from Trojan horses and, to a certain extent, from spam. You should be able not only to defend yourself against an invasion, but also to know how to isolate viruses or neutralize Trojan horses. If you are a network administrator and some cracker writes a virus especially for your network, to steal some information for example, no antivirus program will be able to detect and neutralize it. In this case, the security of your network depends on your knowledge and skills in detecting and fighting cracker tricks.

4.1.1. How Viruses Spread

When we were considering program structure, one of the things mentioned was the executable file header. This header contains the entry point: a program address, from which it starts its execution. When a virus piggybacks on a program, it adds itself at the program's end and changes the entry point to itself, passing control to the old entry point only after the virus code executes. This way, when an infected executable file starts, the virus code executes first, after which control is passed to the program.

Some especially lazy virus-writers do not like bothering with headers. They do it the other way around: They add the executable file to their virus, that is, the virus's body goes first.

This is the main manner of operation of most attachable viruses that were common until about 2000 — MS DOS viruses in particular. The least you can do to protect against this type of malicious code is to check the headers of executable files. A modified header is good cause for alarm, as this may have been done by a virus or a worm. Of course, keeping track of all file headers is a difficult task to carry out manually. At least the size of the main programs, however, can be checked, for it changes when a virus attaches itself to a file.

It is possible, though, for a virus to attach itself to an executable file without changing its header. In this case, the virus code can be contained in another program. The resulting effect is similar to the DLL execution: The infected program loads another program, which contains the executable code of the virus and executes this code.

As already mentioned, viruses of this type ruled until the end of the 1990s. In those days, the Internet was not as developed as it is now, and viruses spread mainly via diskettes or files downloaded from Bulletin Board Systems (BBS), a common means of information exchange at the time. Some viruses infect not programs, but boot sectors of disks or diskettes, and execute as soon as the computer boots. In this case, the virus loads into the memory and starts scanning for executable files, infecting all files of this type on the given computer.

Why infect all the files? The answer is very simple. In the MS DOS environment, there was only one means, by which to start a program during the computer boot: listing the program needed in the autoexec.bat file. This file executes automatically when the computer boots and can launch other programs that are listed in it. But, if all viruses listed the programs they infected, they could easily be detected and neutralized by even the simplest of antivirus utilities. This is why a boot-sector virus would try to infect all of the files on a computer. Launching any program would then also launch the virus.

In Windows, which has replaced DOS as the mainstream operating system for personal computers, viruses have more ways to camouflage themselves. They can also launch automatically when the computer boots, by placing themselves in the Windows' startup utility. So they no longer need to scan the file system in search of executable files to infect: The operating system will itself launch the malicious code every time it boots. But viruses of this type are no longer popular, because effective means of smoking them out of the startup area have been developed.

In addition to numerous ways of launching files automatically, Windows has many files that launch automatically when the system boots – the system Dynamic-Link Libraries (DLL), for example. This makes life easier for viruses. Whereas in earlier times all programs had to be infected because it was not known which would be launched, now it is enough to infect only one of the libraries or an important executable system file. This means no more tedious work scanning for executables.

So, if before the evil could hide only in executable files, now it has spread to dynamic libraries as well. Dynamic libraries have one big shortcoming: Code can be added to them that will execute when the library starts. Adding virus code to an automatically launched library will also launch this virus. Correspondingly, the number of potential loopholes, by which the system can be accessed, has increased greatly.

But dynamic libraries are not the only evils. To make lives of their customers easier, Microsoft has built Visual Basic support into many of its products. Almost all Microsoft Office programs make extensive use of the capabilities provided by Visual Basic. Being able to expand the capabilities of your system and make your life easier is, undoubtedly, very convenient. For crackers, however, it is just another way to get into your computer.

Most Internet users had grown used to the idea that only executable files presented virus infection danger, while virtually nobody could imagine that a threat could be posed by text documents or electronic spreadsheets. This is why the first viruses embedded into Word documents or into e-mail processed by the Microsoft Outlook mail program infected a huge number of computers within a very short period of time. Neither users nor the best antiviral utility developers were ready for this turn of events.

I personally consider writing viruses one of the most stupid pursuits a person can engage in and, therefore, have never approved of it. This is the type of behavior exhibited by some children who, when they see that one of their playmates has a new toy, try to take it away or break it. This is exactly how crackers act in trying to deprive others of their toys or, what is even more threatening, their means for earning a living.

Today viruses spread mostly via the Internet, and diskettes or other removable media are practically never involved. E-mails in general, and mass mailings (read "spam") in particular, are the main vehicles. A typical scenario is something like the following. You receive a letter with an attachment and some intriguing message that leads you to open this attachment. But opening the attachment will launch the virus, which is what it actually is. What it does once it has been launched depends only on how imaginative or sick its creator was. One of its possible actions is to mail itself to all of the addresses in your address book.

4.1.2. How to Protect Yourself

With viruses you never know where the next trouble will come from, but I have never had an antivirus utility in the startup menu of my computer. As for manual scanning for viruses, the last time I did this was about six years ago. Despite this seeming lack of protection, no virus has ever enjoyed the liberty of my system for more than five minutes.

Back in the days of MS DOS, I scanned my disk about once a year — and then only to ease my conscience. As you already know, the main sources of infection back then were BBS and diskettes. I did not use BBS, so there was no threat to my computer from that direction. As for diskettes, I would always scan for viruses any diskette, even one given to me by a close friend, before opening it. Friends simply may not have known that their computer was infected and might unwillingly have brought me an infected file.

Nowadays, I do not use diskettes and do not exchange executable files with friends. I recommend obtaining all software from the original source, that is, from the official Internet sites. Only official sources can give a 90-percent guarantee that their products are virus-free. Of course, there have been incidents of well-known companies inadvertently spreading viruses with their products. However, these are very isolated and rare cases and the Internet community detects and corrects mistakes of this type very rapidly.

Do Not Use Well-Known Software

As already mentioned, the main vehicle for spreading viruses is currently the Internet, or, to be more exact, e-mail. To protect myself on this front, I use The Bat (**http://www.ritlabs.com**) as my mail program. It does not support scripts and does not have Visual Basic for Applications or VBScript embedded (the Visual Basic script language can launch an e-mail attachment). Although most mail clients now have defenses against launching programs by VBScript, cracks are sometimes found in those defenses and viruses gain a back door into the system. Of course, sometimes weak spots are also discovered in this program, but The Bat is not a widely used program, so there are practically no viruses in existence that are designed specifically to exploit its vulnerabilities. My advice is not to use the most popular programs, because they are also the most popular among virus-writers. The fact that there are practically no viruses floating around to wreak havoc on Linux does not mean that this operating system has some unique antivirus properties. It is simply the result of the fact that this operating system is not very widely used, so there are not very many computers to infect. Any cracker seeks to become popular — or at least notorious — among the largest possible audience and, therefore, specializes in Windows as the most widely used among home users. But even if you work with a program that is way down on the popularity list, do not become overconfident in the security it gives you. Different programs can contain the same types of errors, so your computer could become exposed to attacks. Suppose that, in your Internet surfing, you use a simple browser that supports only text and, seemingly, cannot be attacked by viruses. But, in order to receive data from the server, this browser uses the HTTP protocol, which, in turn, is layered over the TCP/IP protocol. Should an error be discovered in one of these protocols that can be used to gain access to your local hard drive, the fact that your browser is 100-percent secure will be of little relevance. In this case, breaking into your system will not be very difficult. But the not most popular products are like a two-edged sword. Suppose that an error was discovered in the browser you use, but the developer no longer supports the product. There will be no update available to correct the error, and switching to another product may cost you both time and money. So, in order to avoid this sort of problem, you should opt for products that are more likely than not to be around for a while. These are usually products from companies that rank second or third on the popularity scale, but not those at the bottom of the list. These weaklings are the first ones to go belly up.

Update Regularly

If the capabilities offered by the most popular programs are a must for you, update these programs regularly. Microsoft is the best with respect to offering updates for its products. For all the flood of invectives in its address, the people at Redmond pay the closest attention to customer support and regularly provide updates to patch errors in their products. Software from every developer has bugs but, because the software from the most popular companies is scrutinized the most, it seems like their software has more errors, which is not the case. Moreover, when such errors do crop up, Microsoft swiftly reacts to reduce their negative impact.

Updating your operating system and the main application software on a regular basis also allows you to protect yourself from viruses. The results of studies conducted by different analytical companies concerning software use vary, but they all show that most Internet users do not update their software regularly. Some users do not do this because of laziness, others because of a weak Internet link, while others fail to do this because they are using pirated software versions. Virus-writers take advantage of this. Very often, when a new vulnerability in some software is discovered, new viruses exploiting this appear virtually at the same instant. So, when an update that fixes an existing breach comes out, don't hesitate to install it in your system. Having said all of this about lazy users and conscientious Microsoft, however, I believe that the greater share of the blame for viruses spreading through the loopholes in Windows security lies not with the former, but with the latter. They put out quite a few updates and it is very difficult to figure out, which of them should be installed. Microsoft ought to inform all of its customers in a timely manner about bugs that have been discovered and announce the most critical ones publicly. In most cases, the company tries not to publicize its errors, which is not a responsible attitude. Crackers are constantly on the look out for vulnerabilities and know more about them than the average user.

Sure, the Microsoft brass may claim that they inform their users via mailings. But this method hardly seems adequate. E-mail addresses change constantly, so this method is not particularly dependable. Other, more reliable methods, such as television or radio broadcasts, should be employed. Only then can computer virus protection be enhanced and the virus activity code permanently turned green.

Trust but Verify

It is a very good idea never to trust e-mail messages you receive. Never, ever open e-mail attachments! Even if your friend's address is in the **From** field, there is no guarantee that the message is actually from your friend. Even if it is, this does not mean that it is safe to open the attachment: Your friend's computer may be infected by a virus that sends messages bearing his or her name to everyone in the address book, meaning that you might become a victim. Virus-writers understand their social engineering very well and go to great lengths to make their messages intriguing enough to get you to open the attachment. I often receive messages with attachments that are seemingly from my friends or partners, with subjects like *"Urgently check this proposal!"*, but I never do this until I make sure it is safe.

Attachments

If you receive an attachment with an e-mail, take the little time involved to check with the sender that he or she did indeed send the message. Viruses can only send messages, they cannot send confirmations.

How can you determine what types of attached files can contain viruses? Text files of the TXT type, images of the JPG, GIF, BMP types, and audio and video files of the WAV, MP3, API types presently pose no danger. However, there is no 100-percent guarantee that files in these formats will not become susceptible to infection in the future. Given certain conditions and using special programs, viruses can infect files of any type. For the time being, hackers are restrained by too many conditions. Nevertheless, when source codes for Windows were stolen, a virus named Angel appeared that infected computers through specially constructed BMP files when users attempted to view them.

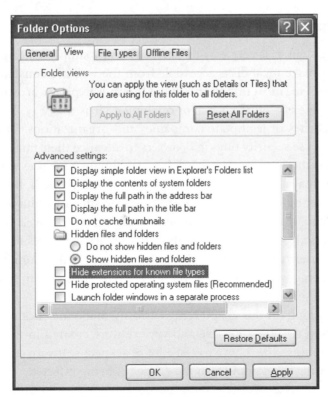

Fig. 4.2. The **Folder Options** dialog window

When examining an e-mail attachment, you have to be certain of that file's extension type. By default, the operating systems of the Windows 9*x*/NT/2000/XP family do not show extensions of the registered file types. That is, if a file has the EXE extension, only the file name will be shown. Hackers take advantage of this fact and give files double extensions. For example, the system will hide the EXE extension in update.jpg.exe, showing only the update.exe part. This can trick people into trying to view the supposed picture and, as a result, launching this file and infecting the computer.

To avoid potential double extension problems, I recommend that you disable the feature hiding extensions of registered file types. This can be done in a number of ways. One of these is to select the **Folder Options** item in **Control Panel**. In the same-name dialog window (Fig. 4.2), select the **View** tab and remove the check mark from the **Hide extension for known file types** box.

Untrustworthy Sites

In addition to e-mail, it is very easy to catch a virus by simply visiting web sites. Because bugs that make local disks accessible from the web are constantly discovered in Internet browsers (most important, in the Internet Explorer browser that is most widely used), there is a good chance of catching a virus this way. I personally visit only the official sites of legitimate companies and organizations. They play by the rules and do not use security bugs in browsers to advance their purposes illegally.

Most personal pages are not used for illegitimate purposes either, although sometimes they may serve as the proving grounds for hackers. If, however, you like visiting sites offering cracks, warez, porn, or other sites of a dubious nature, the chances of picking up something undesirable during your travels increase significantly. In this case, you need to install the latest security updates to your operating system and browser regularly and to keep the antivirus utility running at all times. But even complying with these rules will not prevent your system from rather rapidly collecting all sorts of trash.

As I was working on this chapter, my curiosity made me click on a certain link and, immediately, two files, xxx.exe and yyy.exe were created in the C: drive root. Writing books of this type, I have to test a lot of suspect software and Internet sites, constantly exposing my computer to the danger of being infected.

Once I had to write an article about pornography sites. To gather research material for this, I had to surf the Net quite a bit, after which I had to spend about a week cleaning strange things from my computer. Most of these did not work, because they needed to be started manually, but their mere presence did not make me particularly happy.

My E-Mail is My Castle

I always maintain four or five mail boxes: one for work, one for communicating with the friends, one for the general public, and one for trash. I have had my work mailbox for six years and only my coworkers know this address. During all of this time, I have taken care to keep this address as private as possible and have been successful so far. As the result, the number of viruses and spam messages coming to this mailbox is virtually nil. The address for friends is more widely known and viruses sometimes are sent there. The other two addresses are widely known to general public and I receive megabytes of infected mail in them during periods of heightened virus activity.

Periodically, there comes a time when the amount of undesirable mail I receive on these boxes significantly exceeds the amount of legitimate mail. I then simply obtain new mailboxes for these purposes and start with a clean slate. Yes, it does make things a bit inconvenient for some of my acquaintances, but they understand.

I use the trash mailbox for cases where I need to provide my e-mail address to someone I don't know, such as for registering on an Internet site. This address is instantly spread among spammers and I have to change it regularly. But this does not create any inconvenience for anyone.

With this kind of separation of my e-mail boxes, I am especially careful with messages arriving to my public mailboxes and delete those with attachments at once, regardless of what format they might be in. Even if a file is in a format that, in principle, cannot contain viruses (e.g., TXT format), I delete it without opening it.

Fake URL

Because my addresses are well known to the general public, messages of dubious nature often come to them. Just a short time ago, I received a letter, supposedly from my bank, asking me to change the information used to access my account. The contents of the letter were as follows:

The Letter Asking Me to Change My Bank Account Access Information

Dear SunTrust valued member:

❏ Due to concerns for the safety and integrity of the Internet Banking community we have issued this warning message.

❏ It has come to our attention that your account information needs to be updated due to inactive accounts, frauds, and spoof reports. If you could please take 5–10 minutes out of your online experience and renew your records, you will not run into any future problems with the online service. However, failure to update your records will result in account deletion.

❏ Once you have updated your account records, your online banking account will not be interrupted and will continue as normal.

❏ Please follow the link below and renew your account information. **https://www2.suntrust.com/cgi_w/cfm/personal/account_access/account_access.cfm**.

❏ SunTrust Internet Banking.

Since I do not use this bank's services, it was obvious that something about the message was not right. At first glance, the link to the web site at the bottom of the letter seemed to be real. But placing the mouse cursor over the URL line made the real address, the one that will load if the link is clicked on, appear. For some reason, it changed from **www2.suntrust.com** to **http://211.202.3.208**. Having checked this address, I discovered that the server was located in an entirely different place and was simply made to look like the bank's site.

The hackers made a big mistake using such a simple way to hide the address. It would have been much more effective to register an address such as **www2.santrust.com** or something similar; then the dummy address would not be so noticeable, the difference being just one letter. An IP address immediately rouses suspicions, whereas it is unlikely that anyone would notice a small difference in a domain name given in the text.

Break-ins using domain names that closely resemble the real McCoy were very popular several years ago. When Internet access was still relatively expensive, user passwords were often obtained in this way. For example, a user would receive a message that was supposedly sent by the provider, requesting that the user send his or her password. Suppose that the real address was support@provider.com. The hacker would set up a domain similar to the real one, for example **provader.com**, and the address shown in the message asking for access information would be given as support@provader.com. A large number of users fell for messages like this because they did not notice the small difference in the address.

Attacks of this type were easy to organize before 1995 because, until that point, any domain name could be registered for free. Further, Internet addresses were still a novel concept for many users, so they seldom attributed much importance to these small differences. Now that there is a charge for registration and all of the names that are more or less similar to those of well-known companies have been bought up, it is much more difficult to register a site trying to capitalize on a name similar to the genuine item.

Nowadays, break-ins of this type are a rarity, but there is a danger that this could just be the calm before the storm. Users have forgotten about simple break-in methods like the address swap, so hackers might try to take advantage of their complacency. Moreover, multitudes of new users every day move onto the Internet, many of whom not only have never run into this penetration method, but have not even heard about it. To return to the message asking for my bank account information, had I entered these data at the stated site, there is no doubt that these data would have fallen into the hands of a cracker.

And, while this method was used in the past to steal Internet access passwords, the rising popularity of e-commerce means that this method can be used increasingly to steal financial information.

4.1.3. Treatment

Sooner or later, even the most heavily protected computers, equipped with the best antivirus utilities, become infected. It happens to me all the time. So, if despite all of your protection measures your computer still gets infected, to "cure" it you just have to perform a few regular, simple procedures (in addition to those described in *Section 4.1.2*). This is the preferable alternative to having an antivirus utility running constantly in the background.

As you already know, a program written especially to compromise a particular system contains unique code and, more likely than not, will go undetected by antivirus utilities. In this case, the security of your computer will depend on your skill in correctly identifying and neutralizing the malfeasant program.

The latter is not that difficult: You simply terminate the program and delete all its files. To determine which file to delete is much more difficult.

The System Disk Root

Check the contents of your system disk root regularly. You must know the purpose of each file and folder here and be able to notice any changes. In order to see all of the contents, you must turn on the **Show hidden files and folders** option in the folder settings. This can be done in several ways. One way is to double click on the **Folder Options** item in Control Panel. This will open the **Folder Options** dialog window (Fig. 5.2). Select the **View** tab and put a check mark in the **Show hidden files and folders** box.

There must not be files of the EXE or PIF format in the disk root. The only COM file that has the right to be in the C: disk root is ntdetect.com. All other files should have the extensions SYS, INI, BIN, or BAT. With the exception of the BAT files, these files cannot be executed.

Files with the BAT extension cannot be viruses. They can, however, launch executable files, meaning that they can launch viruses. This is why you should also keep an eye on these files. There can be only one BAT file in the system disk root: autoexec.bat.

To make the task of monitoring the contents of the system disk root easier, never install programs or copy anything to the root. Create separate folders for this.

Startup

Viruses can hide anywhere in the file system, but they most often take up residence in the system folders or the system disk root. If the disk root is easy to keep an eye on (there are not that many files there), the task is much more difficult for the system folders (\Windows, \Windows\system, \Windows\system32) because of the numerous executable files in these directories. Viruses often attempt to get into the startup folder, which makes our task of detecting them easier. Windows 9*x*/ XP/2003 (but not Windows 2000) have a utility called msconfig that can be used to find out what programs start automatically when the system boots.

The utility is started by selecting the **Start/Run** menu sequence and entering *msconfig* in the dialog window that appears. Clicking the **OK** button will open the program's main window. It has several tabs, but we are interested in the one labeled **Startup**. Open this tab, and you will see the window shown in Fig. 4.3.

You should know what all of the programs listed on this list do. Actually, even if some program on this list is disabled, it will not disrupt Windows operation. It may make an icon in the system tray disappear or disable some feature. The former is more likely.

The list is divided into the following three columns:

❑ **Startup Item.** An arbitrary name for the launched program. This is most often the program's name, while it is sometimes even the name of the developer.
❑ **Command.** The executed command of the file path.
❑ **Location.** The location of the program's launcher.

Keep track of the programs in this list. If you see something here that was not put there by yourself or a program that you have installed, delete the line immediately. Strange execution file names should also be scrutinized.

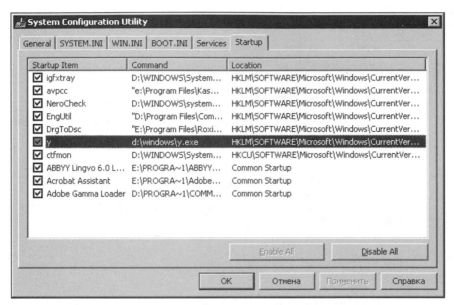

Fig. 4.3. The startup program list window

There is a line in the list shown in Fig. 4.3 that launches a program named *y* and has the file name y.exe. It is highly unlikely that a legitimate software developer would name a program or a file in this manner. This should set off alarm bells. To check the suspicious program, remove the mark from its box and reboot the computer.

The **Location** column shows the location, from which the program is launched. The values in here can be the following:

❑ **Common Startup**. Programs are launched from the **Start/Programs/Startup** menu. These programs are easy to check, even without specialized utilities.

❑ A registry path. In this case, you can check the corresponding registry key, using the **regedit** program.

If for some reason your system does not have the msconfig utility, you will have to check for startup programs yourself in the registry. They can be found in the following registry keys:

HKEY_CURRENT_USER\Software\Microsoft\Windows\CurrentVersion\Run
HKEY_CURRENT_USER\Software\Microsoft\Windows\CurrentVersion\RunOnce
HKEY_LOCAL_MACHINE\Software\Microsoft\Windows\CurrentVersion\Run

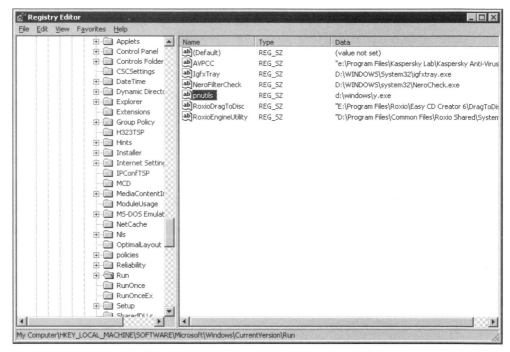

Fig. 4.4. The registry list of automatically launched programs

In Windows 9*x*, programs can be launched at startup by the system.ini and win.ini files. This operating system will always have the msconfig utility, which shows the corresponding files. With the help of the msconfig program or using the registry, we can discover the name of the executable files (Fig. 4.4).

Remember that you have to delete not only the registry reference to the program, but also the file itself. It is possible that there are other ways, by which it can be launched, meaning that everything may be restored.

If the file cannot be deleted, the most likely explanation is that it is being executed at the moment and has to be terminated. This is done as follows:

❏ Press <Ctrl>+<Alt>+<Del>. If you have a server operating system, a window will appear with six buttons representing the actions that can be performed. Click the **Task Manager** button. In a non-server operating system, this window comes up immediately after pressing the three-key combination.

❏ In the **Task Manager**, select the **Processes** tab (Fig. 4.5).

❏ Find the needed process, and press the **End Process** button.

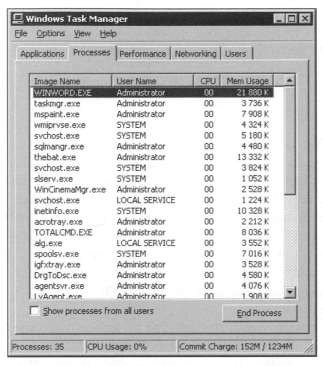

Fig. 4.5. Task Manager: the running processes

When checking what programs are running, pay close attention to every letter in their names. Crackers are very good at disguising their wares. For example, I once wrote a Trojan horse to reboot my boss' computer. I named the file Internat32.exe, and placed it into the startup folder via the registry. For a whole month, nobody could figure out why the computer was acting so strangely. The computer was tested by professional administrators, but not even they could find anything. The system actually has a very important program, named Internat.exe, so none of the administrators even suspected that something might be wrong with the file named Internat32.exe, even though the system contains no such file.

A couple of years later, there was another case, where I was given the task of writing a program to monitor, which programs the employees of our company used on their computers. I called the Trojan scanbisk.exe and, again, no one noticed it. There happens to be a legitimate utility named `scandisk.exe` in the system, used to check disks, and nobody noticed that the impostor had letter *b*, instead of *d*, in its name.

Crackers use the same letter trick to disguise their programs as legitimate software. Letters can be replaced with similar looking numbers. For example, letter O can be replaced with number 0. The difference is very difficult to detect with only a cursory glance at the file name, but this will be an entirely different file. The file is then placed into the same folder as the program it is masquerading as, and nine out of 10 users will be fooled.

Services

In Windows 2000/XP/2003, viruses and Trojan horses have a new way to start at the system boot: They become a service. Services are programs that execute in the background, invisible to the user, and can start automatically when the system is booted.

Many beginners are reluctant to configure Windows services, for fear of accidentally damaging something critical for to the system's own operation. This is why crackers have been devoting more and more attention lately to writing malicious code masquerading as services. Personally, I have not run into viruses of this type yet, but it is probably just a matter of time before one of these unwelcome guests visits my computer. One may have already actually arrived and I may simply not yet be aware of the fact.

The first virus programs camouflaging as services were so-called "spyware" programs, designed to perform illegal information-gathering operations on other people's computers. There are many other varieties of things that go bump in the night, things that can make you lose sleep worrying what they might do to your computer or the information you store on it. So you have to check your services regularly for unexpected, unwelcome lodgers.

The services are controlled from the **Services** utility. To open **Services**, click on **Start**, point to **Settings**, and then click on **Control Panel**. Double-click on **Administrative Tools**, and then on **Services**. The window that opens is shown in Fig. 4.6.

The services list is comprised of five columns:

❑ **Name**: a short name.
❑ **Description**: a description of the service function.
❑ **Status**: if the service is running, it marked as "Started" in this column field; otherwise, the field is blank.
❑ **Startup Type**: the way the service is started. The possible values in this field are **Automatic** (upon the system boot), **Manual**, and **Disabled** (the service cannot be started).

❏ **Log In As**: the account, under which the service runs. If the service has administrator rights specified in this field, it has access to all system resources; if a guest account is specified here, the service has limited rights. Most often, the local system is specified in this field. In this case, the service holds the rights of the account, under which the user enters the system.

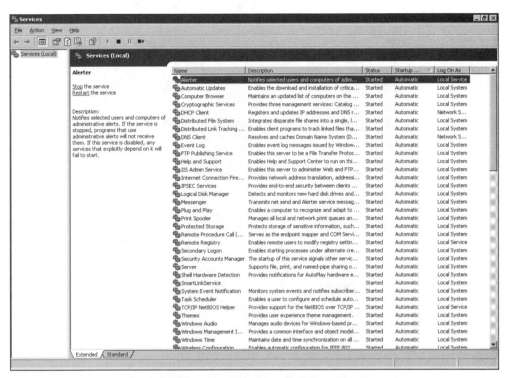

Fig. 4.6. The **Services** window

Don't be lazy. Investigate what each service does. There are currently numerous examples of malicious software that masquerade as services, and you should be able to neutralize these without relying on antivirus utilities.

If you see a service with a suspicious name, double click on it to open the service properties window (Fig. 4.7). On the **General** tab, the following information is available:

❏ **Service name**: a short service name.
❏ **Display name**: the name shown in the service list.

❑ **Description**: a short description of the service. The same description that can be seen in the information panel on the left of the extended service list.
❑ **Path to executable**. The path to the executable file used to start the given service. It is followed by the parameters passed to the service. These cannot be changed here.

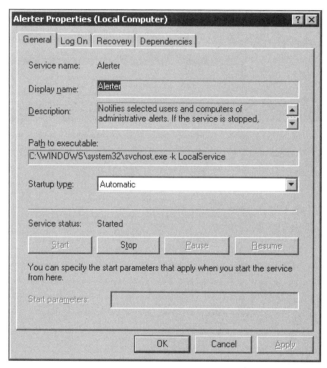

Fig. 4.7. Service properties

Everything displayed in this window is for information purposes only and cannot be edited. But this is what this book is about: To show you how to change things that seemingly cannot be changed. If necessary, any system parameter can be edited without developing calluses on your index finger as a result of excessive mouse clicking. All you need to do is to get into the registry and open the HKEY_LOCAL_MACHINE\SYSTEM\ControlSet001\Services key. All the services are located in this key and you can edit any of their parameters. The functions of the keys cannot be readily guessed from their names, so each key has to be selected and its exact name ascertained in the **DisplayName** parameter.

You can easily modify service descriptions with the help of the registry. If you want to change the startup parameters of a service, you should study the corresponding documentation. Study it closely, because if the parameters are incorrect the service may not start properly. It might not even start at all.

Looking at the registry, you can see that it has many more service keys than are present in the **Services** utility. As usual, Microsoft has provided us with the means to control some things, but has left most of them hidden. The main problem with this is that we cannot use regular means to determine, which services are running. Not all of them are shown. Some services are quite complex and are made up of several parts, possibly having two branches in the registry.

If I had my way, I would break the arms of a few programmers at Microsoft for this, or even better, burn them at stake, because all of this provides lots of places in which malicious code can hide. If viruses and other miscreant code do not use services extensively now, there is a good chance that, barring a good service monitoring facility, they might move from processes to services in a year or two.

The path to the service's executable file and the file name itself are shown in the **Path to executable** field. The service can be stopped by clicking on the **Stop** button, after which the service can be deleted safely. Even if the **Stop** button is not available, the service can still be deleted. In this case, the changes will not become effective right away, but only after rebooting.

A service is deleted from the system by launching the executable file with the /UNINSTALL parameter. After this, the file itself can be physically deleted from the disk.

To facilitate keeping track of changes in services, you can avail yourself of a very useful program called Ad-ware. It can be downloaded from **www.lavasoft.de**. I highly recommend this piece of software because it will hunt down all transgressors in services and the programs automatically launched at startup.

But even automating the malicious code detection process should not lull you into a false sense of security when hitting dubious Internet sites. New programs appear nowadays with the regularity of Microsoft patches that circumvent automated defenses. Consequently, it is a good idea to check the services periodically yourself.

Changing Parameters

If your computer has been infected by a Trojan horse, I recommend that you change all of your passwords after you have removed it from the system. Most

Trojan horse programs are written specifically to steal passwords. The first thing to change should be Windows passwords, then Internet access parameters and, finally, the passwords for your mailboxes. These are the passwords that Trojan horses are most often after.

If time allows, you should also change the passwords to the sites and forums, on which you are registered. It is possible that the Trojan horse had enough time to sniff out the data you entered into the browser and send it over to the author. Your credit card numbers and/or the passwords to your electronic purses may also have fallen pray to the ferreting code. Immediately replacing your credit cards might, of course, be a bit too paranoiac, and the associated expenses might be hard to justify. Do, however, keep an eye on charges on your cards and sound the alarm at the first hint of an unauthorized charge.

4.2. Full System Access Rights

When we considered computer jokes earlier, we often needed access to the victim's computer, with network access being the best option. But many users only share folders with nothing of interest in them over the network. Knowing the administrator's password to the victim's computer gives you automatic access to all of his or her disks. By entering this computer through the network neighborhood, all you can see are shared folders.

How can you access a disk then by knowing the administrator password? Type the following address in the network neighborhood address field: \\Name\c$. Here, *Name* is the name or the IP address of the computer. This is followed by a back slash and the name of the needed disk and the dollar sign. This way we can obtain full access to any disk that does not show up in the network neighborhood.

If your network employs Windows domains, domain administrators have full access rights to any computer in the domain by default. This way they can access any disk in the network in the manner we just described. This is no good.

Once, when I came to work for a company and entered my notebook onto the domain, within five minutes I noticed strange network activity on my computer. This was indicated by the blinking of the network connection icon in the tray, even though I was not sending or receiving anything over the network at the time. In addition, hard disk activity was too high.

Checking the connections revealed that it was a crooked local network administrator trying to rummage through my personal information and download my secret files. I did not have to worry much about him stealing my passwords because they are hidden in places, to which even myself have problems getting access. He could, however, steal the source codes for my programs or the electronic versions of my books. He could then post or sell them on the Internet and reap the profits of my months-long difficult labors. Of course, I am not a Bill Gates, but my source codes are my property and I have the strange notion that my toils must benefit me and not some nosey, sticky-fingered, crooked administrator.

As soon as I discovered that there was an intruder in my computer and determined his identity, I unplugged the network cable from the notebook. This was a simple but very effective way to break the connection and prevent the malefactor from downloading my data. Should you find yourself in a similar situation, you now know a simple way to deal with the problem.

My next task was to find the administrator in person and explain to him that what he did was not particularly nice. The women I shared my office with willingly informed me that the sysadmin's office was nearby and, two minutes later, I was massaging the kidneys of the scrawny youngster who had dared to trespass on my turf. Having finished with introductions, I politely asked him to delete all of the stuff he had copied from my hard disk. I supervised the process personally.

To avoid similar problems, you need to disable network access by outside administrators to you computer. This is done as follows:

❏ Right-click on **My Computer** and select the **Manage** item in the context menu that appears. This will open the **Computer Management** window (Fig. 4.8). Its left panel contains a tree structure for computer components that can be managed.

❏ In this tree, open the **Computer Management/System Tools/Local Users and Groups/Groups** node. A list of all available groups will open in the window's right panel. Locate the **Administrators** group, and double click on it. This will open the **Administrators Properties** dialog window (Fig. 4.9), which lists all accounts with administrator rights on the given computer.

❏ If you use the administrator account, delete all accounts except yours. If you have your own account, leave it and the **Administrator** account.

Now no domain administrator will be able to access your disks, unless he or she knows the password of your local system administrator.

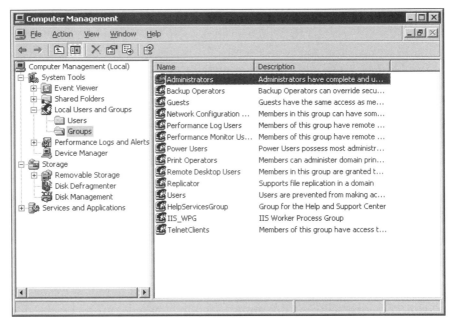

Fig. 4.8. The **Computer Management** window

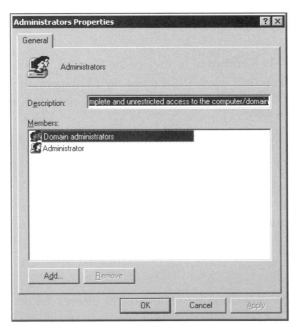

Fig. 4.9. The **Administrators Properties** window

4.3. Viagra for BIOS

When computer performance no longer satisfies our needs or desires, most of us start to upgrade. But it is possible to enhance performance without an additional infusion of funds, by optimizing hardware operations or overclocking the system.

What is the difference between optimization and overclocking? Optimization involves configuring computer devices to allow the hardware to use the available resources to the greatest extent possible. Optimization does not violate the operating parameters recommended by the manufacturer. With overclocking, the hardware is forced to work at the outer limits of its potential, violating the specified operating parameters.

What benefits are there in optimizing the computer? Most desktop computers are supplied with default BIOS settings, which are such that any hardware will operate reliably. But components from different manufacturers may operate at different speeds, and their capabilities may differ. With the default BIOS settings, the hardware operates at the minimum of its potential.

In this respect, it is advisable to buy products from large manufacturers, such as IBM, Apple, Sun, etc. These companies meticulously match the components in their products and configure the BIOS to use the hardware potential to the maximum. As a matter of fact, computers of this type might not even have the user-configurable BIOS option, considering it to be unnecessary.

If, conversely, the computer was assembled in a garage shop, its BIOS will most likely be configured for minimal performance. To shell out a pile of money on a computer and then only use it at a fraction of its potential is not particularly sensible. Therefore, you should know how to squeeze out from the hardware everything it can manage safely.

4.3.1. System Optimization

A system is optimized by configuring its BIOS. The process is rather difficult to describe because there are numerous BIOS versions from many manufacturers, each of which provides different BIOS configuration utilities. Fortunately, the parameters are named in the same way everywhere. I will demonstrate BIOS configuration for the most popular BIOS, from AWARD.

To enter the BIOS configuration utility, reboot the computer and press the key to enter the utility when the system runs the memory check. Which key is this? During the memory testing and IDE drive detection operations, very often there will be written *"Press DEL to enter SETUP"* at the bottom of the screen. So, this will most often be the <Del> key, but it can also sometimes be the <F2> or <F12> keys.

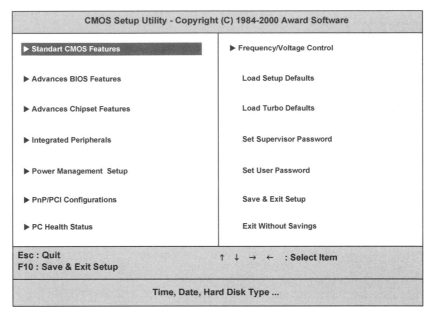

Fig. 4.10. The Award Software BIOS configuration utility

Modern computers often do not display the testing process, instead keeping the screen blackened or placing a logo on it during testing. In such a case, after starting the reboot, keep on pressing the <Del> key until the BIOS setup utility appears. Fig. 4.10 shows the main menu screen for the Award Software BIOS configuration utility.

Some of the described parameters can be different for your computer. In such a case, I recommend that you become acquainted with the BIOS documentation for your computer's motherboard. The motherboard manual should be enough. If you have misplaced this manual, I recommend that you look for the documentation on the site of the motherboard manufacturer.

4.3.2. Fast Boot

The first thing that you need to look at to speed up in your computer is the boot process. Here, the system testing process can be optimized. For example, why do you need to run the memory test three times or check for the presence of the floppy disk drive when you can do perfectly well without these tests?

Selecting the **Advanced Chipset Features** in the utility menu (in some utilities it is simply identified as **Advanced**) opens the parameter list for this section (Fig. 4.11).

In some BIOS versions, the **Advanced** parameters may be divided further into subsections, so your task is to find the necessary parameter in one of the subsections.

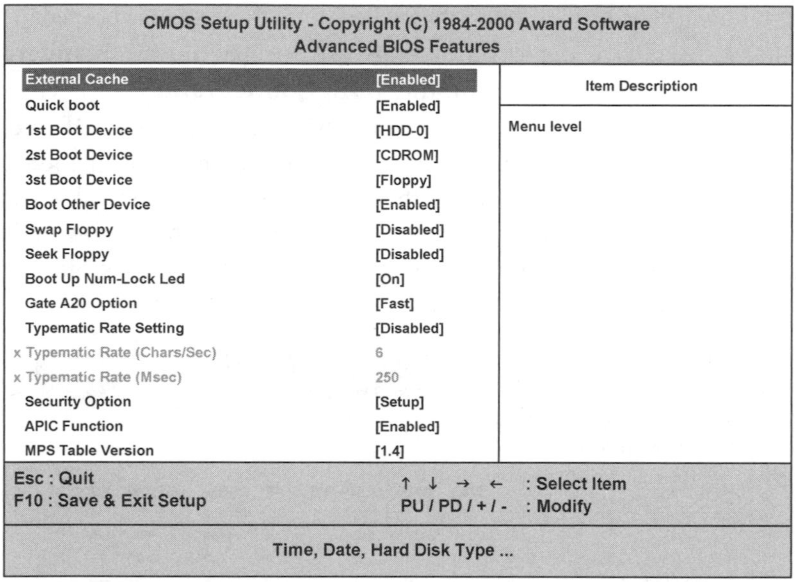

```
          CMOS Setup Utility - Copyright (C) 1984-2000 Award Software
                         Advanced BIOS Features

 External Cache                [Enabled]              Item Description

 Quick boot                    [Enabled]
 1st Boot Device               [HDD-0]        Menu level
 2st Boot Device               [CDROM]
 3st Boot Device               [Floppy]
 Boot Other Device             [Enabled]
 Swap Floppy                   [Disabled]
 Seek Floppy                   [Disabled]
 Boot Up Num-Lock Led          [On]
 Gate A20 Option               [Fast]
 Typematic Rate Setting        [Disabled]
x Typematic Rate (Chars/Sec)   6
x Typematic Rate (Msec)        250
 Security Option               [Setup]
 APIC Function                 [Enabled]
 MPS Table Version             [1.4]

 Esc : Quit                           ↑  ↓  →  ←   : Select Item
 F10 : Save & Exit Setup              PU / PD / + / -   : Modify

                    Time, Date, Hard Disk Type ...
```

Fig. 4.11. The **Advanced Chipset Features** section parameters

The first thing I recommend that you do is enable **Quick Boot**. The parameter values are usually selected using the <PageUp> and <PageDown> keys, and accepted using the <Enter> key. Now, to do away with unnecessary floppy drive access, the **Seek Floppy** parameter can be set to **Disabled**. Modern BIOS may not even have these parameters and, from what I have seen, all of them run the memory check only once and do not look for the floppy drive when booting.

By default, most systems look for the boot loader on the floppy drive first, and then on the master hard drive. If you seldom boot from the floppy drive, I recommend that you disable the floppy boot seek altogether, leaving only the hard drive option. Why check the floppy every time you boot when you are not going to boot from it anyway? Should the need to boot from here arise, you can always easily configure the system to boot from the floppy first.

To change the boot sequence in most BIOS, you need to select the First Boot Device line and, using the <PageUp> or <PageDown> key, change its value to *HDD-0*. There are BIOS configuration utilities, in which the boot sequence is assigned not in the **Device** section, but in a separate **Boot** section.

4.3.3. Detecting Disks

The default BIOS settings are very often set for automatic detection of IDE devices (hard disk and CD-ROM drives). But most of us replace hard disk drives or CD-ROM drives, at the most, once a year, so why detect them every time the system is booted?

The hard disk drive detection settings are located in the **Standard CMOS Features** section (Fig. 4.12) or in the **IDE Configuration** subsection of the **Advanced** section. Here, four IDE devices are listed: two primary IDE and two secondary IDE devices. None of these should have the **Auto** value. If there is a hard drive or a CD/DVD drive connected to the IDE controller ribbon cable, you should specify it explicitly. If there is no device connected to the controller, you should explicitly specify **None** for the corresponding BIOS entry, so as to avoid unnecessary device detection for that channel on startup.

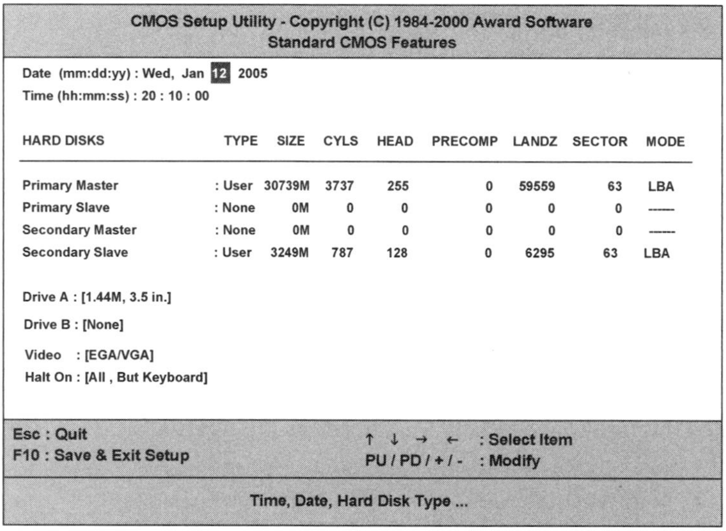

```
          CMOS Setup Utility - Copyright (C) 1984-2000 Award Software
                          Standard CMOS Features

  Date (mm:dd:yy) : Wed, Jan  12  2005
  Time (hh:mm:ss) : 20 : 10 : 00


  HARD DISKS            TYPE   SIZE  CYLS  HEAD  PRECOMP  LANDZ  SECTOR  MODE
  _____

  Primary Master      : User  30739M 3737  255      0    59559    63    LBA
  Primary Slave       : None     0M    0     0      0        0     0    -----
  Secondary Master    : None     0M    0     0      0        0     0    -----
  Secondary Slave     : User   3249M  787  128      0     6295    63    LBA


  Drive A : [1.44M, 3.5 in.]

  Drive B : [None]

  Video   : [EGA/VGA]
  Halt On : [All , But Keyboard]

  _____
  Esc : Quit                        ↑  ↓  →  ←   : Select Item
  F10 : Save & Exit Setup              PU / PD / + / -  : Modify
  _____
                       Time, Date, Hard Disk Type ...
```

Fig. 4.12. The **Standard CMOS Features** section parameters

To specify the connected device explicitly, select **User** instead of **Auto**, and BIOS will try to detect the connected device. If the BIOS fails to determine that the device is connected this could be due to two problems:

❏ No device is connected to the given channel, so **None** should be specified for it.

❏ BIOS cannot automatically determine the connected device. In this case, there should be a separate item in the main menu of the BIOS setup utility for automatic disk detection. Select this item, and perform the device detection again.

4.3.4. Fast Memory

Memory with different technical characteristics can be installed on a computer, and BIOS uses the least performance-oriented values. Memory has three main speed characteristics:

☐ **CAS# Latency** is the most important characteristic. It defines the time necessary to receive requested data. The values for this parameter are 2, 2.5, or 3. The lower the value, the faster the memory. Modern memory can work with no difficulty with **CAS# Latency** values of 2, and there is no reason to set it higher.
☐ The **RAS#** and **CAS#** parameter is the memory read delay. It can have a value from 2 to 4. The optimal value is 3, with which stable operation is guaranteed for any type of memory with any processor. If you are certain of the quality of your memory, you can set this value to 2. If this renders the computer's operations unstable, the value should be set to 3.
☐ **RAS# Precharge** is the time it takes to rewrite a memory block. It can take a value from 2 to 4. Stable operation is usually achieved when this value is set at 3, but quality memory also allows you to lower this value to 2.

The settings for these parameters can be found in the **Advanced** features section, or in the **Chipset Configuration** subsection of the **Advanced** section. Depending on the BIOS configuration utility, these parameters are changed by carrying out one of the following actions:

☐ Setting **System Performance** to **Expert** and **Memory Timing** to **User**.
☐ Setting **Extended Configuration** to **User Defined** and **SDRAM Timing Control** to **Manual-User Defined**.

The essence of the both actions is the same, the difference being only in the names, because manufacturers name BIOS parameters any way they like.

4.3.5. Updating BIOS

BIOS is a piece of software and as such, it can contain bugs that negatively affect system operation. Windows is not necessarily the only party responsible for unstable computer operation. There have been quite a few cases where the culprits were errors in the processor or BIOS design. Both Intel and AMD have recalled batches of their processors more than once.

This problem can be alleviated by updating BIOS, which can also compensate for some processor design errors. Updating BIOS can enhance the system performance if the new version works faster. This is similar to a driver: If it works fast, the system also performs like a sprinter. If it is slow, the whole system will be snoozing, even while performing simple calculations.

It is useless to describe the BIOS update procedure, as the process depends on the motherboard and its manufacturer. Recently, this process has been simplified to launching a utility that reboots the computer and does all of the work automatically. The important thing here is to obtain the right utility for your motherboard. Installing the wrong BIOS version will make it impossible to start your computer. Bringing it back to life will be only be possible in a professional repair shop. If the unsuccessful update is your fault, you will have to pay to get your computer working again.

I recommend that you update BIOS only occasionally, and not right after a new version comes out. New versions also often contain bugs, so it is advisable to wait until other users work them out or the manufacturer itself has tested out the new version thoroughly.

Updating BIOS may allow your computer to operate with modern devices or processors, and may also correct critical errors. One of my notebooks, a Fujitsu-Siemens, refused to boot when running on battery power, while another one refused to recognize PCMCA network cards. Updating BIOS solved the problem in both cases.

4.4. Hardware Overclocking

If the optimization has not resulted in the expected performance, it is time to resort to overclocking and to make the hardware work at the upper limits of its potential, often exceeding the manufacturer's recommended parameters. Some processors can be overclocked by as much as 50 percent. Personally, I overclock my computers to this degree very seldom, and then only for short times, because exceeding the recommended technology limits may cause unwelcome consequences.

If the processor operating frequency is 3 GHz, it is at exactly this frequency that the manufacturer guarantees stable operation. Nevertheless, the quality of AMD and Intel chips is sufficient to allow them to work faster. You must, however, keep in mind that making the system operate in excess of the manufacturer's recommended parameters will void the warranty. The system might also become unstable.

I recall back in 1995, when I was working with a 486 computer and its performance was sufficient to work with main software packages, programming, and playing Doom2. But then a new game came out that lagged on the system and ran a little bit slowly. The game was 3D Action, and lagging by the system with games of this type can affect your eyes badly. I didn't feel like going for a major computer upgrade merely for one game, so I decided, instead, to resort to overclocking.

I raised the processor's operating frequency 66 MHz to 100 MHz. The computer's operations remained stable, and the game performance became acceptable. The processor, however, started overheating. This problem can be addressed in a manner that will be considered later in the book. Everything seemed to be working just fine, until I inserted a diskette into the 3.5" floppy drive. The Front Side Bus (FSB, the bus used to exchange information with the memory and other system devices) was operating at too high a frequency and data exchange with the floppy drive was performed with errors making reading from and writing to the floppy impossible. Any attempt at floppy access produced the *"Why did you break the game?"* message, which the developers had built into the file manager.

As a result, on one hand I could play a very good game but, on the other, I could not use the floppy. In order to do both, I had to overclock the processor to play the game, and then return the clock back to normal to work with the floppy.

I resort to overclocking only occasionally, because it is dangerous for the system, but sometimes the desire to increase performance is too hard to resist.

If you have no experience working with computer hardware, I recommend that you limit your experiments with hardware to optimizing the BIOS parameters and increasing the operating clock frequency only slightly. Serious overclocking may result in damage to the processor, memory, or motherboard.

NOTE

When doing anything that requires opening the system block, do not forget to disconnect the power from the computer. Leaving the computer powered up can be fatal.

4.4.1. Refrigeration

Some computer components heat up during operation. One such component is the processor. When designing a new processor, the developers provide it with a cooling system with a 10 to 20 percent safety factor built in. This is the degree, to which processor can be overclocked for short periods of time.

Old processors burned up when overheated, but modern chips and good quality motherboards have a built-in thermal sensor, which shuts down the processor when it overheats. To prevent this from happening, you should take care to provide sufficient cooling to allow the processor to work at the upper frequency limits, or even beyond them, at maximum workload for a sufficiently period of time.

Horizontal system cases provide insufficient cooling from the start, because the faulty form of the cases means that ventilation is poor. All of the components in these cases are piled one on top of the other, so the air circulates poorly between the cards. The problem is only aggravated if the monitor is placed atop the case. This hinders the flow of heat out of the system. It actually just serves to heat up the surrounding air and the case itself.

Big tower cases are much more effective with regard to cooling. They provide more internal space for the air to cool the components by circulating freely among them.

Two or three fans-coolers are sufficient to maintain a normal operating mode temperature.

❏ The first fan is installed on the processor radiator and should be as powerful as possible. The best solution is to replace the radiator and the fan supplied with the processor with more powerful versions. In this respect, I recommend that you not scrimp and save in this area, especially since you will only subsidize Chinese industry in the process. Instead, install a good, brand name cooler from companies like Thermaltake Technology or Titan. Personally, I prefer the latter, as its "blowers" have yet not let me down.

❏ The second fan is installed on the power supply. This fan is not as critical, especially if you install the additional fans that we will discuss later.

❏ The third fan can be installed on the video chip if it is powerful and the cooling provided by the radiator alone is not sufficient. We will not consider video card overclocking here. Even if you do raise the video card operating frequency slightly, it is unlikely that it will overheat if there is additional cooling of the case.

These fans should be sufficient for regular work. If, however, you are planning to overclock system components, I recommend that you install additional cooling. Fans can now be purchased that can be installed into the 5.25 drive bays and are powered by the standard 12 V computer power supply.

Installing fans of this sort is easier than installing CD or DVD drives. Simply open the case, remove the bay panel, and install the fan assembly in the bay. You should have a free 12 V plug, the kind used to power hard drives and CD-ROM drives, available. Connect the installed fan to this power connector (Fig. 4.13).

If there are no free power connectors, you will have to get a T-adapter. Disconnect the power connector from one of the devices, plug it into the T-adapter, and connect the disconnected device and the fan to the T-adapter.

Fig. 4.13. A fan installed into a 5.25" drive bay

This fan allows the case temperature to be lowered by blowing additional air into the case. Without an additional air supply of this type, the air inside the case gradually heats up, meaning that the components inside the case (the processor, the video card, the hard disk drive, etc.) cannot be cooled to a temperature below this point.

Having installed an inflow fan in a front bay drive, it is desirable to install power outflow fan of the same type on the back panel to remove the heated air from the case.

Intel processor based computers suffer from numerous ribbon cables jumbled up inside the case. Most small companies do not even bother to organize these cables. Generally, only the major manufacturers bundle them up and place them out of the way of air circulation. So it is a good idea to open up the case and try to organize the ribbon cables as best you can. Wide ribbon cables in the path of air circulation disrupt the air flow. I always bundle up the cables and lay them accurately along the edge of the motherboard. This leaves the central part of the case wide open.

But let's get back to processor cooling. As I already stated, it is important to install a powerful processor fan. The fan supplied with the processor may not be powerful enough (with the exception of brand name Intel fans) to provide sufficient cooling. The heat sinks in Chinese made cooler assemblies generally fit poorly to the processor crystal, so they do a poor job when removing the heat.

As I already mentioned, a good alternative are cooling assemblies from Thermaltake Technology or Titan. But even these have shortcomings, and require a bit of finish-up work on your part. If developers think that a powerful heat sink combined with a powerful fan can cool just about anything, they are sadly mistaken.

A big heat sink is only effective if it makes good contact with the processor crystal. This contact is not possible if the heat sink is painted.

Unfortunately, the majority of manufacturers, even the most respectable names, paint their heat sinks. Paint is simply not a good heat conductor, meaning that a painted heat sink does not remove heat well and you can be assured that things will run a few degrees hotter than is necessary. To improve the heat removal from the processor, the heat sink should be taken off the processor and the paint removed from it with fine sandpaper. This should be done very accurately, rendering the heat sink base surface as polished as possible, while avoiding scratching it. Scratches also impede heat removal.

Having removed the paint from the heat sink, blow off the dust that has been produced by the polishing. Now, apply a drop of heat-conducting paste in the center of the heat sink. Applying more does not bring any advantage, because any extra paste will be squeezed out onto the motherboard when the heat sink is attached to the processor. Finding the right paste for the heat sink should not pose a problem: Any do-it-yourself electronics buff has some in his arsenal. Now, simply reinstall the heat sink on the processor.

Be careful when installing the heat sink, because some processors have very flimsy crystal protection. One such processor is the Celeron Coppermine processor. When mounting the heat sink on such a processor, there is a danger that you will simply crush the crystal, because it extends too far above the processor housing.

4.4.2. Some Theory

Before discussing overclocking specific processors, some discussion of overclocking theory is due. The processor operating frequency is determined by two factors: the bus frequency and the frequency multiplier. These two values are multiplied to produce the processor operating frequency. Suppose, for example, that you have a Pentium 3 processor with an operating frequency rated at 600 MHz. Due to design requirements, these processors are supposed to operate at 100 MHz system bus frequency. This means that the clock multiplier should be 6, since 600 MHz = 100 MHz × 6.

The processor speed can be raised in two ways: by increasing the system bus frequency or by increasing the clock multiplier value. I recommend that you start overclocking experiments with the former, because the bus frequency affects not only the processor speed but also the speed of the rest of the system devices. For example, data exchange with the system memory takes place at the system bus speed, so raising this parameter also increases the memory data exchange speed, as well as making almost all other computer components work faster.

For a 600 MHz rated processor, setting the bus frequency to 133 MHz (which is an acceptable frequency) and the clock multiplier to 4.5 produces an operating frequency of 598.5 MHz. The actual processor operating frequency has been lowered a bit, but the performance increase of the other components clocked by the bus produces an increase in overall system performance.

Setting the clock multiplier to 5 produces the actual processor operating frequency of 665 MHz, meaning that not only the bus, but also the processor, are overclocked. The bus frequency and clock multiplier cannot, however, be changed for some processors. These parameters are selected by the motherboard and not every motherboard provides the means to change them manually. Indeed, most brand name computers do not provide this capability, so overclocked computers are usually those from smaller companies or those assembled by the user him or herself.

My desktop computer at home is built around a Celeron 566 processor. This is the first Celeron processor designed using Coppermine technology (which is also used in Pentium 3). Its motherboard is built around the ZX chipset. This is a very old chipset for this processor, and the BIOS is also old. Of course, they didn't take notice of the processor's fixed bus frequency, and determined the processor as Pentium 3. So they automatically set the bus frequency to 126 MHz and the clock frequency to 4.5, with the resulting processor operating frequency of 567 MHz. In those days, the recommended bus frequency, even for Pentium 3, was 100 MHz, while Celerons were supposed to be content with a 66 MHz bus. The result is that my processor works, on average, 15 percent faster than its 66 MHz brethren, without any detriment to the workload or any overheating. While the processor itself may operate with no problems at the raised bus frequency, some devices attached to the bus may fare less well.

The first thing to do before increasing the bus frequency is to make sure that the memory can operate at the intended frequency. If you have PC100 memory installed on your computer, you will have no problems running it at 100 MHz. You might, however, experience problems at 133 MHz. It just so happens that memory manufacturers do not build much reserve performance capacity into their products. If it possible to make the processor work faster by providing more efficient cooling, this is almost impossible to do with the memory.

The bus frequency and the clock multiplier are mainly set by the motherboard jumpers. On modern motherboards, this may be done in BIOS, but not all motherboards provide this capability. Don't forget that processor manufacturers are constantly fighting against overclocking. They want to prevent users from getting more performance for less money. This is clearly not right. I can understand when overclocking protection is used to stop unscrupulous system assemblers from overclocking processors and selling them to consumers at increased prices. There have actually been stories when processors were overclocked, the speed ratings on their cases doctored, and the processors then resold with a faster rating.

But users should have the opportunity to overclock their processors themselves, as long as they are aware that the system's stability will wane in direct proportion to each megahertz, by which they make it run faster. If your system crashes, no manufacturer will be responsible for the data you lose as a result. But, as long as you follow the main rule of overclocking, your data will be pretty safe. The main rule of overclocking is simply this: You should raise the processor frequency in the smallest possible increments, and then carefully test the computer for error free operation before moving to the next rise in frequency. If something goes wrong, turn the computer off immediately and restore the original frequency.

Having mastered the theory, now let's move on to individual processors and to the problems you can run into while trying to overclock them. It is simply impossible to consider all of the possible motherboard/processor combinations, but we will consider the information that will be of greatest use here.

4.4.3. AMD Processors

I seldom use processors produced by this company because I have been burned (quite literally) several times on their quality. While the quality of AMD processors is better today than it used to be, the added attention here seems to have come at the expense of the quality of their technical support. This is evident even when simply installing Windows. There are no problems with installing on any Intel system, but there is always some kind of problem with regard to Athlon systems. Most of the time, these problems are due to raw motherboard drivers, which is even the case with motherboards from such renowned manufacturers as Asus and Gigabyte.

That's why I do not use AMD-based systems. I have, however, had to overclock AMD computers on two occasions and the results were satisfactory. More about this later, but I want to warn you for now that old AMD processors (even the first Athlons) did not have thermal sensors. This means that the processor does not shut off when overheated — it simply burns up. The Intel processors have been equipped with this kind of sensor for a long time and are much safer to overclock without running the risk of frying them.

The K6 family processors can be overclocked by 33 MHz, or even as much as 66 MHz. If you have a 233 MHz processor, you can jack it up to 266 MHz (by setting the bus frequency to 133 MHz and the clock multiplier to 2) or even 300 MHz (setting the bus frequency to 100 MHz and the clock multiplier to 3). Remember, though, that not all memory will work at 133 MHz. If yours does, I recommend that you opt for a lower processor speed and a higher bus frequency. A good option for a 233 MHz processor is to overclock it to 266 MHZ. The heat generated will not be significantly higher, but performance will be enhanced significantly.

If after overclocking the computer will not boot — or it boots, but then hangs — it could be due to either of the following two reasons:

❑ As already mentioned, the memory might not be able to work at the set bus frequency. It must be lowered and a different frequency/multiplier combination used.
❑ There may not be enough power for the processor to work at this frequency. In this case, the processor voltage needs to be raised.

This can be done via BIOS or by using the jumpers on the motherboard. The standard processor power supply voltage is between 2 V and 2.2 V, but it can be raised safely up to 2.4 V. I do not recommend going above this value, because the probability of burning the chip up will increase, while it is unlikely that stable operation will be the result.

Overclocking the new AMD family processors — Athlon and and Duron — is more difficult. On one hand, these processors have enough performance in reserve for overclocking but, on the other, raising the bus frequency creates memory problems. These processors use the Alpha EV6 bus. With the old bus, data were clocked at one edge of the clock pulses, while in the new bus this is done at both edges. This means that the memory data exchange rate is doubled. For example, if your bus frequency is 100 MHz, the actual data transfer will be conducted at 200 MHz. Increasing the clock frequency by 33 MHz means that the actual bus frequency increase is 66 MHz, while the operating frequency is 266 MHz.

The cases where memory can work in excess of its design frequency by 66 MHz are not common. Consequently, if you have an old Athlon 800 lying around and want to breathe new life into it, you will have to update the memory before overclocking the processor. Only then can you seriously think of overclocking it. If the memory is old, the bus frequency can only be raised to 120 MHz. If your motherboard is built around the KT133 chipset, you will not actually be able to raise the bus frequency by any more than this. The KT133A, KT266, and KT266A chipsets can set the bus frequency to 150 MHZ and, given good quality memory, operating bus speeds of 300 MHz can be obtained (150 MHz actual bus frequency, multiplied by the double edge data transfer).

Unlike the K6 series processors, the clock multiplier cannot be changed for the Athlon processors. Therefore, most motherboards do not even have this parameter. This only leaves us with the option of adjusting the processor's supply voltage and increasing the bus operating frequency. The overclocking in this instance cannot be done gradually. But the multiplier is not disabled permanently. The old tooling was obviously left at the plant because the multiplier was not disabled in the first Athlon/Duron versions. The multiplier is disabled simply by cutting the L1 bridges on the processor to prevent hackers from realizing the processor's great overclocking potential. Fig. 4.14 shows an Athlon processor with the L1 and L3 bridge area enclosed in a box.

Fig. 4.14. An Athlon processor from AMD

If you look at your Athlon processor, you will see that all of the L1 bridges are cut. Your task is to restore these bridges. But you do not have to use a soldering iron for this — there is a better way. The only tool you need for this is a soft graphite pencil, which you use to draw the bridges, as shown in Fig. 4.15. Why does it have to be a soft pencil? This is because pencils with a hard lead crumble, so you will have a hard time making the graphite stick. Be accurate when drawing the bridges, so as not to make connections where they are not needed. But don't fret if you mess up, for the graphite can be erased easily. This is also handy if you want to cover the tracks of your experimentation for some reason.

Fig. 4.15. The L1 bridges

The pencil method is expedient, but its results, unfortunately, are not lasting. More likely than not, some time later the bridges will deteriorate, and you will have to draw them again. To make the bridges more reliable, I advise that you use conductive glue. Take a nib, or you can even use a simple needle, and draw the bridges using the glue as ink. These bridges will be more reliable and durable. On the other hand, the glue is more difficult to remove if it ends up somewhere it is not supposed to be.

For the Athlon XP, the overclocking task is even more difficult, because here the bridges are not simply cut, but pits are burned by laser in their places. The circumventing technology is the same, however. Simply drawing the bridges is more difficult, because the pits are harder to fill with pencil. If you have acquired good working skills with glue, you can also use this method here. The important thing is to be as accurate as possible.

For greater reliability, you can fill the pits with non-conducting super glue to obtain a level surface. I recommend that you tape the area around the pits before filling them with glue. This is like painting over a scratch on a car, where you tape the areas you want to keep the paint off.

4.4.4. Intel Processors

I like overclocking these processors because they are more reliable and have a good frequency reserve, provided that they are supplied with good cooling. Their only shortcoming is that, in modern processors, the clock multiplier is disabled on the crystal and there is no way around this. But Pentium 2 and analogous processors do not come equipped with such serious protection and, with a good motherboard, this protection is easily removed.

The official bus frequency for all processor models before Pentium 3 was 66 MHz but, notwithstanding this fact, it was possible on any motherboard to raise this value to 85 MHz, 100 MHz, or even 133 MHz.

I want to remind you that the clock multiplier cannot always be changed and, if you have such a processor or a motherboard, on which there is no way to do this, you will be unable to raise the bus frequency significantly. For example, the Celeron 400 processor has a hard-wired clock multiplier of 6, and its operating bus frequency must be 66 MHz. With the clock multiplier of 6, increasing the bus frequency to 85 MHz increases the processor operating frequency to 510 MHz. From my experience, I can assure you that the system will only work at these parameters with very good cooling. In order to raise the bus frequency, the value of the clock multiplier simply has to be lowered.

With the switch to the FCPGA connector, the overclocking problem for the Intel processors became more substantial. If before the Celeron and Pentium processors differed architecturally, now the only difference was in the cache size and bus frequency. With the switch to the Coppermine technology in the Pentium processors, the bus frequency was raised to 100 MHz, and even 133 MHz in some processors, while the bus frequency for Celerons remained at the same 66 MHz. The reason for this difference was simply commercial: to divide the market explicitly between the Celeron and Pentium systems.

Getting the cheaper Celeron chip to operate at the 100 MHz bus frequency reduces the performance gap with the more-expensive Pentium variant. The remaining difference is due only to the different size of the caches. The performance of the Celeron chip operating at bus frequency higher than 100 MHz almost equals that of the Pentium. This is exactly why Intel tries to prevent overclocking of its processors by installing various forms of protection.

Still, despite all of these protection measures, the example with my Celeron 566 demonstrates that these processors can be overclocked easily, given a motherboard with the means for doing this, and they will operate stably at the performance level of the Pentium chip with the same frequency for practically unlimited periods (4 years in my case). This is possible because the processor operates at what is actually its design frequency and, therefore, does not overheat at all. I could raise the performance of my Celeron even more by making it work at a higher frequency. After all, the motherboard detected it as a Pentium chip and allowed the bus frequency to be raised to 133 MHz.

If you are the lucky owner of a Celeron Coppermine processor, be careful when overclocking it. These processors require different voltages and can work at 1.6 V, 1.65 V, and 1.7 V. The higher the voltage, the better the processor overclocks.

Some manufacturers started producing motherboards for Pentium 3, on which the bus frequency can be increased to 150 MHz, 170 MHz, and even 200 MHz. But most memory is unable to work at these frequencies, and my experience has shown that 150 MHz is the limit. You can, of course, buy the best memory to get that extra hundred megahertz, and shell out a pretty penny in the process, but doesn't it make more sense simply to buy a new processor instead?

Pentium 4 is overclocked in the same way as Pentium 3, but not every processor overclocks equally well. Every day Intel builds in more and more protection mechanisms designed to thwart hackers, making their life more difficult. Nevertheless, it is sometimes hard to resist trying to squeeze that extra 100 megahertz out of even a processor that is already fast.

When overclocking the system, increase the frequency as smoothly as possible. As soon as you notice system operations becoming unstable, lower the frequency by about 100 MHz. You can then work at that frequency with confidence. But do not forget to monitor the temperature within the system case and of the processor. There are many utilities for this purpose.

If you have performed this overclocking during a colder time of the year, pay more attention to the processor temperature when the weather gets warmer. Not only will it often be warmer where the computer sits, but there is often more dust in the air, which also has a negative effect on cooling. Dust clogs up the fan and slows it down, which results in weaker air flow. This requires regular wet dusting around the computer and vacuuming its insides. Dust is always one of the computer's enemies, and this is even more the case for an overclocked system.

4.5. Video Card Overclocking

The most simple and safe way to speed up the video card's operation is to update its drivers. For example, when a new NVIDIA card comes out, its drivers are still raw and do not use the hardware's capabilities to their full extent. This has to do with the fact that the software department always lags behind the hardware developers. The chip is produced first, and only then is the final version of the software for it written. It is impossible to write optimized code for a video chipset while it is in the development stage, so there is a slight delay.

Why not, you may ask, hold back the hardware until there is the proper software for it? Simply put, the harsh realities of business dictate that new products must bring profits and not gather dust in the warehouse. NVIDIA regularly makes fresh driver versions available that improve image quality and raise performance.

There have been cases, however, when a fresh driver version was slower — or did not work at all. A driver version was issued once, in which the necessary complex calculations were only approximated resulting in lower image quality, but faster performance. Therefore, I recommend that you update drivers regularly, but accurately, because doing this does not always produce the desired results. After a new version comes out, always ascertain its operability and quality on a test computer.

There are easy-to-use programs with graphical interfaces that can help you enhance your system's performance by overclocking the video card processor or its memory. One of the most popular programs of this type is PowerStrip. It owes its widespread popularity to its ability to work with all major video cards. Of course, a given video card can be overclocked only if it has this capability.

PowerStrip can be downloaded from the following site: **http://entechtaiwan.net/ util/ps.shtm**. It can be used to configure any graphical parameters, including the video card's processor and memory speed. After installing the program, the computer has to be rebooted. After rebooting, the PowerStrip icon will be placed in the system tray. Clicking on this icon opens the program's menu, in which the **Performance profiles/Configure** item can be selected. This, in turn, will open the performance configuration window (Fig. 4.16).

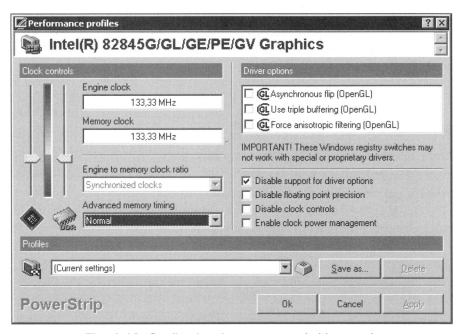

Fig. 4.16. Configuring the memory and chip speeds

The **Engine clock** field displays the current operating frequency of the card's graphics processor. The **Memory clock** field shows the video card's memory clock frequency. At the left edge of the window are located two frequency control sliders. The slider on the left is used to adjust the frequency of the graphics processor; while the right slider controls the memory frequency.

As was the case with processor overclocking, the video card's speed must be raised gradually, in small increments. The frequency increase must be carried out in turns between the processor and the memory. After each change, the system's performance must be tested thoroughly. As soon as system operation becomes unstable, the frequency of the video processor and memory must be lowered to the point of stability and left there.

In addition to adjusting the video card's speed, there are many other parameters that can be changed. I recommend that you familiarize yourself with the program's help file to learn its configuration capabilities.

There are many other programs available on the Internet for adjusting video card performance, but they are generally specialized for specific device versions. For example, Radeon Tweaker (**http://radeontweaker.sourceforge.net**) is a program for tuning Radeon video cards. It has a rather simple Linux-style interface, but not a large number of options.

4.6. Windows Optimization

Even with optimized BIOS and overclocked hardware, the computer resources may not be sufficient for a new Windows version, or you may simply want the computer to work even faster. In this case, you need to optimize Windows for maximum performance.

4.6.1. Keeping Your Disk in Order

After Windows is installed, it starts accumulating various trash, the amount of which is directly proportional to the time that has elapsed since the installation. So, as the time goes by, system performance gradually decreases. One reason for slower performance is file fragmentation. If you have, for example, an 80 GB hard disk in one logical drive, then the operating system, application software, and data files will all be located on one disk. The system can write any file to any location within the 80 GB, resulting in severe fragmentation.

What files are accessed most often? These are, of course, the system files. Therefore, you have to take care to keep them from being scattered all over the disk. This can be achieved by regularly defragmenting the disk. This, however, places a great strain on the hard disk platters and reading heads, as well as overheating them, which may one day prove fatally.

There is another way: Create disk C: as a logical partition of about 5 GB, and install the operating system here. The rest of the physical disk is partitioned into logical disk D, and all application software and data are stored here. Only the operating system and its files should be stored on the first disk. Consequently, the system files will wander only within 5 GB and not over the entire disk. Not only will you need to defragment this disk less often, but it will also take less time. The disk holding data may fragment as much as it wants. There is lots of room and most of its files are accessed much less often. This does not, of course, mean that you should not defragment it at all. You should, however, do this no more often than once every six months.

4.6.2. Windows 2000/XP Services

Any modern operating system has a large number of functions. In this respect, Windows is one of the best operating systems, as it has many things a common user may need, as well as some that he or she may not. Starting with Windows 2000, all of these capabilities are implemented as services, which makes it easy to control them and select only those that are needed.

When optimizing the operating system, I recommend that you pay careful attention to those services that are started automatically by default. We already mentioned services when considering viruses, but now we will look at them from a different angle. Each of the services increases the booting time and wastes valuable memory. The service configuration utility is opened by executing the **Start/Settings/ Control Panel/Administrative Tools/Services** command sequence. This opens the service management window.

This window is simpler in Windows XP than in Windows 2000. You will see two tabs at the bottom: **Extended** and **Standard**. Selecting the **Extended** tab opens a panel to the left of the service list, in which a description of the selected service is displayed. In **Standard** mode, only the service list is displayed. This is the only mode available in Windows 2000.

A selected service can be started, stopped, paused, or restarted using the corresponding toolbar buttons or from the **Action** menu. A service is configured in its corresponding **Properties** window, which is opened by double clicking on the service. One of these windows, for the **Alerter** service, is shown in Fig. 4.7.

Two of the parameters on the **General** tab of the properties window are **Startup type** and **Startup parameters**. The startup type can have one of the following values:

❑ **Automatic:** The service starts automatically upon system start-up. It can then be left running or stopped manually. Only the services you need at all times should be started automatically.

❑ **Manual:** The service is started manually from either the service control utility or the command line. If a service is seldom used, it is preferable to start it manually. For example, you only need MS SQL Server for tasks you perform occasionally. Installing the service every time you need it and removing it afterwards is rather annoying, but leaving it running all the time is inefficient, as it slows down the boot process and takes up its share of the memory. In this case, you should specify manual start for the service and start it only when it is needed. This way you can have your cake and eat it too.

❑ **Disabled:** The service is disabled and cannot be started in any way. If you consider a service potentially dangerous and do not use it, disable it. Disabling a service also disables all other services dependent on it. For example, disabling the basic network service disables all network services.

You can find out what services depend on the selected service in the **Dependencies** tab of the service's properties window. The services that the selected service depends on are listed at the top. If any of these services is stopped or disabled, the selected services will not start. So, in order to ensure that a service operates reliably, all the services on which it depends must also operate reliably.

The lower list displays the services that depend on the selected service. Before disabling a service, check this list carefully so as not to disable a necessary service accidentally.

Now, let's consider some services that can, and sometimes even should, be disabled for greater security and to enhance system performance.

❑ **Automatic Updates.** If this service is started, the computer will automatically download updates from the Internet and install them. If you do not want your Internet traffic to be wasted, switch this service into the manual start mode to prevent it from downloading updates whether you want them or not. If you decide to disable this service, you will also need to disable automatic updates in the system properties. This is done by right-clicking on **My Computer**, opening the **Properties** item, and disabling the automatic update option on the **Automatic Updates** tab. Failing to do this will cause an error the next time the system tries to perform an automatic update, as service will not be running.

- ❒ **Print Spooler.** This loads files into the print queue for later printing. Even if you have a printer installed, this service can be dispensed with. If you don't have a printer, switching this service to the manual start mode is the only thing to do. I very seldom print from my notebook, so keeping the spooling service running constantly is a useless waste of system resources.

- ❒ **Task Scheduler.** I personally never schedule any tasks, so I have no need for this service. Some people like to launch the file defragmenter at a certain time every day. Imagine that you are killing the next monster in a new 3D Action at this time and this drag on the system kicks in. Defragmentation is generally a stupid thing to do (what with all the extra stress on the hard drive mechanism, overheating, etc.) and scheduling this task is even less clever. It is enough to do this once a year. So forget about the scheduler and rid the computer of the unneeded service.

- ❒ **Portable Media Serial Number.** This retrieves the serial numbers of all media devices connected to the system. Do you really need this service? If you do not, switch it to the manual start mode.

- ❒ **DHCP Client.** This is a client for receiving IP addresses dynamically from the DHCP server. If your IP address is specified explicitly, you have no need for this service and can switch it to the manual start. Disconnecting this service altogether is not recommended.

- ❒ **DNS Client.** This is the service for determining the IP address of the computer by its name. If your network employs domains, this client is necessary. Otherwise, the service can be switched into manual start mode. The service is not used to convert Internet site names.

- ❒ **Smart Card.** This service is used for working with smart cards. These devices are most often used in notebooks, although there is nothing to prevent their use, through special reading devices, in desktop PCs. If you have no smart card device, you have no need for this service.

- ❒ **Messenger.** This service is used to transmit net send and alerter messages between servers and clients. This service is vulnerable to message flooding (discussed in *Chapter 3*) and, if you have no need for it (for example, you have no network or use other ways to exchange messages), disable so that it is out of the harm's way.

- ❒ **Terminal Service.** This service is used to allow remote computers to connect to yours and to work with the desktop and applications over the network.

This requires a terminal service server and client. Remote work is often used in large companies to work with so-called thin clients, or for the administrators to control other network computers remotely. There is no need whatsoever for this service for work at home. This is why this service is disabled by default and, unless you need terminal access for some reason, you should leave it that way.

❏ **Remote Registry Service.** The name of the service makes it clear that it is used to change registry parameters over the network. The most interesting thing is that the service is started automatically by default. So switch it into the manual start mode as quickly as possible. It will then only be possible to edit the registry locally.

❏ **FTP Publishing Service.** This service is only necessary if you want your computer to be used as an FTP server. Other network users will then be able to connect to your computer with the help of FTP clients and exchange files.

❏ **IIS Admin Service.** If you do not want your computer to be used for publishing FTP or web pages, this service can be disabled.

❏ **Themes.** This service is needed for using Windows XP themes. If you prefer the classic desktop look, the service can be disabled so as not to waste system resources.

❏ **Telnet.** This service allows remote users to log on to the computer through the command line. Disable it without fail. The overwhelming majority of computers do not use this service, so there is no need to keep it running and give miscreants another way of getting into your system. Should you ever need this service, you can always start it manually.

❏ **Run As.** This service allows applications to be launched in the name of another user.

❏ **ClipBook.** The service allows shared folders on remote computers to be viewed. Set it to the manual start mode, because folders of this type are seldom used, even in networks.

❏ **Fax.** Unless you use the computer extensively to exchange faxes, set it to the manual start mode, or disable the service altogether.

❏ **Distributed Link Tracking Client/Server.** The client sends, and the server tracks, messages about file movement among NTFS volumes. If your computer is not on a network, this service should definitely be disabled. Personally, I disable it even when connected to a network.

❏ **Distributed Transaction Coordinator.** This is used to coordinate transactions involving multiple resource managers, such as databases, message queues, or file systems. When not working with databases, I disable this service.

❏ **Logical Disk Manger.** This monitors the logical hard disks. The information about these disks does not change often enough to require constant monitoring, so the service can be switched into the manual start mode. Do not, however, disable it altogether.

As you can see, the system has quite a large number of services that can waste your computer's resources. Disconnecting them speeds up computer operation and frees up a few megabytes of memory.

4.6.3. Chopping off Dead Wood

The best thing to do with unused programs is to remove them. First, remove unused Windows components. This is done from the **Add or Remove Programs** utility in the **Control Panel**. Let's see which Windows components are needed, and which you can do without.

❏ **Internet Information Services (ISS).** This is a WEB server, which can be installed locally. This is most often done by programmers for debugging their web applications, or by administrators to create a corporate site server. If you are not going to have your own server, this entire section can be disabled.

- **FTP Server** allows you to manage site contents using an FTP client. It is installed by administrators or programmers if they want other network users to be able to update their sites using an FTP client. This is an extra security hole. You can replace files on your hard drive without it. The other local network users can be given a shared folder to use.

- **WEB Server** is the actual page server.

- **Internet Information Services Snap-In** allows the IIS to be administered via the browser.

- **Documentation** may seem innocent at first, but ASP scripts for viewing documentation are also installed along with this client, and all scripts are vulnerable.

- **FrontPage Server Extensions.** There have been numerous weak spots discovered in these extensions. If you do not know what they are used for, there is no need for you to install them. The extensions are used to produce dynamic web pages. However, not all Internet servers can display such pages properly, because most hosting servers run on Unix systems, which do not support these extensions.

- **NNTP and SMPT Services** allow news and mail to be sent from your computer. News services have become of less importance nowadays, so you do not really need the NNTP service. As for the SMTP service, unless you are a web programmer, you do not need it either.

❏ **Other Network File and Print Services.** By default, only the service for working with Windows system resources is installed. Additional services for printing documents from Macintosh and UNIX computers can be installed in this section.

❏ **Terminal Service Licensing** makes your computer a terminal license server providing client licenses. Unless you have the terminal service installed, there is no need to install the licensing.

❏ **Script Debugger** is used by programmers to debug scripts.

❏ **Networking Services.** Most of these are used only on servers and are not needed for client computers.

- **DHCP** allows temporary IP addresses to be assigned to computers. It is used in large networks to make address management easier.

- **DNS** server is used to convert DNS names into IP address. Do not confuse DNS names with computer names, which do not require the DNS service.

- **WINS** is the server for NetBIOS computer names used to register them.

- **Simple TCP/IP Services** support such services as Character Generator, Daytime, Echo, etc. In most cases, even server computers do not need them.

- **QoS Access Control Service** most definitely needs to be removed, because it robs each connection of part of its bandwidth, which naturally slows down the communications. Nobody uses it anyway.

❏ **Indexing Service** is used for fast search in files. It wastes disk space, so if you do not often use the Windows search system, it can safely be removed.

❏ **Windows Media Services** are used to transmit multimedia streams over the network. Unless you transmit audio or video over the network, there is no need to install it.

❏ **Terminal Services** are used to let remote computers connect to the local computer and use local applications. A connected client can see your desktop and start any application on your computer. These services are installed on servers to be used by clients that do not have enough resources to work with applications locally, or to save money on buying software licenses.

❏ **Remote Installation Services** make it possible to install Windows on the local computer from a remote computer.

❐ **Management and Monitoring Tools** will most likely be of no use to a common user, although they can be useful for administrators.

- **Connection Manager Clients.** These are the connection manager itself and a phone book service.

- **Simple Network Management Protocol** monitors the activity of network devices and reports the results to the network console workstation.

- **Network Monitoring Tools** allow for the monitoring of computer connections, files and folders being used, and the data transmitted. They can be used to monitor the traffic in the same manner as sniffer software does. (The latter will be considered in *Chapter 5*.)

❐ **Accessories and Utilities.** This section contains office applications for everyday work. In most cases, they have no effect on computer performance, but do occupy disk space.

- **Games.** These are standard Windows games, such as Miner and Solitaire.

- **Accessibility Wizard** is used to provide special accessibility features for hearing, vision, or movement-impaired individuals. Unless you have some of those disabilities, you do not need these features and can disconnect them to save some system resources.

- **Multimedia.** If you have an audio card installed (and who doesn't nowadays), this section contains mixer, recording, and CD player programs, as well as sound samples. They do not use any resources but do occupy some disk space. For example, removing the audio samples will allow you to save 1 MB of disk space.

- **Communications.** This section contains programs for communicating with remote computers. The HyperTerminal program is one such program. It can be used to connect to other devices via a COM port, or to communicate with your friends directly via modem without connecting to the Internet.

- **Accessories.** This section contains such standard Windows programs as Paint, WordPad, Calculator, clipboard, and others. Deleting any of them will save you some disk space, but it will provide no increase in performance.

The list in the **Add or Remove Programs** utility, however, is far from complete. There are many programs that are hidden from deleting. In order to see these,

the sysoc.inf file in the Windows\Inf folder has to be edited. All installed components are described after the [Components] line in this file as follows:

```
WBEM=ocgen.dll,OcEntry,wbemoc.inf,hide,7
```

Take a look at word hide before the last comma. This is the parameter that makes
the given component invisible and impossible to delete. So, to be able to delete the
given program, this word needs to be deleted, leaving only the following string:

```
WBEM=ocgen.dll,OcEntry,wbemoc.inf,,7
```

Delete the word hide in all lines and all corresponding components will become
visible and available for deletion.

4.6.4. Startup

Many other programs besides services can be started automatically upon boot up,
and all of these eat up the system resources. Open the command line by executing
the **Start/Run** command sequence, and execute the **msconfig** command. This will
open the **System Configuration Utility** dialog window (Fig. 4.3). We already discussed this utility when considering viruses. Open the **Startup** tab, where all the
automatically launched programs are listed. Make sure that only those programs
that you use relatively often are checked for automatic start.

For example, if you have Microsoft Office installed, a utility to start office programs faster will be on the list. This utility loads certain libraries when the computer is booted, to save time when loading office applications. This is all fine and
well, but what if you use the computer mostly to play games and only occasionally
to write reports? In this case, you will be wasting resources every time you boot.
You will be better off to remove this utility from the startup and let the office application take a little longer to load.

4.6.5. Memory Dump

What else can be improved? By default, when the system crashes, it dumps memory
to the disk before rebooting. This means that all contents of the operating memory
are saved to a separate file. This information is needed for programmers to determine the cause of the crash. But we are not programmers and have no need to
scrutinize the dumped binary code. Therefore, I recommend disabling this feature
and not wasting your time dumping the memory to the disk (which takes quite
a bit of time), and save some disk space to boot.

This is done by right-clicking on **My Computer**, and selecting the **Properties** item in the window that appears. In turn, this will open the system properties dialog window. Select the **Advanced** tab and click on the **Settings** button in the **Startup and Recovery** section. In the **Startup and Recovery** window that appears (Fig. 4.17), select **(none)** in the **Write debug information** field.

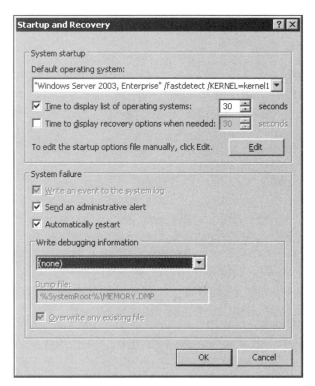

Fig. 4.17. The **Startup and Recovery** window

4.6.6. Embellishments

When we install a new version of the operating system, we want to see all of its bells and whistles, leading us to enable many features just for the sake of seeing them. These embellishments, however, do not always add to convenience of use of the system or improve its performance. To increase performance, sometimes these unnecessary frills have to be sacrificed. Doing this may increase the computer's efficiency, as the deluxe form of the operating system may be too much for it to handle.

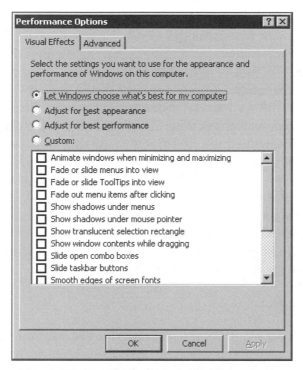

Fig. 4.18. The **Performance Options** window

To disable the unnecessary effects, right-click on **My Computer** and select the **Properties** item in the menu that appears. This will open the system properties window. Open the **Advanced** tab and click the **Settings** button in the **Performance** section. If your operating system is Window XP or 2003, the **Performance Options** window will open (Fig. 4.18). On the **Visual Effects** tab in this window, select the **Adjust for best performance** radio button. This will remove the check marks from all of the boxes in the effect list underneath.

This will disable various visual effects, but will allow the computer to work faster and just as productively.

But these are not all of the effects. Right click anywhere on the free desktop area, and select the **Properties** item in the context menu that appears. This will open the **Display Properties** dialog window. Here, open the **Appearance** tab and click on the **Effects** button. If your operating system is Windows 2000 or older, go straight to the **Effects** tab. Here, all the effects used when displaying program menus or icons are listed.

Painting the desktop also takes some time. Suppose you have several programs launched and you want to start another one by clicking its shortcut on the desktop. Clicking on the **Show Desktop** icon, you can see how long it takes the operating system to redraw the desktop. This is especially noticeable when the system does not have enough memory or is engaged in a resource-intensive process. Then it simply does not have enough resources for redrawing the desktop. The best way to speed up this process is not to use the background image, using a single-color background instead.

But, as we already discussed in *Chapter 1*, working on a bare desktop is not particularly pleasant, and embellishments are sometimes simply a must. But the background image must be chosen carefully. If you work with the 1024×769 display resolution, but use a 800×600 image for the background, every time the system places it on the screen it has to stretch it to cover the entire screen area. This is especially noticeable when JPEG images are used, because this requires enabling the voracious Active Desktop technology. The best thing to do in terms of performance is to use a BMP image of the same size as the screen resolution.

4.6.7. Extra Copies

Windows 2000/XP has many features that make life easier for the user. For example, when the operating system is installed, all drivers are copied to the hard disk. This is very convenient, because right after the operating system is installed it quite often turns out that not all devices have been found and new drivers need to be installed. Moreover, it might be that some devices were not connected during the installation (printers, scanners, removable disks, etc). The first time such a device is connected, the system finds its driver in the disk cache and installs it. The old way was to use a disk containing the device drivers, but these are all now stored on the hard disk.

All of this is fine if you have a 150 GB hard disk. But what if all you have is meager 30 GB, like I do, which is gobbled up by voracious applications in a very short time? The driver cache needs to be cleaned up because it takes up too much disk space. Doing this, of course, is not going to enhance performance, but there is no such thing as too much disk space.

So, after Windows has been running for a certain time and has installed all of the necessary drivers, the driver cache may be cleaned up. If you install a new device, its driver can be installed from the accompanying CD. The driver cache is located in the following folders:

❏ WINDOWS\Driver Cache\i386. Here, more than 70 MB of the most common drivers are stored. The main file here is driver.cab. This is the one that takes the most space.

❐ WINDOWS\System32\dllcache. Here, mostly uncompressed files from the driver.cab archive in the WINDOWS\Driver Cache\i386 folder are located. If the archive itself may be kept, the expanded version is not necessary, because it can take up as much as 500 MB.

Before deleting files, the system needs to be told that the file cache size is 0. This is done by executing the following command:

```
sfc /cachesize=0
```

If you are a relatively advanced user and do not remember the last time you resorted to the Windows help service, you can also delete the help files. They take up quite a bit of disk real estate (more than 30 MB), but contain very little useful information. It is easier to find pertinent information on the Internet than in Windows help.

There is a hidden folder, called System Volume Information, on each disk. This contains the system restore point files. What does this mean? When installing unsigned drivers, the system regularly creates a restore point. In this case, if something goes wrong with the installation, it can be rolled back. This is quite a powerful innovation in Window XP, but I personally have been saved by it only once. The latest operating system from Microsoft is quite reliable and when it does crash, it is most often for good.

When the operating system has just been installed and is being tuned up, the restore points are quite necessary. But once all the snags have been worked out and the system is running smoothly, the chances of its crashing are reduced to practically zero. The restore points take up quite a bit of disk space. This space can be recovered by manually cleaning up the System Volume Information folders on each disk. It is better, however, to use the System Recovery utility to delete these points. I advise you, after deleting all of the restore points, to create one restore point — just in case.

You can also disable automatic restore point creation. Right click on **My Computer**, and select the **Properties** item in the context menu that appears. In the **System Properties** window, open the **System Restore** tab and place a check mark in the **Turn off System Restore on all drives** box. Now the responsibility for creating a restore point rests squarely on your shoulders.

4.6.8. Speeding up the System Shutdown

Often, a situation when some program does not want to terminate arises at a system shutdown. In this case, there ensues a long and tedious wait (by default, 20 seconds) wait for this program to terminate. Most often, this time is wasted, because the fact that a program does not want to terminate usually means that it has hung.

However, if it is taking a long time to terminate a process on a server, waiting may be justified, in order for the process to terminate correctly. For example, if a database started processing a long query at the moment there was an attempt to shut the computer down, it is worth waiting for the processing of the query to be completed correctly.

But home computers seldom have this type of service, and user programs are usually terminated manually both before rebooting and when shutting down. Therefore, the wait time can be reduced. This is done by opening the **HKEY_LOCAL_MACHINE\SYSTEM\CurrentControlSet\Control** registry key, and changing the **WaitToKillServiceTimeout** parameter value from 20000 to 5000, that is, to five seconds. For home use, this should be more than enough.

4.7. Protection

We have already discussed two subjects related to the system security — virus protection and Windows optimization, so we will not go over them again. What we will consider here is how these two subjects are related.

Implementing all of the security and optimization measures described does not guaranty total security. You should be well aware of the fact that Windows settings are not always optimal. What is good for system security is, in most cases, detrimental to system performance. Implementing maximum security requires performing numerous checks, encryptions, audits, etc. All of these operations tax system resources, and enabling all available security features will put such a drag on the system that the efficiency of even the most powerful computer may drop below 50 percent.

Consequently, before getting protected, you need to have a clear idea of how important your data are for you. If their safety is important, you need to define the most important data and provide them with the maximum protection. All of your data should be grouped according to their importance and given protection based on this level of importance. This subject will be discussed in more detail later.

4.7.1. Viruses and Trojan Horses

Everything said previously about protection from viruses is equally applicable to Trojan horses. A Trojan horse is a program that is most often spread in a manner similar to those used to spread viruses (in e-mails with a come-on subject to pique the user's curiosity enough to get him or her to launch the attached file). Launching the Trojan horse program installs an automatically started program that opens a back door to the system for the hacker. Using this door, the hacker can access your computer and control it. Another variety of Trojan horse only looks for passwords, and then sends them to a specified e-mail address. The only way, in which Trojan horses differ from viruses, is that they seldom spread by themselves, as viruses usually do, and are sent with the express purpose of compromising a specific machine.

By following all virus protection rules, you also reduce the chances of being infected by a Trojan horse. Most antivirus programs scan not only for viruses, but also for these. This also testifies to the similar natures of the two.

4.7.2. Optimization

As for optimization, a lot has been said about the fact that the list of programs automatically launched at system boot need to be optimized, so that programs are not launched that won't be used. Every program has bugs, because programs are written by people, and, as we know, to err is human. If a hacker can locate a mistake in a program running on your computer, it may be used to enter your system or to do something else, about which you may not be particularly thrilled. This is why you should run only those programs and services that are really necessary. This is especially important in the case of network programs.

4.7.3. Strong Passwords

As if with one voice, all computer security specialists ask their users to use strong passwords. Unfortunately, their advice is rarely heeded. It is a bad idea to use names, legible words, or birthdays as passwords. These passwords can be compromised easily by a simple dictionary search method and, if there is already a dictionary of likely passwords available, this search will not take long.

It is advisable to generate random passwords containing lower and upper case letters, as well as digits and various other allowable characters. A password should be at least eight letters long, twelve being much more desirable. In the latter case, it will take much more time for the hacker to pick it.

When I need to generate a password, I start a word processor (the standard Notepad will do) and randomly hit the keyboard keys, periodically switching between the upper and lower cases. But how are you to remember such a password, you might well ask? You don't have to. I have a special text file, in which I save all of my passwords, along with the corresponding descriptions what each password is for.

Even though many security professionals recommend that you not save passwords in text files, I have no problems doing just this. The important thing here is to hide this file so that it can't be found by people who are not supposed to see it. How can this be done? Some recommendations on how to hide important files are provided later in the chapter.

But what I strongly urge that you do not do is save passwords using system means. People who trust Windows to remember must enjoy living dangerously. The protection built into this operating system is good enough, but hackers already know where to look for passwords (these locations are fixed in Windows), and they can first steal the encrypted file, and then decipher it on their computers at their own leisure.

Starting with Windows 2000, all passwords are stored in the SAM database, which cannot be opened. But this protection provides a false sense of security, because the file format can be determined easily, after which it can be found in the memory without much difficulty. Moreover, Windows protection against accessing such files can be circumvented easily. But no one even needs to waste time doing this, because the exact same SAM file is located in the Windows\Repair folder. This is a backup copy of the main file, with the important difference that it is absolutely unprotected. This is a huge oversight on the part of the developers.

There are many hardware solutions for storing passwords. For example, special encryption-protected removable media, access to which is further protected by a password. In this case, you only need to remember the password to this device.

The security provided by physical authentication devices is extremely strong. If a password that you enter when starting the computer can be easily stolen and used, a physical device is much more difficult to circumvent. Consequently, using specialized physical devices for protecting your computer is much more effective than relying on the built-in Windows password-protection methods. Without the physical devices the computer will not even boot, while a computer protected by a Windows password can be booted from a diskette or a CD. I recommend using physical devices to protect notebooks, in particular.

Passwords can be made more difficult to compromise by changing them frequently. Many companies recommend changing your passwords every month. Why? Changing passwords this often offers two security advantages:

❑ If the password is stolen somehow, the miscreant can only use it until the next password change.
❑ Picking the password is made more difficult. Many automated security systems can easily detect an attempt at password picking by several unsuccessful

authorization attempts, usually three, in a row. To circumvent such protection systems, hackers insert a delay before trying the next password. This makes the break-in process longer, but, unless the password is difficult and changed periodically, the attack will ultimately succeed. If the password is changed periodically, the possibility of picking it before the next change becomes very low.

For example, suppose that the password contains only numbers. Further, suppose that the password is 7000000. Using a brute force search, the hacker has tried the combinations from 0 to 6000000, when the password is changed to 5000000. Attempts at picking using further combinations can go on indefinitely without any success, because the range, in which the new password is located, has already been passed.

Real-life passwords are made up of letters and, if professional advice is followed, from combinations of letters and numbers. This produces many more possible combinations, consequently making a brute force password search much lengthier. Changing the system password every month makes picking it even more difficult.

4.7.4. Default Passwords

There is another aspect concerning passwords. This one should already be clear. The system must have no default user accounts or passwords. For example, Microsoft SQL Server has an administrator account named *sa* (System Administrator), without a password. If the administrator does not change this, any measures to enhance system security will be useless.

Windows 2000/XP has a guest account, but, fortunately, it is disabled by default. Do not enable it unless you really need it. When you do make it available, never give it full access rights, especially disk write rights.

Suppose that an acquaintance wants to send you a file over the network. Since you trust this user, you see nothing wrong with giving him or her write access rights. But suppose that this individual shares an account with another dozen people? Who is to guarantee that one of these people will not decide to delete all the folders? Even with only two users, the other one may turn out to be a scoundrel or joker.

4.7.5. Updates

As I have already mentioned, all operating systems have holes. The difference is that these holes are found in some systems, while nobody even bothers to look for them in others. Windows is the most widely used operating system, so this is the system that hackers are always trying to compromise and in which they are constantly looking for bugs to exploit. The discovery of such a bug ultimately allows the hacker to gain entry to the system.

Lately, Microsoft has been paying significant attention to Windows security and trying to minimize the adverse affects of the bugs it contains. In connection with this, they regularly issue updates and patches for their operating systems and application software.

As mentioned earlier, updating programs helps protect against viruses. In exactly the same way, updates help protect against hacker intrusions. Security is always security, regardless of whether you are trying to protect against viruses or hackers.

4.7.6. *Open Resources*

When working within a network, you want to be able exchange information without leaving the monitor. Nobody is satisfied any longer with the methods of our grandfathers — carrying diskettes from one computer to another. Moreover, diskettes are notoriously unreliable and fail constantly.

Windows 95 introduced a very handy file-exchange tool using shared folders. While this is convenient, for some reason users do not like protecting these folders with passwords, which makes them accessible by anyone. Some especially lazy users share entire disks when they need to share more than one folder. If I were the Windows developer, I would never allow users to share a folder without protecting it with a password. Protection against empty or simple passwords should be implemented at the operating system level.

Starting with Windows 2000, resources have become more difficult to access. Now you have to know a user login and password to get onto the computer. Moreover, disks can no longer be made common resources. But many people now allow users to enter their computer using one account (this is most often the default Guest account) and allow full access to the folders to everyone. The reason given most often for these actions is that you never know what may be of use and when. This is clearly the wrong approach.

You should strictly delimit access rights and create a separate account for each user of the system. When sharing a folder, allow only specific users or groups to access it. I have only one folder with full access rights to all users on my computer. I call it the common folder. If a user needs to access some other folder, I open it for reading only, and only for this specific user. If a user needs to write something to this folder, he or she first must write whatever it is to the common folder, after which I move the material to the intended destination.

Try not to give excessive access rights, even for temporary use. This reminds me of the time when I obtained almost around-the-clock access to the Internet for only $4.00 per month from one of the best providers in my hometown. A few years ago, when I was still in college, the best Internet access was at night. For only $12 per month, you could get unlimited access from midnight to 8 a.m. I did not need that much time, so two of my friends chipped in and we took turns surfing.

Some time later we discovered that all three of us could log in at the same time, because the server did not check for a multiple access from one account. But even this was not all. Once, at the end of a workday, I called the support service to get a problem of getting through to the server sorted out. The call was made at 5 p.m. I was given lengthy instructions and then an opportunity to check them in practice. For this purpose, the cutoff time was changed from 8:00 a.m. to 6:00 p.m. But this was the end of the workday and the administrator simply forgot to reset the cutoff time back to the earlier value. So, for two months, the three of us had unlimited Internet access from midnight till 6:00 p.m. Then we forgot to renew the agreement, and our account was simply closed.

The moral of the story is quite simple: Do not give access to more resources than the user has rights for, and, if you need to for some reason, don't forget to restore them to the original setting once this reason is no longer an issue. In my case, I did not break into the system, and the provider could not accuse me of any wrongdoing, but I think that it is highly unlikely that the administrator held on to his job for long.

There have been many books written on the subject of user and resource control. If you are an administrator or have to allocate access rights on your computer, it is vital that you read at least some of the trade literature. The advice I have provided here is only in the form of general recommendations based on my personal experience.

4.7.7. Close the Barn Door

Window 9*x* has one serious shortcoming: Local folders and files that are made common network resources by default could be shared through Internet connections. Because the access rules are very simple (you either have it or you don't, with the possibility to use a password, an option that no one ever selected), this is a wide gate for a hacker — with "Welcome" written on it in huge letters.

Suppose that you are working on a local network and have made a folder a common resource. This renders this folder accessible not only from the local network, but also from the Internet. If you do not want the folder to be accessible via the Internet, you need to disable this feature.

Right click on the **Network Neighborhood** icon and select the **Properties** item in the context menu that appears. Windows 2000/XP users need to right click on the Internet connection icon. This will open the protocol configuration window (Fig. 4.19). The **This connection uses the following items:** list enumerates all protocols and services that can be used to access the network from the computer, and vice versa. Clear the mark from the **File and Printer Sharing for Microsoft Networks** box. The service is now disabled, and the open local resources cannot be accessed via the Internet.

For Windows 9x, you also need to open the **Server Type** tab and clear the check mark from the **Enter the network** box. This way, when establishing an Internet connection, the computer will not waste time registering on the network, which means that the connection will be set up faster and will be more secure.

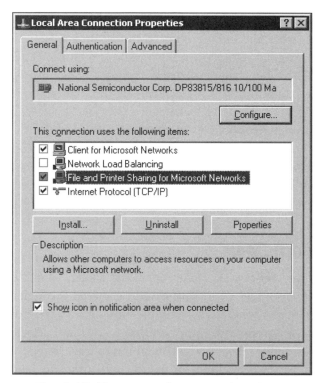

Fig. 4.19. The connection properties window

4.7.8. Settings

Now let's consider certain Windows settings that can be used to enhance system security. When the operating system is installed, some of its parameters are configured for high operating efficiency, but not for high security. This makes sense for a workstation, but for a server, where more important data is stored, these settings are ineffective.

The biggest oversight that needs to be corrected in the default settings is the path to the explorer.exe file. Open this registry key :

```
HKEY_LOCAL_MACHINE\SOFTWARE\Microsoft\Windows NT\CurrentVersion\Winlogon.
```

Note that only the file name is specified in the **Shell** parameter. So where is this file located? It is assumed that it should be located in the system folder. But this is not always the case. If a file with the same name is placed in the root of the system disk, this file will be executed, and not the one in the system folder. This problem is easy to fix: Simply change the parameter value to the full path, that is, to C:\Windows\explorer.exe.

The same is true for Windows 9*x*, only there the **Shell** parameter is stored in file system.ini in the Windows folder.

I remember a couple of years ago, when one of my coworkers was getting on my nerves with his music, which was not simply a little louder than I would have liked but, for good measure, not anything I would listen to myself. It is not particularly pleasant to spend eight straight hours listening to trash. To preserve my sanity, I wrote a little program deleting MP3 files, gave it the same name as the default screen saver, and slipped it into my colleague's system. Most users use the default screen saver. My friend was not an exception. When the time arrived for the screen saver to switch on, my program promptly took over and efficiently cleaned the disk of all of his torture instruments. Now I am the department's DJ, so I play what I like.

The moral: Never use default screen savers. They are easily substituted and any Trojan horse or virus can substitute for this file, and do whatever it wants while you are not watching.

When the system runs short of actual memory, it stores unused pages on the disk. When the computer is shut down, not all of this information is deleted. These memory pages written to the disk may contain very important data and hackers can read them. To prevent this from happening, it is best to delete these pages from the disk when the computer is turned off. Open the following registry key:

```
HKEY_LOCAL_MACHINE\SYSTEM\CurrentControlSet\Control\
Session Manager\Memory Management.
```

There should be a parameter named **ClearPageFileAtShutDown**. (If there is no such parameter, then you should create it yourself.) By default, the value of this parameter is set to 0, and the page file is not cleared. To fix this oversight, set the value to 1. This will prolong the shutdown time, but now there will be one fewer way to compromise your data.

4.7.9. Hiding Things

For starters, go to the Windows\System32 folder and check out how many files there are. Lots, huh? I would even say too many. Most of these files have the DLL extension. If you stick one more file with this extension in here, the chances are excellent that no one will ever notice. Just do not call it passwords.dll. Give it some innocent name, chkprofit.dll, for example. The name is not much of an attention grabber, so it is unlikely that anyone will notice it.

I remember reading a recommendation somewhere, advising people to name files they want to hide kernel.dll. There is already a file named kernel32.dll in the system, and any hacker knows that there should not be files with names like kernel.dll or kernel16.dll. So it is advisable to come up with a name that won't arouse suspicion. It should be similar to other names, but should not differ simply in the fact that it contains numbers.

Even though the file has the DLL extension, it can be opened and modified with any text editor, including Notepad. Because only you know the name of this file, anyone else will have problems locating it among more than two thousand system files.

Password files can be hidden not only in the Windows\System32 folder, but also in any other system folder in the Windows or Program File folder. The only requirement is that the folder contains as many different files as possible, which will make finding the password file difficult.

The final result is a well-hidden text file. There is a more effective way to hide a password file, but it costs $19.00, or, to be more exact, the price tag for CyD Archiver XP (Fig. 4.20). This is a great archiver for the bona fide hacker.

A file is hidden using this program by executing the following steps:

1. Create a text file, in which to save your passwords. This file can be given any name.
2. Using the CyD Archiver XP program, create an archive of the file. This is done by selecting the file and executing the **File commands/Add to new archive** command sequence. This will launch the new archive-creating wizard. Name

the archive following the same rules described earlier for hiding files. This means that the file must have the DLL extension and arouse no undue interest. CyD Archiver XP pays no attention to extensions, so the file can have any name.

3. For even greater security, you can protect the file with a password.
4. Move the archived file to the **Windows\System32** folder.

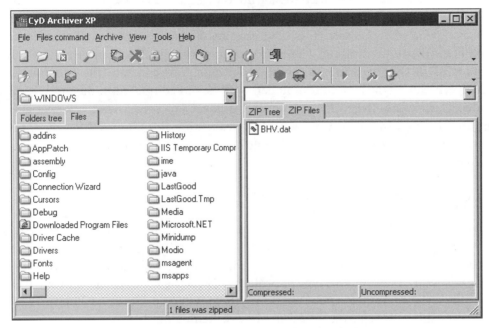

Fig 4.20. The CyD Archiver XP main window

Now the file is lost among thousands of other files and cannot be read in a text editor. Most archivers will not be able to open it, because of the changed extension, but CyD Archiver XP will open it with no problems.

There are some archivers that do not take the extension into account, but even they will not be able to open the file. I would not recommend CyD Archiver XP if it did not offer one neat feature: soft archive corruption. Any ZIP archive starts from a header, the first two characters of which must be letters PK. Launch CyD Archiver XP and select the **Break/Restore** command. This will open a window, in which you need to specify the archive name. Clicking on the three-dot button opens the standard file-open window. Use it to find the archive you created. Now, click on the **Patch** button, and the program will replace the first two characters (the file signature) with two random characters.

All the archivers that I have worked with before opening a file check to be sure that its extension is ZIP and that the signature is PK. If one of these conditions is not satisfied, the file is not considered to be an archive, so it is not opened. The CyD Ardchiver XP program does not perform these checks, and can even open an archive with a corrupted signature, and regardless of the extension.

CyD Archive XP can be used to hide not only individual files, but also entire folders. The main thing to remember is to give files plain names and keep their size small.

Following these simple rules, you can create well-protected files that hackers will have difficulties finding. There is one thing, though, that can give away a file protected in this manner: its modification date. Most system files do not ever change, meaning their modification dates will be old compared to the modification date of our camouflaged file. The problem is easy to solve using any specialized utility, or the same SyD Archiver XP (by executing the **File/Set file access time** command sequence in the latter). Simply do not forget to change the file modification date after editing the file.

4.7.10. False BIOS Protection

Practically all BIOS have an option to protect the entrance to the system with a password. The good thing about this protection is that, if a potential perpetrator does not know the password to the system, he or she will not be able to enter it. But this is an undependable type of protection, because it can be circumvented easily. When the computer is powered down, the power to preserve BIOS information is supplied by a battery on the motherboard. Removing this battery for a few seconds, with the main power disconnected (you can also short the battery connectors to make sure), clears all BIOS settings, including the password.

With older BIOS versions (such as AWARD), you did not even have to remove the battery, as there were many universal passwords for them. Starting with version 4.51, there are no more universal passwords, but the system security provided by the BIOS password has not been enhanced greatly.

A BIOS password can only provide even minimal protection if the system unit is well protected. Locking it in a safe in another room is one option.

4.7.11. Encryption

Encryption is one of the most reliable ways of protecting information, especially if the key is well protected. The key must be protected not only by making it as long as possible, which increases the code's resistance to the brute force breaking method, but it also must be stored in a place where hackers cannot get their hands on it. Stolen data will be impossible to use without knowing the key. The reason is that, in most cases, the missing key can be obtained only by breaking it using the brute force approach (using all of the possible key combinations), which may take too much time and/or computing resources. This, in turn, may not be worth the data that the key is needed in order to gain access.

Notebooks are very easy to steal, and this theft is a regular occurrence all over the world. Quite often, the information stored in a notebook is worth many times more than the notebook itself. Unless this information is encrypted, it becomes an easy prize for the thief.

But, for the encryption to be effective, the key must be properly designed. Otherwise, encryption produces a negative effect, because it can be easily broken and it does not provide the necessary level of security. But, because encryption uses computer resources and slows down the computer, the only effect achieved as a result is a waste of resources, while producing only minimum protection.

Most modern encryption programs generate random keys of maximum length. In this case, the system itself forces you to use the maximum protection. If your encryption program does not have a key-generation function, meaning that you have to make it up yourself, follow all of the recommendations provided in the Strong Password section. The main thing that I emphasize is that you should make the key as long as possible.

Practically all modern operating systems can encrypt entire disks. There are also specialized programs for this purpose, and these often offer more features. But it makes no sense to encrypt all of the data on all computer disks, because the encryption process consumes computer resources and its operation slows to an unacceptable level.

You have to classify information properly and encrypt only that data that actually requires it. If your encryption program can only encrypt disks, the best solution would be to create a separate disk for confidential data and encrypt only this disk. If you store your data or confidential files on the system disk (for example, in the My Documents folder), the entire system disk will have to be encrypted.

The built-in Windows encryption service can encrypt individual folders, and even files. But it cannot encrypt system folders, which I consider to be a serious minus. Consequently, if you intend to employ the built-in Windows encryption services, you should under no conditions store your confidential data in the system folders.

To encrypt a folder or a file, right click on it, and select the **Properties** item in the context menu that appears. Open the **General** tab, and click on the **Advanced** button there. This will open the advanced attribute window. Put a check mark in the **Encrypt contents to secure data** box. This will make it so the data is automatically encrypted in the background. Other users will not be able to read the data from the encrypted folders or files.

The encryption feature is available only if your disk is formatted as NTFS. The service does not work with disks formatted as FAT32.

Do not forget to regularly create a backup copy of the encrypted data. If the operating system becomes corrupted and will not boot, it will be impossible to restore the encrypted files. The backup copy must, of course, be stored away from unauthorized eyes, because it makes no sense to encrypt data that can be obtained easily from the backup copy.

You should encrypt not only disks, but also the information transmitted over networks, especially information transmitted over open Internet channels. The Internet was designed as an open system and there are many ways to intercept data sent over it. One of such methods is in the form of sniffer programs. They monitor traffic and intercept data belonging to others. For these programs to work, they must be installed on a computer handling third-party traffic.

Installing a sniffer program on a local computer with dial-up Internet access will allow you to see only your own traffic. You will not be able to see third-party traffic. However, installing a sniffer on the server of your Internet provider will allow you to see the data of all of the provider's clients.

By default, all e-mail messages are sent unencrypted. If you are worried about someone reading your mail, you should encrypt it yourself. Most mail clients already have a built-in encrypting tool based on Pretty Good Privacy (PGP) or OpenPGP technology. This is open-key encryption technology. Let's take a look at how PGP works.

You start by generating two keys: a public key and a private key. The public key is used to encrypt data. To decrypt it, you use the private key, which is not in any way related to the public key and cannot be picked by employing simple algorithms. You publish the public key and any user can use it to encrypt a message. Now, even if the message is intercepted, it cannot be decrypted without the private key, which you have safely stored somewhere.

Keep your private key in a safe place and you can be sure that your correspondence is 100-percent secure, because the only way to break the key is by trying all possible combinations. Even if the most powerful computer is used for this endeavor, the average time to find the correct key using this method will take an amount of time that is incommensurably larger than the value of the information. Unless you are sending top-secret government papers, Windows source codes, or credit card numbers for million-dollar accounts, no hacker will assemble these kinds of resources in order to break your private key. If all that is available to the hacker is a home computer, even the fastest that money can buy, he or she will grow old before being able to read your message. It's unlikely that the information will still be of much value by this point.

4.7.12. Login Accounts

To enter a computer running under Windows 2000/XP/2003, you need a user name and the corresponding password. By default, only one account is active when the system is first installed: the administrator account. If you are the only one who uses the computer, this is the way it should be. My only recommendation in this respect is that you rename the account and give it, for instance, your own name.

The administrator account is the most important account, and it possesses full access rights. Leaving the default account name — Administrator — makes the job easier for someone trying to compromise your computer. In this case, he or she has only to pick the password. If you use a simple password, you can kiss your computer security goodbye. It will be a cinch for a professional hacker to pick it by the dictionary method with the help of special utilities.

User accounts are controlled using the **Computer Management** utility. It is launched by executing the **Start/Settings/Control Panel/Administrative Tools/ Computer Management** command sequence. The Computer Management utility window is shown in Fig. 4.21.

In this window, open the **Computer Management/System Tools/Local Users and Groups/Users** section. Rename the administrator account. This is done by right clicking on the administrator account and selecting the **Rename** item in the context menu that appears.

You must ensure that only accounts that are actually used are active. I have heard many stories of corporate servers that were broken into using the accounts of fired employees. Employees that are fired often do not take the event easy and look for ways to get even for what they consider an unfair twist of fate.

Unused accounts can also be used to compromise home computers. For example, an account can be created by one of your friends, by a Trojan horse, or even by a virus. It is not even necessary to create a new account, as one that already exists will do. For example, Windows XP has an account called **SUPPORT**. This account is used for troubleshooting the computer from a remote computer, over the network. If you do not use the Microsoft support service, instead of simply leaving it disabled (which is its default state), you can delete it altogether, thus removing any temptation a hacker may have to try to use it.

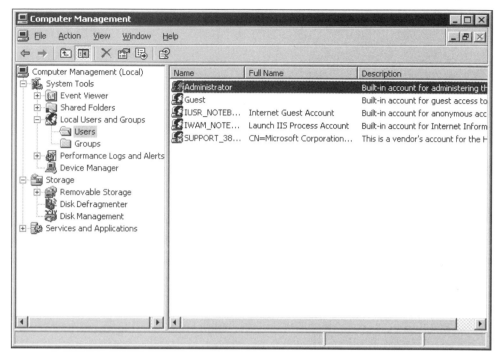

Fig. 4.21. The Computer Management utility window

Network administrators should pay close attention to accounts and use policies to make their life easier. This is too complex a subject for this book, so we will not go into it further.

4.7.13. Physical Access

I have already mentioned that a break-in can be either remote or local. To prevent unauthorized physical access to servers, they are often locked in a separate, alarm-protected room. This way nobody will be able just to get at the keyboard of a protected server and gain access to its resources. The administrators themselves manage these servers over the network, and a malefactor can also only break into them remotely.

It is a different story with notebooks. Where a desktop computer is quite bulky and heavy, a notebook is light and portable. It is no problem to take it home with you. No wonder that notebook theft continues to proliferate all over the world.

Most notebooks today are equipped with a connector for attaching a security cable, called a Kensington Lock. This cable is used for securing a notebook to the desk or to some other bulky piece of office. A notebook secured in such a way cannot be moved farther than the length of the cable, unless you have the key to the lock (or a good pair of bolt cutters).

4.8. Restoring Lost Data

Everyone who has worked with computers long enough has undoubtedly run into the problem of losing data. Files can be lost due to an electrical supply failure or simply because the wrong file was deleted. Whatever the reason, if the lost data is the fruit of long and tedious labor, the natural wish is to restore it, instead of doing all the work anew.

In my days as an administrator, I knew many young typists who could do as many as 150 words per minute (although what came out was often gibberish☺). These persons sometimes move faster than they think, and their fingers often reach out for the <Delete> key before their brains even realize what they are doing. The result is sometimes that hair-raising wail with which we are all familiar, something of the sort of: "Oh my God! I deleted the quarterly report! What am I going to do now?!" Indeed, what can be done? Create the report anew? I don't think that will be necessary. The data can be restored, and doing it right away increases the chances that the restoration will be successful without the need for lots of time and effort.

Data can also be lost because of the physical failures of the information-storage media. For example, with time, hard disks develop bad clusters, from which data can no longer be read, or at least not by conventional methods. There is also the danger that data will be destroyed by viruses, the number and variety of which have been increasing almost exponentially of late. Should a virus appear that can penetrate the system in some unique way (e.g., via a hole in Windows security), it can destroy all of your data.

4.8.1. File Deletion Mechanism

When a file is deleted, it is moved by Windows to the **Recycle Bin**. The **Recycle Bin** is simply a hidden folder. Each disk has this folder and when a file is deleted on a particular disk, it is moved to that disk's recycle bin so that time is not wasted moving files from one disk to another. Consequently, the deletion process is rapid and reversible. You can dig into this computer equivalent of an office waste basket at any time, and pull out things safe and sound that you did not intend to throw away in the first place. They won't even be crumpled, unlike the case with paper materials rescued from a real waste basket.

The file is gone for good when it is deleted from the recycle bin or when it is deleted while holding down the <Shift> key. But, even then, files are not physically deleted from the disk. They remain where they were, but the disk sectors they occupy are simply marked as available. In FAT16, when a file is deleted, the first letter of its name is changed to the character ~. Undelete utilities work by replacing this character with any letter in the name of the file that needs to be restored.

In FAT32, the deleted file name is not changed, and the entire name can be seen with the help of undelete utilities. The idea, however, is the same: When a file or a folder is deleted, it is not deleted physically, but its first sector is simply marked by the operating system as available. New data can then be written to it.

Consequently, a deleted file can be restored completely only if the operating system has not written to the sectors it used to occupy. The chances of complete recovery are quite high if you have a high capacity hard disk and no disk writing operations, such as system rebooting, large scale copying, or program installation, have been performed following the deletion. Each operation of this kind reduces the chances of successful recovery, so you must get down to the undelete business posthaste. Also, no matter how much real estate your hard disk may boast, the less free space that is left, the greater the chances that the operating system will write something into the released sectors of a deleted file.

4.8.2. Complete Deletion

So, as it turns out, deleted data are not actually deleted and can often be restored. But what if the data is confidential? Suppose that you want to get rid of an old hard drive and do not want that whoever ends up with it to see your data. So you confidently delete all your confidential files and folders, remove the drive from the computer, and sell it, donate it to a young hacker club, or simply throw it away. Whoever then gets their hands on this drive will have no problems restoring all of the data you had deleted, because the disk has not been written to after the deletion. So the peace of mind the deletion of your confidential data gave you is absolutely false.

Consequently, if you do not wish the data on a disk you are going to dispose of to be compromised, I recommend you carry out the following sequence of steps:

1. Delete all of the files you do not want others to see.
2. Fill the disk to 70 or 80 percent of its capacity with garbage data.
3. Defragment the disk.

Even if some of the files are not overwritten in step 2, the defragmentation procedure will take good care of that. During this process, many read/write operations are performed all over the disk, with the 20 percent of free space used as temporary data storage for these operations. After the defragmentation, you can be 99-percent certain that the data cannot be restored.

There are special utilities for the secure deletion of data from hard disks, which write garbage into the sectors occupied by the deleted files or folders. These utilities are easy to use, but make the deletion process longer. Where conventional deleting simply involves marking the deleted file sectors as available, secure delete utilities also have to fill these with other data, which takes some time, even though what is being placed here is just garbage.

I do not personally use secure delete utilities because, in my opinion, they just waste resources, with little payback. I also do not trust programs whose developers say that the products overwrite deleted files more than once. Why isn't writing garbage once enough? Could it be that they are simply duping us and the data are not overwritten? I can't say one way or another for sure, but I do hope that these utilities work as advertised.

4.8.3. Data-Recovery Utilities

The easiest way to restore data is to use a program developed especially for this purpose. These programs have a simple graphical interface, most often resembling Explorer. You simply search through the folders looking for the data you want to restore and, when the necessary file is found, click the restore button.

As you already know, after data have been deleted, there should be as few disk writing operations performed as possible before an attempt at recovery. Therefore, you should be prepared for such contingencies. Suppose that you have accidentally deleted a file and want to restore it, but you do not have the necessary utility. You urgently connect to the Internet and download and install a recovery utility. However, what guarantee is there that, while you are searching the Internet for the utility and then downloading and installing it, the clusters you want to recover will not be overwritten?

If you want to recover data, but do not have a recovery utility installed, do not download and install it to the disk where the file you want to recover is located. Disk writing operations must be kept to a minimum so as not to overwrite the clusters containing the data you want to recover.

The best option is to be prepared for such a contingency and have a recovery utility already installed. I will try to help you select the right one by describing a few of the best recovery utilities.

EasyRecovery

The address of the developer is **http://www.ontrack.com/**.

This is the most powerful utility of its type, and its distribution package is also the largest: more than 30 MB. The program is quite expensive; however, the capabilities it offers are sometimes simply a must-have and losses incurred as a result of lost data may be many times more than the program's price.

In addition to data-recovery capabilities, the professional package includes tools for repairing damaged Microsoft Office files. Suppose that your hard disk has developed a bad cluster. In this case, the file containing the cluster cannot be opened. Using EasyRecovery, the file can be brought back to life. Of course, the data in the bad cluster will most likely be lost, but the remaining part of the file will be recovered successfully. In most cases, the recovered material only needs to be patched up slightly (e.g., styles reformatted, missing text restored, etc.) to be ready for use again.

The professional package contains many diagnostic tools and utilities for repairing various storage media. It can even be used to restore e-mail messages.

Working with the program, you immediately feel that this is one of the best utilities available, as every detail has been thought over so thoroughly and so many features are offered. The only drawback is its biting price. It is up to you to decide whether your data is worth the price of this program. If so, you should have already bought it yesterday.

File recovery

The address of the developer is **http://www.lc-tech.com**.

This is a very simple and easy-to-use utility. It supports the main file systems: FAT12, FAT16, FAT32, NTFS, and VFAT. The utility even works with compressed or encrypted NTFS volumes and folders.

The most basic license costs $25.00, while the most expensive version goes for $99.00. This is quite reasonable for a product of this quality that can save you in the event of important data loss.

4.8.4. Manual File Recovery

Next, we will consider manual data recovery. Sometimes data cannot be recovered with special recovery utilities. In such a case, you can try to locate the lost file or its fragments on the disk, and restore it manually. Situations may arise when data has not been saved to the disk at all or the clusters involved have already been overwritten. For example, imagine that you are working on an annual report or a term paper when, suddenly, there is a power failure or a fatal system crash. In principle, your last changes (or the entire work, if you are not in a habit of saving the document every few sentences) have not yet been saved to the file, so these programs will be of no help to you here. They only recover deleted files. It looks, at first, like you will have to kiss this data good bye. Don't despair yet. There is a way out, and there might even be more than one. First of all, Word automatically stores your current work in temporary files. In addition, your work is always saved in the swap file. To recover your data from here is a test for your hacker skills.

The latest Word and Excel versions can restore unsaved data from the temporary files themselves. But this does not always work, and I have often encountered situations where automatic recovery was not successful.

If you are trying to recover text data, this will not take you that much time. You might not be able to recover everything, but recovering at least some, or even most, of what is lost is a realistic proposition. Exactly how much is recovered depends, of course, on how much disk writing has been done since the time, at which the data were lost.

For this work, you will need a good disk editor utility. Because I work with Windows 2000, I personally use DiskProbe utility, which is a part of this operating system. Those of you who are still plugging away under Windows 9x/ME will have to use some other utility. I recommend WinHex (**www.winhex.com**) or, even better, PTS DiskEditor (**www2.PhysTechSoft.com**). The latter utility is preferable, because it has a sector-search option, which is very handy for searching the disk for the lost data to be recovered.

Which of these programs to use is for you to decide. I will demonstrate a recovery example using DiskProbe, because I spend 99 percent of my working time in Windows 2000 and see no reason to pay for other utilities. I have Windows 9x installed, just in case, but it is not even configured properly. If you have a Windows 2000 distribution package, you can even install DiskProbe on Windows 9x/ME.

Installing Disk Probe

Insert the Windows 2000 installation CD into the drive, and open the **Support/ Tools** folder. Here, find and launch the Setup.exe program. It will install the utility on your system. Needless to say, it is better that the utility is installed before you lose the data.

Having installed and launched Disk Probe, you are now ready to embark on some practice recovery experiments. You will have to find sectors containing some test-file text on your hard disk and save a piece of the text into another file. All of this has to be done without resorting to the file system but, instead, by using Disk Probe to work directly with the disk sectors.

This should be good practice for you, for, when a disaster strikes, you should already know how to handle it.

Recovery

If you are ready to start, launch DiskProbe (Fig. 4.22). If your operating system is Windows 2000, the utility is launched from the **Start/Programs/Windows 2000 Support Tools/Tools** menu item.

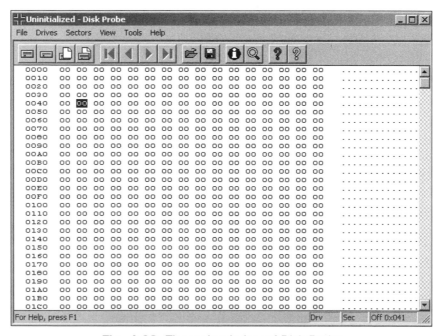

Fig. 4.22. The main window of Disk Probe

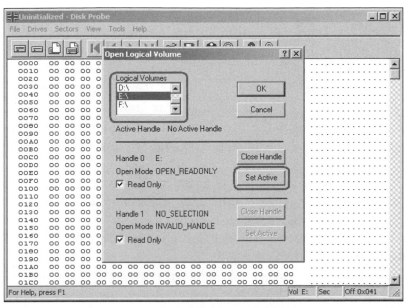

Fig. 4.23. Selecting a disk

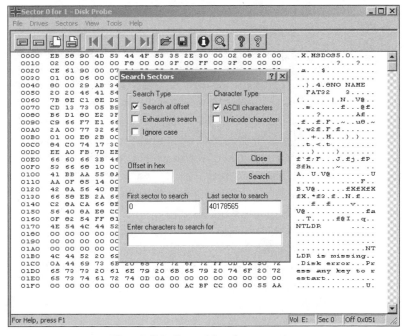

Fig. 4.24. Searching for a sector

You now need to select the disk containing the data you want to recover. This is done by selecting the **Drivers/Logical Volumes** menu item. The window that opens (Fig. 4.23) contains a list of the system's disks. Double click on the required disk, and click on the **Set Active** button. Finally, click on the **OK** button.

Next, select the **Tools/Search Sectors** menu item. This will open the **Search Sectors** window (Fig. 4.24). To search the entire volume, place a check mark in the **Exhaustive search** box. If the case of the text is not important, or if you simply do not remember it, place a check mark in the **Ignore case** box. You will also have to specify whether the text is in ASCII or Unicode coding. This is very important, because the text will look different in different codings. Now, enter some text from the file you are trying to restore in the **Enter characters to search for** field, and click on the **Search** button.

Try to use words in the text that are not too common, to avoid having DiskProbe stop every couple of seconds.

The search may take as long as five minutes. It depends on the volume size and the spindle speed of your hard drive. It took DiskProbe almost 20 minutes to search through my 5 GB logical disk at 7,200 rpm.

When the program finds the text, it issues a request for a new search. Refuse the request. Click on the **NO** button and check the found text. The contents of the sector are shown in hexadecimal format in the larger area on the left of the window. In the smaller panel on the right, the contents are shown as text. Check it to ensure that the text is from the right file.

If you are not satisfied with the results, resume the search. If this is the text you are looking for, check if the entire file has been found. If not, execute the **Sectors/Read** command sequence. In the window that opens, enter the starting sector (this will be the one that you have found) and the number of sectors to read. Read about 10 sectors. If this does not cover the whole text, increase the number of sectors to be read.

After you find the entire file, execute the **File/Save As** command. Save the found text using the file save dialog window that opens.

The main drawback of the manual search is that it is so complex and work-intensive. The most difficult task is restoring large files. Here, the main problem is that a file can be saved in non-sequential sectors, and large areas of the disk have to be searched. This makes search for and saving the found data more difficult, but at least some of these will be found.

4.8.5. Restoring Data on Removable Storage Media

Data are not physically erased on diskettes and rewritable CDs either, but only the sectors they occupy are marked as available. Consequently, the same data-recovery techniques can be used to restore data on them. Some programs issue a direct warning that the erased data can be recovered. Also, serious CD-writing software packages contain utilities for recovering erased data. Fig. 4.25 shows an example of such tool for Roxio Easy CD and DVD Creator 6.

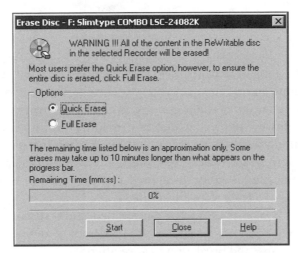

Fig. 4.25. The disk-erase window for Roxio Easy CD and DVD Creator 6

By default, all CD-writing programs (at least those that I have tried) use a quick-erase method, which does not physically erase the disk. If you want to dispose of a disk containing important information, use the full-erase method. I personally supplement the full erasure by putting a few deep scissors scratches on the disk.

4.9. Reanimation

Too many times I have seen computer components being thrown away that could have been put back in working order with minimal expense. One of my acquaintances collects components of this kind and brings then back to life. He has two big boxes at home filled with hard drives, CD-ROM drives, and various expansion cards that he has repaired. Looking at his computer, you are reminded of Frankenstein's monster, as not a single screw has been bought new. Every piece of hardware present has been restored after being removed from another machine. His room gives you the impression of a survivor of World War III — a motif that is often popular among hackers.

It is indeed cheaper to throw some components away than to repair them, but the process of reanimating dead hardware can be interesting and educational. The most important thing, however, is that you can boast to your friends that you have repaired this or that part all by yourself.

4.9.1. Fans

With time, any fan will wear out and start squeaking and making other unpleasant noises. Many users get scared when they hear this noise for the first time, but there is no need for undue alarm. First, get your ear close to the system block and try to determine the exact source of the noise. If it is emanating from behind the system block, it is your power-supply fan that is providing the musical entertainment. If the noise is coming from inside the system block, then the soloist is the processor's cooler fan. Both problems can be solved, but the latter is easier to deal with, because the processor fan is easier to remove. Getting to the power-supply fan will require the removal of a large number of screws.

If the source of the noise cannot be determined, but it disappears after a while, it was most likely your processor's cooler fan. Processor cooler fans are more fragile than power-supply fans, and break down more often.

Why do fans begin to make noise? There are two reasons:

❏ Its lubrication has dried up or become clogged up by dust. Consequently, the friction has increased.

❏ The spindle in the bearing sleeve has worked loose and is beating against the walls.

Both problems are easily repaired by applying a couple of drops of simple lubricant to the spindle. While this represents a long term solution to the former problem, it is rather short-lived in the latter case. The computer case constantly collects dust and needs regular vacuuming and cleaning. But human laziness is one of our greatest failings, and we seldom open the case for maintenance cleaning.

But, if your processor fan starts acting up and you cannot get it serviced or replaced, you can solve the problem yourself in no time at all. Open the system case and take the fan off the processor heat sink. Clean the dust off it and give it a good looking over. There should be a small hole in it, as shown in Fig. 4.26.

Fig. 4.26. The lubricating hole

In the Intel fans, this hole is often hidden under a sticker. Peel off the sticker to gain access.

Having found the hole, put a couple of drops of lubricant into it and put the fan back in place. If there is no such hole, try to put the oil on the fan's shaft and let it seep down into the bearing. This simple therapy should help the fan work like new.

Power supply fans are repaired in a similar manner, but it takes longer to remove them and they usually have no holes for lubrication.

Even if your processor fan is not making too much noise, it doesn't hurt to lubricate it when you open the system block for some other purpose. Doing this will not take that much time, while the fan's life time will be extended and it may even begin to work more quietly.

4.9.2. DVDs and CDs

The surface of these disks is quite fragile and deteriorates over time. Repairing a disk edge is the most difficult task. It is very thin and, if it is not well protected, moisture from the air gradually penetrates the disk and gradually destroys the disks surface to the point that it becomes unreadable.

The reverse surface of the disk, the one with the picture or printing on it, is also important. It serves as a reflector for the laser beam and, if it is scratched, the disk will read with errors or may become altogether unreadable. This side on both CDs and DVDs can be repaired by painting the scratches over with simple, dark colored nail polish. I have restored quite a few movie disks this way.

The working surface is also rather easily damaged, and any scratches reduce its reflective quality. Needless to say, nail polish won't do here. So, how can you fix these scratches? If the scratch is not too deep, it can be polished out. How is this done? Take some toothpaste and a piece of soft cloth and buff the scratch. This often works.

4.9.3. CD Drives

Imagine yourself sitting peacefully, working busily, and listening to some music from a CD, or simply copying some data from it, when, all of sudden, there is a loud bang from the system block. From personal experience, I can tell that the sound is loud and unexpected enough to shake you up a bit. Fortunately, it is rather harmless, as it is just the CD departing to the greener pastures. Going out with a bang, so to say.

Why did it explode? Modern CD drives spin disks with speeds up to 52x. Old CDs were not designed for speeds of this magnitude and their material cannot withstand the load, so they start to develop tiny cracks. Scratches on the disk surface also contribute to the development of cracks. As time goes by, the cracks get bigger, eventually becoming big enough that the disk can no longer handle the load, resulting in you jumping from your chair in fright that this guy in the next office cubicle must have decided to finally make good on his promise to blow your head off if you play that Grandma-got-run-over-by-a-reindeer song again.

Most audio disks are not designed for high speeds either, because the 2x speed is enough for quality audio reproduction with the prefetch read to the buffer. So music centers and other audio disk players do not spin disks at these high speeds. Consequently, even cracked disks, which might explode in a computer CD drive, can safely be played on these.

Post-Explosion Cleanup

After an explosion, the pieces of the destroyed disk must be removed from inside the drive. For a start, try to remove the CD drive cover. If this fails, look for a small hole on the front panel of the drive. Straighten a paper clip and insert it into the hole. With the end of the clip, try to feel for a part, which yields to being pushed, with moderate force by the clip. The indication that you have found the right part is that the CD drive tray will open slightly, after which you can open it fully by yourself.

Now you can try to remove the remains of the disk from the drive. If the disk blew up at a slow revolution speed, there is a good chance that it cracked into a few large pieces that will be easy to remove. If it blew up at high speeds, it will most likely have been reduced to sand. In this case, the CD drive cannot be cleaned without performing an autopsy.

Before opening the drive, you will have to disconnect the power cord from the computer and open the system block. Disconnect all of the cables from the drive

(I recommend that you map out how they are connected on a piece of paper to ensure that you can actually put them back properly) and remove the screws holding the drive in the drive bay. There may be warnings on the drive case against opening it, but pay no attention to these, as you have no choice but to open it. Just make sure that its power supply is disconnected before you do.

Remove the screws holding the cover in place, and remove the top cover and the front panel. Clean all of the disk pieces out of the drive and put everything back together. If the lens has not been damaged or moved by the accident, the drive should work as if nothing has happened.

Cleaning the Lens

As they get older, CD drives develop problems reading disks. The main culprit here is dust. Over time, the lens that focuses the laser beam becomes dirty and the laser may not read all disks.

This is easily fixed by special CD drive cleaning kits. These are regular CDs with a brush attached at the business surface. When the drive tries to read such a disk, the brush cleans the dirt off the lens.

But cleaning disks do not always help. If the lens is covered with grime, you need to open the drive and wash the lens yourself. Use cotton wool and warm water for this task. Do not use alcohol-based cleaners, because they can tarnish the lens.

4.9.4. Hard Disks

Hard disk drives have become less reliable of late. I have three hard drives made at the end of the 1990s and they are still working like new and have no bad sectors. But, as write density has increased, disk sectors have become so small that their quality leaves a lot to be desired. It often happens that data cannot be read from bad sectors, and are lost.

What makes bad sectors develop? As a matter of fact, even brand new disks have bad sectors. Because the sectors on the disk are extremely small, any miniscule dust particle or a wrong move by the reading head kills them. Manufacturers anticipate a certain percentage of defects in disks and leave spare sectors·on them. While the supply of the spare sectors lasts, data from the bad sectors that develop during disk operation are moved to these sectors without the user even noticing. However, when the supply of the spare sectors is exhausted, the developing bad sectors can be observed with the help of special programs.

Most users employ the standard Windows scandisk utility for checking their disks. When it encounters a bad sector, it marks it as such and moves all its data to a spare sector. But a month later, or even sooner, another bad sector will develop next to the old one. This process will just continue.

Bad sectors most often develop at the end of the disk, so reducing its size by 10 to 20 percent will make the disk work for a long time without developing bad sectors.

Disks can sometimes be restored with the help of specialized diagnostic and repair utilities from the disk manufacturer. But, in my experience, repairs of this type have only a temporary effect and, some time later, the disk will start developing problems again. Therefore, this should be seen only as a temporary solution, such as, for example, when a new disk cannot be obtained at the present time.

In order to use a utility of this type, you should know the exact disk model and find a corresponding utility on the manufacturer's site. Also, before using the utility, familiarize yourself with the accompanying instruction manual.

4.10. Cracking Programs

There is a never-ending war between programmers and hackers: The former are trying to protect their programs while the latter are trying to break through the protection. Programmers want to receive financial rewards for their labors, which is quite natural. Everyone has to make a living one way or another, so few people can afford simply to give away their work for free. If a person has selected programming as his or her profession, then earning a decent living should be one of the rewards.

Only people for whom programming is a hobby and not their main profession can afford to give away their programs. But they do not provide their users with any follow-up support worth mentioning, and generally distribute their wares on an "as is" basis. Some companies distribute their software free-of-charge on purpose, after which they earn their money by providing support (as is often the case with the Open Source software) or from other associated products or commercials.

Hackers refuse to pay for their programs flat out. A person can be forgiven if he or she cracks a program because of the lack of money to pay for it. But doing this with pecuniary motives, or just for the hell of it, is a crime and should be punished.

In this book, I will consider only the principles used by hackers to break programs. This information is given for educational purposes only, and it is not recommended to actually use it, especially for commercial or self-serving purposes.

Although only simple methods are going to be considered, I hope that you will find the information useful and educational.

4.10.1. Why People Crack Programs

Most shareware software works for only a certain period of time or for a certain number of launches. In this case, they are protected by a most simple launch counter, or a simple date check algorithm. These forms of protection are often quite easy to circumvent for even an inexperienced user.

Why is the protection in many cases so simple? Because the average next-door programmer will not spend a lot of time and effort on designing protection. To make a program really difficult to break, the author has to come up with some original method. But thinking up program-protection methods will leave him or her no time for working on the program itself. Then he or she will not be able to compete with corporate software monsters, which have large protection experience and algorithms that are already worked out.

Programs created by corporate software teams have stronger protection against simple cracking methods, but this does not mean that they cannot be broken. A beginner might be thwarted by these, but a professional who has cracked several products from the same company will be familiar with the protection methods and algorithms used in its products and will quickly find the changes and bypass them.

Note that prior to the introduction of activation for Windows XP, even Microsoft used to protect its software products by the simple serial number method. The algorithm is as simple as the ABC, because it makes no sense to devise a complex variant that can be broken just as easily. There is no protection that cannot be circumvented.

If a program is too difficult to crack, a cracker who buys one license will spread it all over the world. Although you might think that it should be easy to find out who made his license code available to everyone, this is not the case, since the standard practice is to place only those licenses that have been purchased with a stolen credit card on the Internet. The culprit can never be traced.

It makes no sense to spend all the time and effort devising protection that will be broken anyway. It would be much more prudent to make buying licensed software more advantageous than stealing it. The software price must correspond to the content, and then buyers will not begrudge spending their hard-earned money on it. If software writers follow these conditions, people will buy their programs instead of breaking them or using cracks.

Some companies have tried to protect their products with built-in keys, encryption, or equipment binding, but these protection schemes have ultimately ended up being broken anyway. A program too difficult to break will not become popular. Windows has become so popular thanks to its simplicity, user-friendliness, and the ease with which it can be broken. Sometimes, cracks for new versions appear on the Internet before the operating system's official release. Consequently, the number of people using this operating system becomes large, with some users liking it so much that they ultimately buy a licensed copy. Word of mouth from users is the best form of advertising. The more users (legal and otherwise) a product has, the greater popularity it generates. Fighting hackers is useless and, sometimes, simply unnecessary. Software developers should make people pay money for their products by producing quality programs and not by means of strong protection.

Let's take a look at the various protection techniques and how hackers get around or break them. For shareware programmers, this information will be of help in devising more effective protection for their products.

4.10.2. Extending the Usage Period

The easiest method for cracking a program is to extend its usage period. As already mentioned, most shareware programs are protected by primitive number, launch, or day counters. The latter protection is the easiest to bypass. The reason for this is that programmers often work with this method in a clumsy way. A program with this type of protection records the installation date to the registry. At launch, it checks the number of days, by which the current date exceeds the installation date. If this is greater than the set value, it determines that the free-use period has expired and applies some method of preventing its further use. This is where the error lies. Change the computer system date to, for example, January 1, 2015 before installing the program. After installing the program, set the date back and you can use it for 10 years plus whatever its trial-use period is. During this time, it will not only become obsolete, but may simply no longer be needed. Technologies change every couple of years, but, here, you have given yourself 10.

Too bad, only beginners make this kind of mistakes with their protection. Professional programmers in shareware producing companies long ago designed more effective methods to check how long a program has been used. The simple clock change will not work on their products.

4.10.3. Jacking Up the Counter

If changing the system date does not do the trick, or if the protection is based on counting the number of launches, another technique may be helpful. This is called registry monitoring, and a tool to work with this can found at the following site: **www.sysinternals.com**. The program is called Regmon for Windows NT/9*x*, and is available as freeware.

Let's consider how Regmon operates using a program called Window Shell as a guinea pig. This program is no longer sold, so we will not deprive the developer any sales by showing how to crack it. Start Regmon, and then start the program you want to crack. All instances of accessing the registry are displayed in the Regmon window. The access messages are divided into the following column fields:

- ❑ #: the message number
- ❑ Process: the program accessing the registry
- ❑ Request
- ❑ Path
- ❑ Result
- ❑ Other: additional parameters

The first things you need to look for are the lines, in which the value of the **Process** field is *deskt* (this is the name of the executable file) and the value of the **Request** field is *SetValueEx*. When programs are loaded, they usually read the parameters and settings from the registry, while *SetValueEx* is the registry-write operation. But what can a program write to the registry while being loaded? Only the counter value. Look at the *Other* field: It contains the value written to the registry. In the example shown in Fig. 4.27, its value is 18. It is written to the following address: **HKEY_CURRENT_USER\Software\ Desktop\ProductID**.

Now, look a little higher. A value of 19 was read from the same address earlier. This means that we have a countdown counter here and, when its value reaches zero (or perhaps even a negative value), the program will no longer start. But you can now increase the value of this counter manually, allowing the program to work indefinitely. In some programs, this counter can be set all the way to 10,000 without the program noticing it. If the protection is a count-up counter (say, to 100), you can set its initial value to −10,000 and, again, enjoy unlimited use of the program.

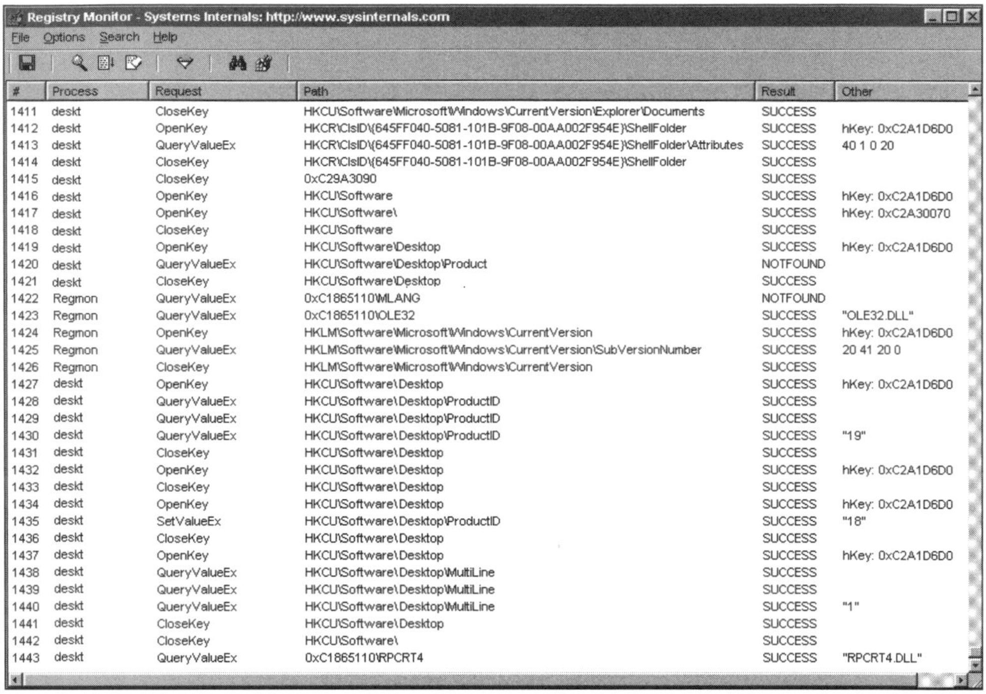

#	Process	Request	Path	Result	Other
1411	deskt	CloseKey	HKCU\Software\Microsoft\Windows\CurrentVersion\Explorer\Documents	SUCCESS	
1412	deskt	OpenKey	HKCR\ClsID\{645FF040-5081-101B-9F08-00AA002F954E}\ShellFolder	SUCCESS	hKey: 0xC2A1D6D0
1413	deskt	QueryValueEx	HKCR\ClsID\{645FF040-5081-101B-9F08-00AA002F954E}\ShellFolder\Attributes	SUCCESS	40 1 0 20
1414	deskt	CloseKey	HKCR\ClsID\{645FF040-5081-101B-9F08-00AA002F954E}\ShellFolder	SUCCESS	
1415	deskt	CloseKey	0xC29A3090	SUCCESS	
1416	deskt	OpenKey	HKCU\Software	SUCCESS	hKey: 0xC2A1D6D0
1417	deskt	OpenKey	HKCU\Software\	SUCCESS	hKey: 0xC2A30070
1418	deskt	CloseKey	HKCU\Software	SUCCESS	
1419	deskt	OpenKey	HKCU\Software\Desktop	SUCCESS	hKey: 0xC2A1D6D0
1420	deskt	QueryValueEx	HKCU\Software\Desktop\Product	NOTFOUND	
1421	deskt	CloseKey	HKCU\Software\Desktop	SUCCESS	
1422	Regmon	QueryValueEx	0xC1865110\MLANG	NOTFOUND	
1423	Regmon	QueryValueEx	0xC1865110\OLE32	SUCCESS	"OLE32.DLL"
1424	Regmon	OpenKey	HKLM\Software\Microsoft\Windows\CurrentVersion	SUCCESS	hKey: 0xC2A1D6D0
1425	Regmon	QueryValueEx	HKLM\Software\Microsoft\Windows\CurrentVersion\SubVersionNumber	SUCCESS	20 41 20 0
1426	Regmon	CloseKey	HKLM\Software\Microsoft\Windows\CurrentVersion	SUCCESS	
1427	deskt	OpenKey	HKCU\Software\Desktop	SUCCESS	hKey: 0xC2A1D6D0
1428	deskt	QueryValueEx	HKCU\Software\Desktop\ProductID	SUCCESS	
1429	deskt	QueryValueEx	HKCU\Software\Desktop\ProductID	SUCCESS	
1430	deskt	QueryValueEx	HKCU\Software\Desktop\ProductID	SUCCESS	"19"
1431	deskt	CloseKey	HKCU\Software\Desktop	SUCCESS	
1432	deskt	OpenKey	HKCU\Software\Desktop	SUCCESS	hKey: 0xC2A1D6D0
1433	deskt	CloseKey	HKCU\Software\Desktop	SUCCESS	
1434	deskt	OpenKey	HKCU\Software\Desktop	SUCCESS	hKey: 0xC2A1D6D0
1435	deskt	SetValueEx	HKCU\Software\Desktop\ProductID	SUCCESS	"18"
1436	deskt	CloseKey	HKCU\Software\Desktop	SUCCESS	
1437	deskt	OpenKey	HKCU\Software\Desktop	SUCCESS	hKey: 0xC2A1D6D0
1438	deskt	QueryValueEx	HKCU\Software\Desktop\MultiLine	SUCCESS	
1439	deskt	QueryValueEx	HKCU\Software\Desktop\MultiLine	SUCCESS	
1440	deskt	QueryValueEx	HKCU\Software\Desktop\MultiLine	SUCCESS	"1"
1441	deskt	CloseKey	HKCU\Software\Desktop	SUCCESS	
1442	deskt	CloseKey	HKCU\Software\	SUCCESS	
1443	deskt	QueryValueEx	0xC1865110\RPCRT4	SUCCESS	"RPCRT4.DLL"

Fig. 4.27. The Regmon program window

Dates can be corrected in exactly the same way. For example, it is possible to modify one registry parameter for The Bat program in such a way that the program will work, for all practical reasons, indefinitely, indicating that you have –5,000 days left.

If you ran into problems obtaining the necessary information using registry monitoring, deleting all the information pertaining to the program you are trying to crack may help. The program may sometimes have to be reinstalled after this lobotomy.

If the protection counts the number of launches, instead of the date, bypassing it can be made even easier. When the program is installed, it will write the initial parameters to the registry. Launch the registry editor, and look for those parameters at this registry key: **HKEY_CURRENT_USER\Software**, plus the name of the company or the program. Select the key and export it to a file. When the number of launches runs out, simply import this key, overwriting the old one. This will restore all of the settings to their initial state and you will be able to use your favorite utility again. Repeat this process when necessary.

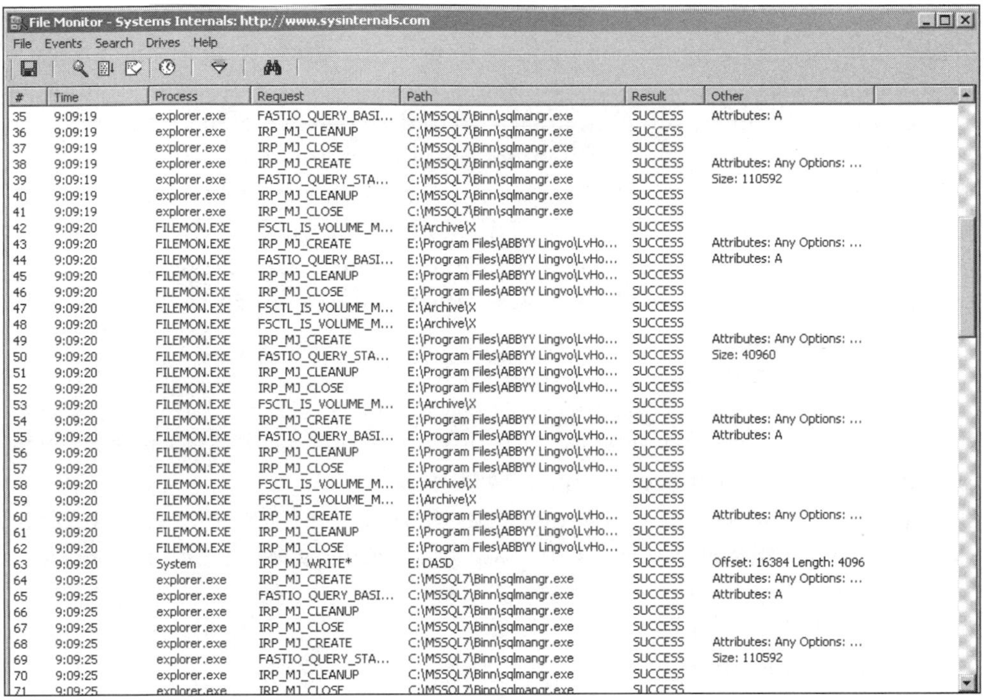

Fig. 4.28. The Filemon program window

Why have we only been talking about the registry? Because writing to it is the most common and convenient method for storing program parameters. But this is not the only method. Some modern, and most old, programs use regular files to store their parameters.

A file-activity monitoring utility can be downloaded from a site that should already be familiar to you: **www.sysinternals.com**. It is called Filemon, for Windows NT/9x.

Working with Filemon (Fig. 4.28) is the same as with Regmon, the only difference being that it monitors writing and reading various parameters to files.

Finally, I would like to point out that the counter may be updated not only when the program is started, but also when it is shut down. The date counter may not change at all, but you can also try to figure them out.

4.10.4. Total Crack

If you want to get rid of all registration nag screens and enjoy the program's features, you can create a fake registration. Here, however, you will have to have at least basic disassembler and assembler skills, as well as knowledge of machine code. A disassembler is a program that converts the machine code for the program into assembler code, which is more convenient for humans to work with. In order to program in assembler, you need to have a good knowledge of its commands, but a very basic knowledge will be sufficient for breaking a simple protection system.

We will consider only the fundamentals of cracking using disassembler, without going into the subject too deeply. The information presented will be enough for an experienced programmer to crack quite sophisticated protection systems. However, if you are just a user, this information will be enough to crack only the most simple protection methods.

You will need the following programs:

❑ W32dasm, preferably a version no earlier than version 8.9. It can be downloaded here: **www.expage.com/page/w32dasm**.

❑ Borland Turbo Debugger. It comes with development environments. It is advisable to use the DOS version supplied with earlier versions of programming languages from this company — Borland C++ 5.02, for example.

❑ A Disk Editor. Any type will do, but I prefer that from Norton (**www.symantec.com**).

Now, it is time to move from talk to action. Start W32dasm. Select **Open file to Disassemble** from the **Disassembler** menu item. Open the necessary EXE file. For demonstration purposes, I will use the same Windows Shell program. The W32dasm will convert the machine code of the program into assembler code and display it. You need to have at least some basic assembler skills to be able to understand at least some of this code.

Now, let's move on to the actual cracking. For a start, you can try to find the codes. Select the **Search/Find Text** menu sequence. Enter the word **Regist** into the **Find what** field and click on the **Find Next** button to start the search. When a word similar to the one specified is found, take a good look around it. If you do not see anything interesting, continue the search. What, you may ask, are we looking for? What we need to find is some sort of text message associated with program registration, a message that the registration has been successful or that it has failed, for example.

The results of my search are shown in Fig. 4.29. W32dasm found the text: "*Enter registration code*". This might be just what we need. If you are familiar with assembler, you can examine the commands. If you have problems with this, look for lines starting with the asterisk (*) character.

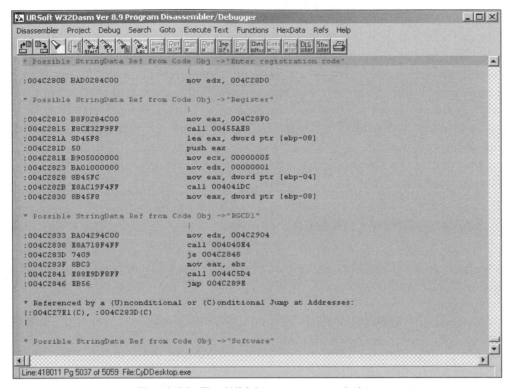

Fig. 4.29. The W32dasm program window

Examine lines like those below. The next line does not tell us a lot. The next one states:

```
* Possible StringData Ref from Code Obj ->"EGCD1"
```

You don't have to be "fluent" in programming to figure out that the code asked for in the first asterisk line will be compared to the string "EGCD1." This is easy to guess, because a message "Enter registration code" is found first, followed immediately by a string of random characters. What is to prevent you from checking this string to see if it is the registration code?

If you are blessed with some programming skills, you can tell by the code that the first five characters of the key must be "EGCD1." Any characters can be entered for the rest of the code.

But this is the perfect case, when a simple check is made. It is more difficult when the key code is checked using some mathematical formula. Here, you will need very broad experience. But let's see what happens next. In the disassembled code, you will find three more asterisk lines: "Software," "Desktop," and "Product." To me, these look like the registry key that we already saw when monitoring the program using the Regmon program. **Software\Desktop** is a registry path and **Product** is a string parameter. Why a string and not some other type? Because there is the string "sdjFE2fih3erj3J" even lower down. This means that, if there is such string in the registry, the program is considered to be registered. That's it. Even if the code is checked using a mathematical formula, you can bypass it if you find something of this sort.

But all these are the simplest protections. Nevertheless, despite their simplicity, they are used quite often.

4.10.5. Sophisticated Cracking

If the protections are not like those described above, you will need sophisticated debugging tools to crack them. You will have to launch a debugger (I personally prefer Turbo Debugger) and trace the program's execution, looking for the registration code.

I will not go into detail here on how this is done but, instead, will provide a couple of recommendations that will be sufficient for programmers.

❐ First, try to find all calls to the `MessageBox` functions. At least one call to this function will often be close to the registration code. It is mainly used to indicate that the registration was successful.

❐ Look for program exit-code sequences and check where they are called from. If the program has exhausted its trial period, it will not start. This means that there must be a call to the routine that shuts it down. If you find this routine code, look a few lines higher in the code to find the jump instruction. It must exist, because there is always some sort of an algorithm of the type "If the program has not been registered, then exit; otherwise, proceed with normal work." Your task is to replace the conditional jump to an unconditional one at the continued execution address.

Turbo Debugger is a handy program for editing code. You can add new code to the program at any time while you are working with it. Simply right-click on the code line and select the **Assembler** item in the context menu that appears. In the window that opens, enter the new assembler instruction, and Turbo Debugger will add the corresponding machine code to the selected line. There is one huge shortcoming, in that the modified code cannot be saved. To do this, you have to remember the code you added and the address, at which it was added. Then use any HEX editor to make the changes permanent (I personally find Disk Editor very handy for disk-editing tasks).

No matter how sophisticated the registration check may be, it almost always ends with a simple check of the type "If the registration has been successful, then continue execution; terminate otherwise."

❏ About 10 years ago, I bought me a game. For some reason, the registration code printed on the box did not work, and it was too late at night to call the support service. But the desire to try out the new game was too keen and, without thinking for long, I loaded it into the debugger. I did not understand anything in the code that checked the registration. At that time, I was only familiar with assembler at the level of basic instructions, and could not figure out the verification algorithm. But, continuing my examining the code, I discovered the prized cmp check and the conditional jump to continue the game. My task was then to replace the conditional jump with an unconditional one. The whole process took just five minutes.

In this way, I was successful in my first, and only, crack of a game — and this despite the fact that I had paid for it fair and square. The next day I discovered how to register the game, but I continued to use the cracked executable file because it was too annoying having to enter the code every time I started the game. I paid my money to have fun with the game — not to bother with codes.

In conclusion, I would like to point out that I have not shown you how to break everything you can lay your hands on, nor have urged you to do so. People should be paid for their labors and the fact that you are using the fruits of someone's labor shows that it is of value. You pay for value. Some users complain that the software prices are too high for them. If that is the case, there is always an alternative to cracking. Nowadays, you can find many free or inexpensive programs. Use those that you can afford, but do not engage in cracking. The purpose of this chapter was simply to show you how programs are cracked. The fact remains that doing this for commercial gain is illegal.

Chapter 5: Internet Hacking

In this chapter, we will consider Internet hacking. No, I will not teach you how to break into sites and steal information. This is illegal and punishable under law. Stealing is stealing anywhere, whether on the Internet or somewhere else. What we will consider is home computer security. Protecting servers and corporate networks is a more difficult undertaking, but everything considered here is equally important for providing server security.

In addition, you will learn how to play tricks on people with the help of the Internet, as well as how to make better use of your surfing time. You will learn how web site voting systems are padded up, and ways to fool registration systems.

You should consider the information presented here with two purposes in mind: using it for your own purposes and making sure that it is not used against you. We will, for example, consider how to jack up the numbers on web site vote counters. If you are a cracker, you can use this information to boost your own vote count. If, on the other hand, if you are a web programmer, this information can be of help to you in writing voting scripts that cannot be tricked into providing false results.

The information introduced by discussion of methods for improving a security system can also be used to compromise that security system. It is akin to advertising a wonderful new and effective lock that can only be foiled using a pair of bolt cutters. On one hand, we are providing information on making the door secure while, on the other, we are telling you how to bypass the security created. Any security information can be used to both enhance and compromise security. Any security information made available in this book is intended to be used for the former purpose. The reason for this is that it is much more difficult to create something invulnerable than to destroy what has already been created.

Any information about hacking techniques can be used by programmers and administrators to devise methods of protection against these techniques. You cannot defend yourself properly unless you know what you are defending against. On the other hand, you must know how a piece of software that you want to crack or play pranks with is built and works. You will not be able to crack it unless you know these things.

5.1. Speeding up the Internet

We always want to optimize our Internet surfing. Even with modern modems, the bandwidth of a dial-up Internet connection does not generally get above 56 Kb/s. Actual transfer rates achieved seldom reach this maximum, falling mostly between 30 Kb/s to 40 Kb/s. Even in order to obtain the rates that modest, the communication protocol must operate efficiently and the communication line be of a good quality.

The bandwidth of a dedicated phone line is utilized much more effectively. Even with a 64 Kb/s channel, which is not a significant increase on the theoretical 56 Kb/s dial-up bandwidth, maximum transfer rates are much easier to achieve and the speed increase is more noticeable. But, where you usually pay for the time spent online with the dial-up access, with dedicated lines you have to pay for the amount of information downloaded, so you want your incoming traffic to be optimized.

One problem common to all connections is that they can simply disconnect. If you were simply loading a web page at the moment, there will be no problem reloading it after the connection has been restored. But if you had completed downloading 90 percent of a 100 MB Windows update, you would have to agree that the prospect of downloading everything again isn't particularly appealing. To avoid such a situation and to save money on traffic, you can make use of download managers, such as GetRight (Fig. 5.1) or Reget, to name just two examples. We will consider these in detail later.

For now, we will discuss various ways to enhance Internet communication efficiency to achieve greater transfer rates and reduce traffic.

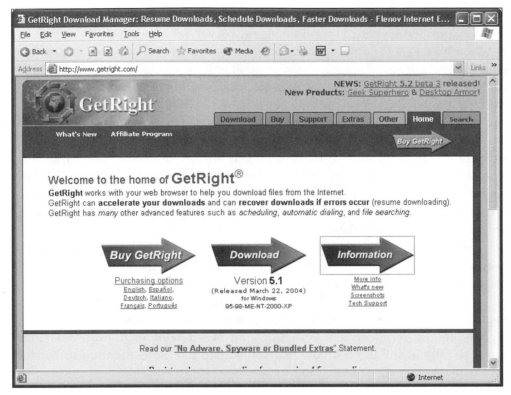

Fig. 5.1. The GetRight site

5.1.1. Protocol Optimization

The foundation of information exchange is the protocol used. The most commonly used protocol is TCP/IP. We will not go into the specifics of this protocol, but will consider some of its theoretical principles.

TCP/IP defines how the connection is to be established and how data transfer is to be conducted. Data are exchanged in packets, whose maximum size is determined by the operating system settings. In addition to the data, each packet contains service information, such as sender and recipient addresses, port information, packet lifetime, etc.

Suppose that the maximum size of a packet is 2,000 bytes. If the data are sent in 1,000-byte portions, or, even worse, in 500-byte portions, the packet size potential is not fully utilized. On the other hand, waiting for a packet to fill up will cause transmission delays. We cannot, however, control the packet filling process, so the protocol must be optimized by modifying the packet size.

Transmitting 10,000 bytes at once, the information is broken into several 2,000-byte packets, that is, it is sent with maximum packet utilization. On the receiving side, all of the packets are assembled in the original order, resulting in rapid transmission of the information. But it is rare for the network to have ideal parameters, and packets sometimes get lost. In this case, in order to complete the assembly, the lost packet has to be resent, which means additional time and traffic expenses.

Sending smaller packets will provide for more effective information transmission. This will be less effective, however, when transmitting large volumes of data, because more packets will be needed. Also, because each packet contains service information, the proportion of overhead traffic increases. This again means increased time and traffic expenses.

There are many other settings that affect payload traffic that we will consider in the process of studying the Windows parameters that can be controlled. Along the way, we will also get to know the theory necessary to select the correct parameter values.

TCP/IP works relatively efficiently in Windows 2000/XP, so, if you are the lucky owner of such an operating system, you can read the following description of registry tuning for general information and self-development purposes alone. However, if you still use Windows 9x, you should pay close attention to the following material.

Optimizing Transmitted Packets

All TCP/IP settings are stored in the registry and can be edited using the standard Windows registry editor, *regedit*. Start by opening the registry key: **HKEY_LOCAL_MACHINE\SYSTEM\CurrentControlSet\Services\Class\NetTrans\ 0000**. The last zeros in the key represent the profile. You can have more than one profile, so the key can end not in 0000, but in 0001, 0002, or even 0022. In this key, you need to create a string parameter named MaxMTU and give it a value of... Well, let's see to what value this parameter should be set.

The name Maximum Transmission Unit (MTU) is self-explanatory. But, as usual, Microsoft developers went their own way and renamed it MaxMTU: the maximally maximum transmitted unit ☺. In Windows 9x, the default value of MaxMTU is 1,500 bytes.

Of course, the larger the packet, the more data received. With MaxMTU set to a large value, the modem can send large packets, meaning more data at one time. But, if the quality of the communication line is not up to scratch and packets are lost regularly, the modem will have to resend the lost packets. You may end up spending more time on resending and receiving lost packet than on transferring new data. There is also another problem: For a long time, the standard MaxMTU value for routers has been 576 bytes. This makes the routers tear up the packets. Therefore, it is best to lower the MaxMTU value.

The possible values that MaxMTU can take on are 552, 576, 1,002, and 1,500. This does not mean that other values cannot be used. It has simply been established experimentally that these values work the best and are used most often. The reasons for this are beyond the scope of this book, so we will not go into them. I direct your attention to the values 552 and 1,002. Try to experiment with these values to see, which produces better communication.

Packet Size

While lowering the MaxMTU, keep in mind that not only the payload data are sent in a packet, but also its header and the service data, which account for 40 bytes. In real terms, this means that, for a MaxMTU value of 1,500 bytes, only 1,460 bytes of data are actually sent. With a MaxMTU value of 576, the actual data are only 536 bytes. In the latter case, service information losses are three times those in the first case, because it takes three 576-byte packets to transfer 1,500 bytes, of which 120 bytes will be service bytes. Consequently, lowering the overhead caused by packet losses increases the load on the network due to service data overhead.

But all is not as bad as it may seem, for it is better to send an extra 40 bytes of service data than 1,500 bytes of a lost packet. With quality communications lines, however, the maximum packet size should be used.

The actual data in the packet, excluding service data, is called the Maximum Segment Size (MMS) and equals MaxMTU minus 40 bytes. This value is set in the **HKEY_LOCAL_MACHINE\System\CurrentControlSet\Services\VxD\MSTC** registry key in the DefaultMSS string parameter. Should this parameter be absent, you should create it yourself.

Closing the Window

All the parameters considered next are located in the **HKEY_LOCAL_MACHINE\System\CurrentControlSet\Services\VxD\MSTC** registry key. Therefore, in discussing them I will reference only their name, type, and function.

The next string parameter considered is DefaultRcvWindow: Receive Window (RWIN). When a request is sent to the server, it can send the RWIN number of bytes without waiting for acknowledgment of successful reception. Making the `DefaultRcvWindow` value equal to the `DefaultMSS` value will cause the server to wait for acknowledgement after each packet is sent. In this case, delays are greatest. Setting `DefaultRcvWindow` equal to 20*`DefaultMSS` lets the server stop to wait for acknowledgment after sending 20 packets.

If the packet-loss rate is low enough, data can be sent in large batches before stopping to wait for acknowledgment. If the packet loss rate is high, a large `DefaultRcvWindow` value will cause long delays due to retransmissions of lost data. For high-quality communications lines, the largest possible `DefaultRcvWindow` value should be used.

This can be calculated using the formula `DefaultMSS*N`. The `N` value can be set to 4, 6, 8, or 10. In my opinion, 8 is the optimal value, although it might be different for your network. As I already said, it depends on the quality of the communications lines.

The next string parameter is `DefaultTTL` (TTL: packet time to live). A packet can sometimes fall into an endless loop shuffle between two nodes and cannot be delivered to the recipient. The `TTL` parameter's function is designed to prevent this from happing. Every time a packet passes through a node, the value of this parameter (contained in the packet's header) is decremented by one. As soon as this value becomes 0, the packet is considered to have entered an endless loop and is destroyed.

By default, the `DefaultTTL` value is set to 32. Lowering this value can only degrade communications, while raising it can decrease the packet-loss rate. The latter is due to the fact that some packets can be destroyed simply because a router may decide to send them in a roundabout way. This does not happen often, but I still recommend that you set this value to 64, since it will do no harm anyway. Although the transfer rate will increase slightly, that this is the fact is difficult to ascertain by any tests. But it is a fact that traffic can be reduced by not having to resend packets destroyed by being sent by a long route.

Monitoring Parameters

As a rule, monitoring parameters have a negative effect on communications. Judge for yourself.

Consider the `PMTUDiscovery` (Path Maximum Transmission Unit Discovery) parameter. Setting this parameter to 1 makes TCP/IP look for the path with the highest MTU before making a connection. With `MaxMTU` properly configured, this parameter only slows the protocol down, as a result of the extra time taken by the search.

Setting PMTUBlackHoleDetect parameter to 1 causes the initiation of a search for dead routers on the way to the server before making the connection. I do not recommend setting this parameter, because it slows down the protocol. Dead routers are not frequent occurrences and the time spent on searching for them is not justified. Consequently, I recommend that you don't monkey around with this parameter.

A Black Hole

All operations to configure TCP/IP involve editing the registry. Paying insufficient attention may mess up your communications to the point that they are non-functional. Should you ever get to this stage, perform the following steps to restore communications:

1. Reboot the computer.
2. After the POST, but before Windows starts loading, press and hold the F8 key. This will open the boot option menu.
3. Select the **Command Prompt Only** option. The computer will boot in DOS.
4. In the command line, enter the scanreg /restore command. This will launch the registry-restoration program.
5. You will be offered a choice of copies of working registries for the last four days.
6. Select the one you want, and press the <Enter> key.

All of these procedures apply to Windows 9x. Windows 2000/XP do not have the DOS subsystem, and these actions cannot be performed. But there is no need to fool around with the registry to the point where it becomes corrupted and needs to be restored. As I have already pointed out, the TCP/IP protocol is set up much better in these operating systems and there is no need to try to improve it.

5.1.2. Speeding up DNS Operation

Every time you want to visit a site, for example, to download a new version of a CyD Software Labs program, you enter the site's address as text data. In the case of our SyD Software labs, this will be **www.sydsoft.com**. But the actual site address is not the text name, but an IP address. An IP address (as used in the most common 4th version of the IP protocol) consists of four groups, each of three numbers, separated by periods.

Consequently, before the site can be loaded into whatever browser you are using, its IP address must be determined by its symbolic address (name). To get the IP address, the computer sends a request to the DNS server to translate the user-friendly name into the IP address. Only after the computer receives the IP address of the server of the site from the DNS can the connection be established and the site loaded into the browser. The address translation process can take some time, so the delay can be noticeable.

Why are DNS address-translation operations needed? Because humans are not particularly good at remembering numbers. It is much easier for us to remember meaningful text names, especially if they are associated with what we are interested in. Machines, on the contrary, use numbers in their operation. So, to build a bridge to connect humans and machines, the DNS system was designed to convert human-friendly text names into the numerical IP addresses used by computers.

When you visit a site for the first time, you — or rather, your computer — have to go through the DNS system. However, if you visit a site regularly, it would make sense to dispense with the DNS system.

The IP addresses for most servers on the Internet change very seldom, if ever. Generally, only underground servers disseminating illegal information change their IP addresses often, as their owners try to stay ahead of the law. Official and legal sites don't usually need to change their IP addresses. This fact can be used to eliminate the unnecessary requests to DNS servers.

All of the sites in my **Favorites** folder use IP addresses, rather than text names. Consequently, a selected site is connected to and starts loading immediately, without having to spend time on going to the DNS system to find out its IP address.

You can also do the same with your **Favorites**. Here is how:

1. Launch Internet Explorer.
2. Select the **Favorites** item in the menu. Select the site for which you want to specify the IP, right-click on it. Select the **Properties** item in the context menu that appears.
3. This will open the site's shortcut **Properties** dialog window (Fig. 5.2). Remember or, even better, write down the site's address in the URL field. This is the part between the double slash and the single slash. For example, the URL shown in Fig. 5.2 is for **http://www.cydsoft.com/**, from which we need the **www.cydsoft.com part**.
4. Execute the **Start/Run** command sequence and execute the cmd command (command.com for Windows 9x). This will open the command line window.

Enter command ping Site Name (e.g., ping www.sydsoft.com) and you should see text similar to that below:

```
Pinging www.cydsoft.com [62.118.251.15] with 32 bytes of data:
Reply from 62.118.251.15: bytes=32 time<1ms TTL=128
Reply from 62.118.251.15: bytes=32 time<1ms TTL=128
Reply from 62.118.251.15: bytes=32 time<1ms TTL=128
Reply from 62.118.251.15: bytes=32 time<1ms TTL=128
Ping statistics for 62.118.251.15:
  Packets: Send = 4, Received = 4, Lost = 0 (0% loss),
Approximate round trip times in milli-seconds:
  Minimum = 0ms, Maximum = 0ms, Average = 0ms
```

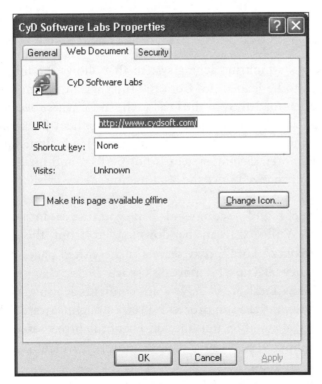

Fig. 5.2. A shortcut properties window

The four groups of digits separated by periods in the square brackets in the first line are the site's IP address. This is what you need to put in the space the **www.cydsoft.com** address occupies in the site shortcut properties windows. Consequently, the URL will appear as follows: **http://62.118.251.15**. However, before you carry out this replacement, I recommend that you test the IP address by entering it in the browser's URL window and trying to load the site. If you run into problems loading the site, it may be due to the fact that the site has no static IP address, or that you are working via a proxy server that did not let the IP address through.

If executing the ping command produced an error instead of the address, this may be due to the fact that this command is not available on your network. This occurs in corporate networks where only certain protocols can access Internet and the ICMP protocol used by the ping command is unavailable. In this case, you can use the site **http://www.rus.org/cgi-bit/nph-ping.cgi**. Just enter the address in the only field there, and click on the **Enter** button.

5.1.3. Local Caching

Internet Explorer has a built-in caching system that allows the information from already visited sites to be loaded not from the Internet, but from the local cache. The things most often loaded from the local cache are images. Because images involve much more data than text information, loading them from the local cache saves significantly on Internet traffic, and lets them be loaded much more quickly. But the Internet Explorer caching system is not perfect, and images contained in the local cache and unchanged since the last time the site was visited are quite often loaded from the Internet.

To improve caching, I recommend that you use a local proxy server. One such server, WinProxy, can be downloaded from the following site: **http://www.winproxy.cz/**. Local proxy servers cache visited pages much more effectively, although they take up a bit more disk space.

Let's consider how local proxy servers are configured, using WinProxy as an example. The program installation process is pretty straightforward. The only thing you have to pay special attention to is the address of the proxy server. By default, it is set to **http://localhost:3129**. **3129** is the port number, which may change in future versions of the program.

Now, launch Internet Explorer and enter **http://localhost:3129** into the URL address field. This will open the server configuration dialog window (Fig. 5.3). Actually, you can start working with the program right away, but I do recommend that you familiarize yourself with the available configuration settings. You may want to change or improve something.

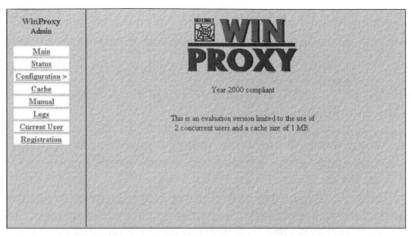

Fig. 5.3. The WinProxy configuration window

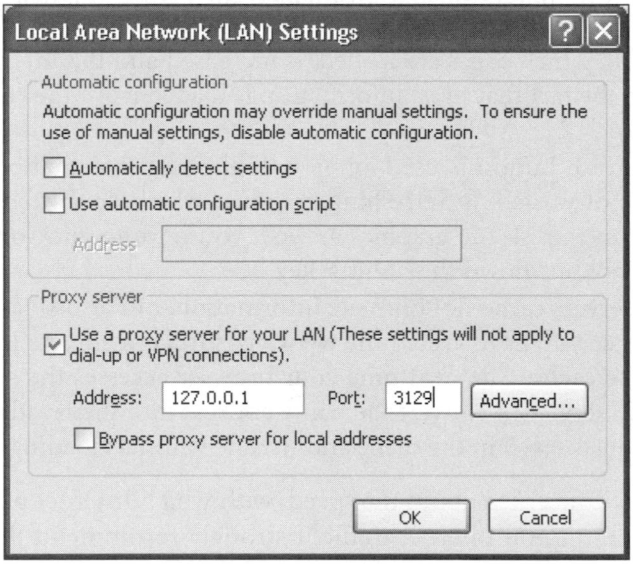

Fig. 5.4. The LAN configuration window

To make Internet Explorer work via the proxy server, you need to start Internet Explorer, open the **Tools** menu, and select the **Internet Options** item there. Open the **Connections** tab in the window that opens, and click the **LAN Settings** button. This will open the local area network configuration dialog window (Fig. 5.4).

Put a check mark into the **Use a proxy server for your LAN** box; enter 127.0.0.1 into the **Address** field (this address always specifies your computer); and enter 3129 in the **Port** field. Save the changes. Now your browser will connect to the Internet via the local proxy server.

Using a local proxy server has its advantages and disadvantages. The main disadvantages are the following:

❑ Extra disk space is used for storing the proxy server cache. However, this can be overlooked, as today's disks are quite large and relatively cheap in terms of storage space per dollar.

❑ When a site is visited, it is not always the newest contents that are displayed. Most proxy servers do not check for changes to the requested page, but simply return it from the local cache. In order to receive the updated page, it has to be retrieved from the Internet by clicking the **Refresh** button.

But there are also unquestionable advantages, such as the following:

❑ The speed, with which pages are loaded, is increased and the Internet traffic reduced, due to the fact that most information is loaded from the cache of the local proxy server.

❑ When the **Refresh** button is used, often only the text information is refreshed and traffic is not wasted on refreshing graphics, which do not change very often. In order to refresh the graphics as well, you have to click on the **Refresh** button while holding down the <Shift> key.

❑ Good proxy servers cache not only site information, but also IP addresses. This means that once you have visited the **www.cydsoft.com** site, its IP address will be saved to the cache. The next time your browser accesses the site, it will not go to the DNS service to convert the name address into the IP address, but will use the IP address saved in the cache and the site will start loading right away.

If you are very concerned about the speed, with which Internet pages load, and are trying to economize on Internet traffic, I strongly recommend that you install a proxy server on your computer. It will most definitely save you time and money.

5.1.4. Get Rid of Images

The bosses at my company are penny pinchers and limit Internet traffic to 50 MB per employee, per month. What is 50 MB nowadays? This trifling amount gets used up in the space of a week simply by viewing web pages. Trying to download something with this limit is like trying to pass a camel through the eye of a needle. Windows updates alone are larger than 50 MB.

To make this pittance of traffic last me a month, just for viewing web pages, I had to disable displaying images on the loaded web pages. As I already mentioned, graphics represent the lion's share of Internet traffic. While text information on most sites does not exceed 10 KB, their graphics can hog up 100 KB.

Displaying images in Internet Explorer is disabled in the **Internet Options** window, which can be opened by executing the **Tools/Internet Options** menu sequence. Open the **Advanced** tab, find the **Multimedia** item in the list, and remove the check mark from the **Show Pictures** box. Without pictures, most sites will not look very pretty, but this sacrifice can save you as much as 70 percent in total traffic.

I also disabled images back in the days of slow modems. They are not really that informative and, in most cases, you can live without them.

Fig. 5.5 shows the **www.cydsoft.com** site with labeled place-holding rectangles for images. If you want to see an image, all you have to do is to right-click on the corresponding rectangle and select the **Show Picture** item in the context menu. In this way, you can still view images, but only those that you specifically want to.

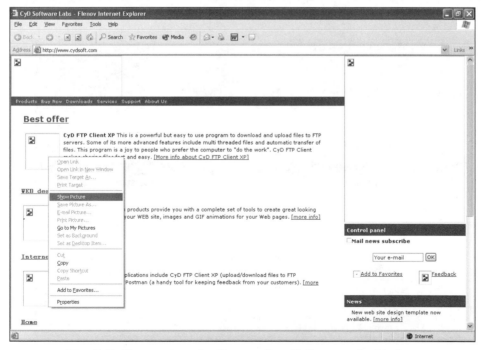

Fig. 5.5. The **www.cydsoft.com** site with images disabled

5.1.5. Enhancing Downloads

A bad Internet connection that constantly breaks down makes downloading anything more or less sizeful very problematic. Because of frequent disconnections, downloading has to be repeated over and over again from the beginning. This means wasted money that could have been better used, for example, to buy a six-pack.

The implementation of the file transfer process in Internet Explorer is not very effective. Even when your communication lines are of good quality, the data-transfer rate can be increased by splitting the download into several streams. Microsoft provided only the absolutely necessary download features in its browser, which are far from sufficient.

I would recommend that you install a download manager called Reget whose window is shown in Fig. 5.6 (**www.reget.com/en**). It will allow you to use your connection with maximum efficiency. When starting a download, the program automatically searches the site mirrors and selects the one with the best communications, or downloads from several mirror sites simultaneously. Even if your communication lines are in the perfect condition, the server, from which you want to download the file, can be overloaded. Mirror sites allow you to download with maximum efficiency and save a lot of time.

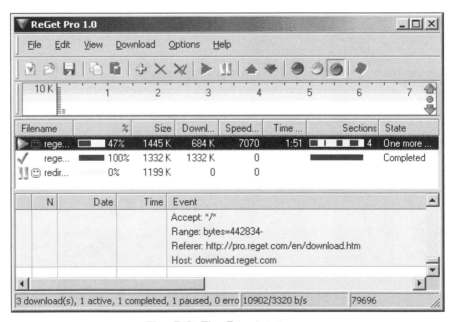

Fig. 5.6. The Reget program

You can find the Reget 4.0 installation package on the accompanying CD in the Chapter5/Reget directory.

The program is pretty easy to work with. All you need to do is to install it. Now, when you click a download link in the browser, the file will be downloaded not by the Windows built-in means, but by Reget.

Should the Internet connection be broken during the download, after it is restored Reget resumes download from where it was interrupted. Imagine yourself downloading a file 1 GB in size and the Internet connection going down right when there is only 1% left to go. With just Internet Explorer you have no choice but to start the download again. Even with the lowest Internet pay rates, you will spend more for the repeat download than on the most expensive Reget license.

These are the main, but far from all of the features of the Reget program. A complete listing and descriptions can be found on the **http://deluxe.reget.com/ru/features.htm** site. All that was said above Reget was not intended as a free commercial, but to save you time and money.

5.2. Jacking up Voting Results

Voting systems on different sites are constantly developing and programmers are trying to devise protection against visitors jacking up the voting counters. Suppose that you have decided to take a part in a poll conducted by some site and want your preferred answer to prevail. How can this be done? There are many ways. The one to employ depends on the program used to conduct the polling.

Let's consider one vote-boosting method, using the **www.download.com** site as an example. Here, visitors can vote for their favorite programs. When you see that your favorite program is way down in the ratings, you naturally want to lift it up and help the developers.

In order to know how to pad the votes, you must know how they are counted. The simplest methods use cookie files. These are files, in which web servers save any useful for them information. Each web site has its own file, which only it can read. No site can read cookies created by other site servers. When you cast your vote for some cause or issue, the server saves the information about your vote in a cookie file. Let's consider the steps performed when registering votes:

1.   A packet with an answer to the question is sent.

2. The server processes the answer and sends an acknowledgement.
3. The local computer saves the acknowledgment in a cookie file.

Consequently, if you attempt to vote again, the server checks your computer hard disk for a cookie file with the vote acknowledgement and, if it finds one, it will not let you vote again. But this method is used only by the least experienced voting-program developers. We will now consider how to circumvent this kind of protection.

5.2.1. Vote-Padding Method #1

Five years ago, the voting system on site **www.download.com** had no protection of any kind against vote padding, and votes could be padded by the simple rapid-click method. You enter the site, select the answer you want, and start clicking rapidly on the **Send** button.

If your are using a dial-up Internet connection, sending your answer and receiving an acknowledgment for it (i.e., a cookie file) takes some time. If the **Send** button is clicked again during the sending/receiving process, the previous send is considered aborted and is cancelled, so a new sending-the-answer/receiving-the-cookie session starts. When the acknowledgment for a previous click, with a request to update the cookie file, arrives at your browser, the browser declines the request, because the session was aborted.

Consequently, rapidly clicking on the send button causes your answer to be sent to the server, which processes and accepts it. That is, steps 1 and 2 are carried out. Your computer, however, will refuse to accept the acknowledgments, and step 3 will not be carried out until one of the following events occurs:

❑ If you stop the rapid clicking of the **Send** button, the browser will accept and save the cookie file for the last send.
❑ If your trigger finger is too slow, the server may manage to process the first sending between two consecutive clicks, send the acknowledgement, which the browser will receive. The ensuing results will be the same as in the previous case.

On high bandwidth dedicated lines, the answers to the server and its acknowledgments travel at high speeds, and your next click may be not fast enough, meaning that the evil cookie file will be created. In these cases, another method may work.

5.2.2. Vote-Padding Method #2

When voting system programmers noticed that their system was being fooled by method #1, they started protecting against it. The simplest protection technique employs Java script to disable the **Send** button right after it has been clicked. So, if the voting-system programmer is no stranger to Java Script, your fast index finger will do you no good, and you will have to look for other ways to advance your cause.

This method can also be used when you want to boost your vote by simply voting again, but cannot because of the cookie file. Since this file is stored on your computer, what is to prevent you from simply deleting it? Open the **\Documents and Settings\User Name\Cookies** folder (**User Name** is the account name, under which you logged into the system). Cookies files are stored here in simple text files and named in **User Name@site address.txt** format. The part of the name after sign @ is the address of the site that sent the cookie. Find the cookie from the site in question, and simply delete it. This will enfranchise you again and let you cast another vote. Repeat as often as necessary.

5.2.3. Vote-Padding Method #3

The hardest defense to get around involves the use of the IP address. Simply put, if the server sees that a vote has already been cast from your IP address, it will not let you vote again. If you have a dial-up Internet connection, you are allocated an IP address every time you establish a connection. Disconnecting and then reconnecting will most likely result in the allocation of a new IP address, thus enabling you to vote again.

If you connect via a dedicated line, you are allocated a static IP address and the only way to circumvent this protection is to resort to anonymous proxy servers. There are plenty of proxy server addresses on the Internet, so you need to compile a good list, and then use each server on the list to cast one vote.

The IP and cookie protection methods are often used in tandem to fight vote padding. In this case, the corresponding cookie file also needs to be deleted. Otherwise, the vote-counting program will notice your attempt at pulling a sly one with the IP address switch.

Organizing vote-padding protection based on the IP address is a difficult task. This is because there are many network users who connect to the Internet via the same IP address. For example, some corporate networks may comprise over a thousand of computers, all of which use one proxy server and one IP address to connect to the Internet. If only one employee on such a network casts his or her vote on a site that uses this protection, the other network users will be deprived of this opportunity.

This is why IP addresses are only used by voting systems to detect vote padding, but are not saved in the database for long. You will be able to vote from the same address some time later with no problems. For long-term voter identification, the cookies protection method is the one employed most often. As you know, these can be deleted and, if their format is known, edited as well.

5.2.4. Vote-Padding Method #4

The following vote-padding method requires at least basic knowledge of HTML. For a demonstration example, I have picked the most difficult protection method (commonly used on large portals), where voting is conducted in a window frame. This method is very convenient for the voters, because only the voting frame, and not the entire page is refreshed after you cast your vote. Russian hackers have a reputation as some of the best in the world. They really are. But they are also humans like the rest of us, and also make mistakes. To demonstrate how you can take advantage of these mistakes in padding votes using method #4, I picked the site of a Russian hacking magazine, called, imaginatively enough, Hacker. The site and the magazine are designed and produced by some of the best Russian hackers, but you will see that even they make mistakes.

After I cracked the voting system on this site, I informed the site administration of the breach, so it has since been closed. But this does not mean that there are no remaining flaws. There are. You just need to know how and where look for them. To help you in this endeavor, I will describe the logic I used to discover the mistake, on which I capitalized. You can use it as a guide for your own explorations.

Open site **www.xakep.ru** in your browser. I picked this site because its programmers did a good job with their voting system. There is always some survey taking place on the home page of this site. Take notice of what is there before and after the voting part. In this instance, there is a **Survey** header just above the voting section, and a material archive right below it.

You will have to open the source code of the page. This is done by executing the **View/Source Code** menu sequence, which will open a **Notepad** window containing the source code. Search for the word **Survey** in the source code. Let's consider the following chunk of the source code following the word **Survey**.

```
<span class="textHeader1White"> Survey</span></td>
<tr>
<td height="1" class="decorCellWhite"><img src="i/fon.gif" width="1"
height="1" ></td>
```

```
</tr>
<tr>
<td valign="middle" align="right">
<table width="98%">
<tr><td><span class="textBodyHome">
<iframe src="/code/common/vote3/include/iframe_vote.asp?site=SVT5"
ID="anIframeRez3" NAME="anIframeRez3s" scrolling="no"
frameborder="0" width="100%" marginwidth="0"
marginheight="0"></iframe>
</span></td></tr>
</table><br>
</td>
</tr>
<tr>
<td height="1" class="decorCellWhite"><img src="i/fon.gif" width="1"
height="1" ></td>
</tr>
<tr>
<td class="decorBodyCell1">
<table border="0" width="100%" cellpadding="0" cellspacing="0">
<tr>
<td class="textHeader1White" height="30" valign="top">/MATERIAL
ARCHIVE/</td>
```

The first line contains the word Survey, while the last line contains words MATERIAL ARCHIVE. This means that somewhere between them should be a reference to the voting mechanism. If the voting mechanism is implemented in a frame, the reference to it will be enclosed by the <iframe> tags. Find the line containing the word iframe, and you will see the following construction:

```
src="/code/common/vote3/include/iframe_vote.asp?site=SVT5"
```

The address of the survey frame is in the quotation marks. Because it starts with a slash, the site's name — **http://www.xakep.ru** — needs to be added in front of it. If the address started with **http://**, nothing would have to be added.

Thus, the address of the survey frame appears as follows:

```
http://www.xakep.ru/code/common/vote3/include/iframe_vote.asp?site=SVT5.
```

Entering this address into the browser's address will open the frame as a separate page in the browser's window (Fig. 5.7).

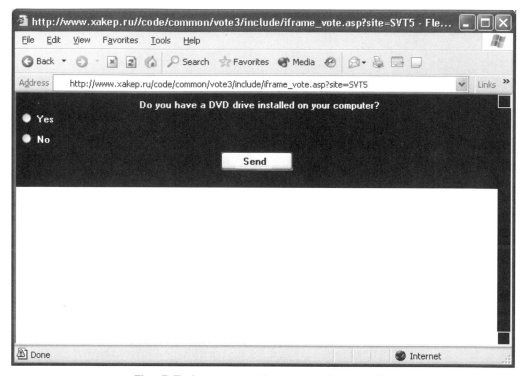

Fig. 5.7. A survey on the **www.xakep.ru** site

Open this page again as the source code in Notepad (**View/Source Code**) and examine it (Listing 5.1).

Listing 5.1. The source code of the survey file

```
<html>
<head>
<meta http-equiv="Content-Type" content="text/html; charset=windows-1251">

<meta name="keywords" content="cracking, computer security, hacker, data security, Linux, programming, trojans,protection from break-ins, viruses, vulnerabilities, operating system, Deface, password picking,e-mail cracking, sniffer, intercept">

<link rel="stylesheet" href="../../../../local/include/main.css" type="text/css">
```

```
<script language="JavaScript"
src="../../../../local/include/scripts.js"></script>


</head>
<body background="" bgcolor="#FFFFFF" marginwidth="0" marginheight="0"
topmargin="0" leftmargin="0" rightmargin="0" bottommargin="0">
<table bgcolor="#FFFFFF" width="100%" cellpadding="0" cellspacing="0"
border="0"><tr><td>
<table cellpadding="3" cellspacing="0" border="0" id="votationholder">
  <form action="../vote1.asp" method="post" target="_top">
  <input type="hidden" name="VoteID" value="VVT1051">
  <input type="hidden" name="userip" value="80.80.99.95">
  <tr><td colspan="2" align="center"><b class="textVoteTitle">Do you have
a DVD drive installed on your computer?</b></td></tr>
  <tr><td width="10px"><input type="radio" name="VoteOptionID"
value="OVT1816"></td><td width="100%" align="left">Yes</td></tr>
  <tr><td width="10px"><input type="radio" name="VoteOptionID"
value="OVT1817"></td><td width="100%" align="left">No</td></tr>
  <tr><td colspan="2" align="center"><input type="submit" name="s1"
class="decorVoteInput" value="Send"></td></tr>
  <tr><td colspan="2" align="center">[<a
href="../vote_results1.asp?site=SVT5" target="_top"
class="textVtrezlink">results</a>]</td></tr>
  </form>
  </table>


    </td>
  </tr>
</table>
 <script language="JavaScript">
 <!--

   document.domain= "xakep.ru"
   parent.adjustFrame(window)
  //-->
 </script>
</body>
</html>
```

Here, we are looking for text `<form action=`, followed by the address of the script that processes the survey answers enclosed in quotation marks. In the present case, this is `../vote1.asp`. The two periods in front of the address mean that it is located a level above the current address.

The current address is:

```
http://www.xakep.ru/code/common/vote3/include/iframe_vote.asp?site=SVT5.
```

The part after the last slash is the page name and its parameters. Delete it. This leaves this address:

```
http://www.xakep.ru/code/common/vote3/include/.
```

Now, move up one level. That is, delete everything after the penultimate slash. This leaves the following address:

```
http://www.xakep.ru/code/common/vote3/.
```

Add the text in the quotation marks found after the code `<form action=` to this address. The result should look like this:

```
http://www.xakep.ru/code/common/vote3/vote1.asp.
```

This is the address that has to be specified in the source code in the quotation marks after the code `<form action=`. You should get this string:

```
<form action="http://www.xakep.ru/code/common/vote3/vote1.asp"
method="post" target="_top">
```

Now, examine the code in Listing 5.1 again. This time, we are looking for lines containing the text `input type="hidden"`. Tag `input` means that this is the input field, for which the contents are passed to the script. Parameter `type="hidden"` means that the field is hidden. Of greatest interest here is the second line, containing the following code:

```
<input type="hidden" name="userip" value="182.181.19.5">
```

This is the parameter used to pass IP addresses. In the present case, the IP address is 182.181.19.5. Your task is to change the IP address in the page source code manually and send your answer to the server with the new IP. How is this done? Easily. You need to carry out the following steps:

1. Save the modified source code (Listing 5.1) on your computer in a file with any name, but with extension HTM.
2. Launch this file, and send your answer.
3. Change the IP address in the file, and repeat step 2.

In this way, you can send as many answers as you wish, but the server will think that they all come from different IP addresses. Despite the fact that the survey is well set up, the programmers made a mistake by determining the IP address not during the script's execution, but before, when the page is formed. It is just that this is an ASP-type page and its code is formed dynamically during the access to the server.

This example shows you how knowing the basics of HTML can be used to change your IP address for certain purposes. But this error does not happen too often, and comes in different varieties. HTML knowledge can also be used to put the JavaScript that disables **Send** buttons out of action and boost your votes using method #1. By the way, the source codes that I found on the **www.xakep.ru** site contain such JavaScript, but it is not used. It looks like the developers put their faith in the IP address protection.

5.3. Social Engineering

Social engineering is the most powerful hacker tool. It was used to perform the most scandalous break-ins and to disseminate the most notorious viruses. Recall the Anna Kournikova virus, when users received a letter offering to her picture, supposedly contained in the attachment. Here is a good example of curiosity killing the cat, or rather, of it enticing men (who comprise the bulk of Internet users) into launching the enclosed file, infecting their computers, and, consequently, helping spread the virus.

Social engineering is based on human psychology and exploits its weak spots. With its help, hackers make victims do what they want them to: infect machines, obtain passwords, etc. One of the areas, in which social engineering is used, is obtaining credit card numbers and other information, with the help of standard e-mail messages. A user receives a letter asking him for the account password because, for example, the bank's database has malfunctioned for some reason. Despite the fact that people are explicitly warned by bank personnel under no circumstances to reveal their password to anyone, there are still people who do!

Nowadays, hackers seldom come up with new break-in methods, instead opting for tried-and-true old techniques in most cases. Despite the simplicity of many of these, there are always some gullible souls who fall for the old tricks. I have been surfing the web for a long time and receive dozens of letters every day that invite me to launch some file to update my computer-security packages, to check out something interesting, or fall for some other come-on. Most of these letters come not directly from their authors, but from computers that have already been infected. There are users who open these files and infect their computers.

Despite the fact that there are numerous antivirus programs and software security complexes available and in widespread use, the number of viruses is not getting any smaller. Numerous new users join the World Wide Web every day who do not yet know anything about its dog-eat-dog nature and destructive potential. It is the new users that most often fall for these tricks.

Social engineering could actually be viewed as a security matter and, thus, more fitting for consideration in *Chapter 4*, with the rest of the threats and protection measures. However, in the present case, we will talk about Internet social engineering, which is why the subject is covered in this chapter.

I myself have used social engineering on numerous occasions to play new computer jokes on my friends or co-workers. The techniques described below will help you to pass along the prank programs described in *Chapter 3* to the victims' computers through e-mail messages.

So, let's consider some tricks used by hackers. This will help you to understand these techniques and to see the difference between social engineering and regular communication with people. Remember that social engineering is extremely effective on the Internet, where you cannot see your interlocutor and determine whether or not he or she is a hacker.

5.3.1. Cheese in a Mousetrap

I have already mentioned e-mail messages asking to open attached files. I have also warned you not to open any attachments where there is the slightest doubt about their source. No stranger will waste his time entertaining you by sending you pictures over the Internet. In most cases, these pictures are well-camouflaged executable files: viruses.

Not long ago, information was made public about a Windows security bug involving BMP file processing, and, just the other day, I heard about a security flaw in the JPEG format. It is possible to attach executable code to an image file that can be executed under certain conditions by certain programs. Internet Explorer is one such program. Now you can get catch a virus or Trojan horse by simply viewing web pages.

Don't think twice about deleting e-mail letters that have files with the extensions SCR, BMP, JPG, EXE, COM, PIF attached.

Pay special attention to e-mails with attachments named Mail Delivery. Messages with these attachments are sent when an e-mail for some reason could not be delivered as addressed, the attachment being the original message. Many users open these attachments to determine, which message did not get to its recipient.

That's a bad move. The attachment should not be opened, as viruses have started camouflaging themselves as Mail Delivery messages. Without opening the attachment, simply look for the address of the returned mail addressee in the body of the returned mail message. If you have indeed sent a message to this address, ask the addressee to confirm receiving it. If the addressee has not received the message, resend it.

Remember that software developers never send updates by e-mail. I often receive e-mail message offering to update Windows or some other program. Microsoft and other software developers do not engage this sort of mailing. They always place updates on their official sites, from which anyone can download them.

While surfing the net, you often come across bright and vivid banners asking you to click on this or that hyper reference. When you yield to your curiosity and do as asked, a message appears on your screen asking for permission to install a program on your computer. Supposedly, this program is needed to show you some famous movie or pop star in all of his or her beauty. Those who swallow the bait and allow the installation to proceed end up with a virus installed on their computer.

Remember that in 90 percent of all cases, alluring references and insistent requests are fronts for malicious code. Lately, I have been noticing that more viruses lurk on pornography, non-mainstream, and other sites with dubious content that are not professionally designed and contain lots of commercials. To be fair, it is possible to explain this not as the result of malicious intent, but as a result of simple negligence on the part of the site's administration. Internet resources designed and created by amateurs are also maintained and serviced by amateurs, so they can have all kinds of junk on them.

5.3.2. Password Change

Lately, the old break-in method using the password change ruse has been making a comeback. I have been getting more letters asking me to update my personal data on a bank site. The hyper reference to the supposed bank's site points to an entirely different site. If I were to fall for this trick and fill out the form, my personal account data would fall into the hacker's hands.

Recently, I received a message employing a very old and long-forgotten social-engineering technique. The contents of the letter were as follows:

Dear Mr. Flenov: I am the administrator of the ABC hosting company. Our data base has been attacked by hackers and we fear that some data may have been corrupted. Could you please review whether the following personal information about your site is correct. Should you discover any inaccuracies, please provide us with the correct data so that we could restore them in our database.

This was followed by a list of my personal data that could easily have been obtained from the Whois service. Any domain registration site has this service to determine domain owner names. The hacker used this service and listed all of the information that was provided to him or her in the letter. In addition, the hacker supplied two more pieces of data: the user name and the password. Of course, the hacker could not know these, so this information was wrong. At this moment, many users would panic that their site is under the threat of imminent shutdown and rush to tell the sham administrator that the user name and password are wrong, to please get them right, and please make sure nothing bad happens to their site.

Another variation on this technique is to send the letter not to the user, but to the hosting support service. Suppose that you want to break into a hosting server. You either call or send an e-mail to the support service, asking why you cannot connect to the internet or to the mail server from such-and-such an account. The account you provide must be correct, but the password can be any jumble of characters. There is a good chance that the support service employees' conditioned reflex to help will kick in and, seeing that you have the wrong password, he or she will correct you either on the spot or by sending you an e-mail telling you the proper one.

The main thing when communicating with support personnel by e-mail is to fake the e-mail address of the user into whose account you want to break. Support-service personnel often accept on faith the sender's address, which can be faked very easily. The SMTP does not need authorization and allows any sender's address to be specified.

This technique is effective because it lulls the reader into complacency and gains his or her confidence by providing the correct information before asking for the needed piece of data. Thus, if the victim has not been burned by this social-engineering stratagem before, the chances of obtaining the password are quite high. The slew of resonant break-ins during the 1980s is good proof of this. Nowadays, old users may still remember this method, but it is fresh and can turn out to be dangerous for many new users.

5.3.3. Forgotten Password

Another effective way to obtain someone's password is to forget it, sort of. They say that what is known to two people is known to everyone. The same applies to passwords: If two people know it, a professional hacker will get it. The forgotten-password method was one of the favorite techniques used by phreakers. A phreaker would call one of the people in possession of the password, pass him or herself off as a friend, boss, or subordinate of the other password holder, or even the holder suffering from a sudden case of amnesia, and ask for a reminder of the password. The phreaker could also claim that his or her computer had burned out, the hard drive crashed, the open sesame would not work for some reason, etc. Whatever the case, the password was needed urgently.

A site belonging to some of my friends was once broken into this way. The site was being developed by several people living in different parts of the country. They communicated via e-mail and had never seen each other. One day, one of the developers received a letter from another, supposedly, developer asking for the password, which had been lost because of a hard disk crash. The sender's address was faked to look like the genuine article, but the address to send the password to was entirely different. No one, however, paid attention to such a "minor" detail, and the villain received the site administrator's password and destroyed all of the important information located there.

5.3.4. I Am No Stranger

I can get into most secure buildings with little or no problem at all. Some time ago, I worked for a company that had four security departments, each performing a different security function. At a glance, the security was excellent, with access to any place being restricted by a system of passes and other modern security measures. The net effect, however, was negligible.

The company was sort of divided into two parts: the downtown office and the production facilities on the outskirts. The production facilities were surrounded by a barbed-wire fence, with guard towers, surveillance cameras, guard dogs, etc. on every corner and with a sand strip several meters wide behind the fence, on which prospective trespassers would leave their footprints. The only entrance was equipped with a metal detector that would make most airport detectors green with envy.

Despite all of these security measures, the workers stole from the plant, and will continue to steal, because they are not paid enough. What can the metal detector detect? Only metal objects. But the metal content in most diskettes and CDs is not high enough to trigger the metal detector. There is more metal in a coat button. If the metal detector were adjusted to sense this little metal, it would label everyone as a thief. Moreover, there was a fax in the communications office above the entrance. The fax machine operation triggered constant false alarms and, for this reason, the metal detector was turned off during the business hours. It only worked in the morning and in the evening.

The results are not hard to guess. Non-metal articles and information carrier media could be taken out in the morning and in the evening. Metal things were carried out during business hours, when the metal detector was turned off and half of the security staff was out to lunch.

There were numerous bans and prohibitions in effect at the production plant. Cellular phones, for example, could not be brought in. But for two months I had no problems brining in my cellular phone without anyone noticing. How did I manage this? Very easily. I kept it in the most conspicuous place in my briefcase. The security personnel simply paid no attention to it because they were searching all of the hidden places without noticing what I was not hiding. Of course, I was caught eventually, but this was done by a new guard who was still following his security-school instructions.

The situation was no different at the office. The 14-story office building was located downtown. In addition to ours, about 20 other companies had offices in the building. There was a guard at the first floor entrance, who checked passes, which looked different for each company. No guard would notice that a pass printed on an office printer looking remotely similar to one of these passes and flashed from a distance of three or four yards was not the genuine thing.

When I was still trying to get a job with the company, I had to visit the office several times. Since I did not feel like going through the lengthy procedure of obtaining a temporary pass, I simply got hold of a similar-looking card and showed it at the entrance. I didn't have to copy anything. The lazy guards never bothered to take a close look at my "pass," and always waved me in after glancing at it from their comfortable chair.

After I was hired, I was seldom at the office — about twice a year. During one of these infrequent visits, I noticed that not all of those entering the building showed their passes. Some people would just stroll in past the guard. After I quit my job there and turned my pass in, I had to come there one more time to get my severance pay. In order not to go through the procedure of obtaining a temporary pass, I simply put my best brazen look on and went through as if I had been an everyday visitor. The security guard either did not notice me, or my self-assured look made him think that I was some big shot.

So it is quite often enough to look as if you belong, and no one will ask you to show your pass. Police and security services reflexively notice and check out only those people who act conspicuously or simply show fear, which in turn makes them act conspicuously. Bold and confident attitude is the best pass to 90 percent of all secured places.

5.3.5. Green and Stupid

A good number of computer systems have been broken in by hackers impersonating a new and stupid employee. To employ this ruse, you need to know the name and login of a low-ranking company employee. You simply call the system administrator, pass yourself of as this person, and say that you were just hired and, for some reason, cannot log in to the server. Most administrators usually have overinflated egos where their administrative powers are concerned and, if you stroke that ego the right way, they will demonstrate those powers by telling you how much they know about the system, including the way to log in.

5.3.6. Why Social Engineering Is So Effective

The task faced by a hacker is to worm him- or herself into the defending side's confidence and to con that person into revealing the access passwords. They do this by employing various psychological techniques to influence people's minds. Humans have three inherent weaknesses: curiosity, trustfulness, and fear. Any of these weaknesses can by exploited by hackers.

Because of our excessive curiosity, we yield to the temptation and open e-mail attachments, infecting our computers with our own hands. Hackers take advantage of our desire to trust others and dupe us into revealing secret information to them. But the greatest weakness is fear. Hackers make us believe that we are in danger of loosing our data, and this fear makes us to hand out our access passwords to them on our own, winding up in our actually losing what were trying to protect.

Hackers make very effective use of social engineering. You will never see the wolf in sheep's clothing, and will dutifully open the door to your house.

In order to avoid becoming a victim of social engineering, you should always be well informed of the techniques used to break into computer systems. Hackers think up something new every day, and you need to stay on top of them.

5.4. Hiding Your Net Identity

Every time you visit any site, this fact, all your actions on this site, and, most importantly, your IP address are logged into the server's operation log. If you access the Internet via a dedicated line, your home address can be figured out by the IP address in a matter of minutes. If you use a dial-up connection, you get a different IP address every time you connect. However, it can be established easily to whom the given IP address was assigned by the time the site was accessed and the phone number used to dial the connection. Needless to say, knowing someone's phone number is the same as knowing his or her home address.

So hackers need to hide their identity, meaning their IP address, when engaging in activities like breaking into sites. To this end, they use various methods of hiding their real IP address, or replace them with another.

Even if you are not a hacker, you don't want your IP address known to everyone and allowing hackers to attack your machine. As you can see, keeping your IP address hidden is a part of the security measures that should be in place to protect your computer.

If you hang out in chat rooms or visit IRC channels regularly, I recommend that you use proxy servers to hide your IP address. People come in all varieties, not all of them good. If someone does not take to what you said in a chat room, he or she may try to break into your system or do some other nasty things to you.

One of the easiest ways to hide your IP address is to access the Internet via a proxy server. This is a tried and true method and has many advantages and disadvantages, each of which deserves deeper consideration.

5.4.1. Proxy Servers

The original purpose of proxy servers was to cache web pages. In the early Internet days, web site channels sometimes could not handle all the requested traffic and, moreover, the transmission costs were quite high. To save on downloading the same information over and over again, Internet providers made use of proxy servers. Now, when a site was accessed for the first time, its contents were cached by the provider's proxy server. The next time this site was requested, its contents were downloaded to the requester not from the original site, but from the provider's proxy server's cache. In this way, providers conserved line bandwidth, while users benefitted from decreased response times, especially in the case of sites located on servers in distant parts of the world.

Enhanced Internet work efficiency is not the only advantage of a local proxy server. In terms of providing information about the packet sender, proxy servers are divided into anonymous and transparent types. Transparent proxies simply forward user packets to the web server, leaving your IP address intact. These proxy servers provide no additional protection.

Anonymous proxy servers operate differently. When you send a request for a site to a proxy server, it forwards this request to the web site server from its own name, and also receives the requested information in its own name. The received information is then relayed to the actual requester. Consequently, hackers can only obtain the IP address of the proxy server, and not yours. Don't worry; these servers are much better protected than your own computer. But even if the hackers succeed in breaking in, what do you care? It's the server administrator's problem, not yours.

So far, only the advantages of proxy servers have been considered. But they also have some shortcomings that are rather difficult to fix. Let's consider the following main shortcomings:

❑ The original purpose of the proxy servers was to service HTTP, with POP, SMTP, and FTP added later. But, even with these additions, the list of the supported protocols is rather limited and it is difficult to make a proxy server work with other protocols. This problem is partially solved by using SOCKS servers, which are similar to proxy servers. We will discuss these servers later.

❑ Not all software can work with PROXY/SOCKS servers, which necessitates software updates or replacements. The problem can also be aggravated by the fact that there are several versions of SOCKS servers and your software may not support the needed version. In such a case, you have to look either for another SOCKS server or another program. The less expensive option is usually the best bet.

❑ As already mentioned, not all proxy servers provide anonymity. The task of locating necessary proxy servers is facilitated by a large number of programs available on the Internet. Even if the proxy server is supposed to hide IP addresses, you should make sure of this before using it. I could give a list of the servers I use in this book, but this information would be useless by the time the book was published, because proxy servers constantly go out of service and new ones appear. I could recommend that you visit the **www.atomintersoft.com/product/alive%2Dproxy/online%2Dproxy2Dchecker** site. There, you can obtain information about proxy servers and check their capabilities, such as transfer rate, anonymity, SSL support, etc.

NOTE

To help you with entering the site's address to check the next proxy server, I placed the proxy.url file in the Chapter5 folder on the accompanying CD. Simply launch it, and the site's address will be entered for you automatically.

But don't think that using a perfectly anonymous proxy server means that you can't ever be found: Secret services and hackers can do this easily. The thing is that proxies keep logs of all their activities, including the IP addresses, from which requests are made. Secret services can have this information summoned by a court order. A court, of course, will not give hackers this information, but they don't need the court's help anyway. They will simply break into the server or obtain it by some other means, social engineering, for example.

But the long arm of the secret service is not long enough to summon information from a server located in some Third World country, with which your country has no diplomatic relations and in which the secret service has no pull — Zimbabwe, for example. How can you find out, in which country the server is located? The easiest and cheapest way is to use the Whois service. I personally use this service at the following site: **www.nic.ru/whois/en/** (Fig. 5.8). Load the site in your browser, enter the IP address into the **Information about IP address** field, and click on the **OK** button.

This will display information similar to that shown in Listing 5.2.

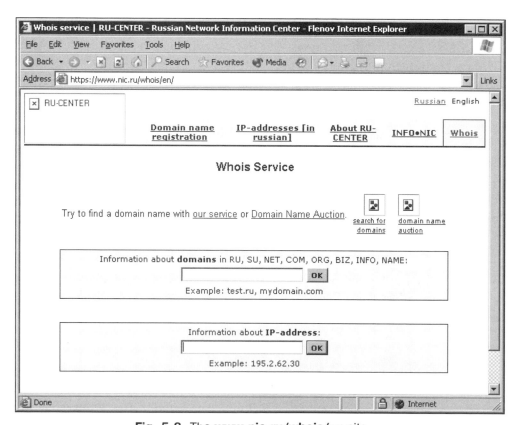

Fig. 5.8. The **www.nic.ru/whois/en** site

Listing 5.2. Information about an IP address

```
OrgName:    Ford Motor Company
OrgID:      FORDMO
Address:    P.O. Box 2053, RM E-1121
City:       Dearborn
StateProv:  MI
PostalCode: 48121-2053
Country:    US

NetRange:   19.0.0.0 - 19.255.255.255
CIDR:       19.0.0.0/8
NetName:    FINET
NetHandle:  NET-19-0-0-0-1
Parent:
NetType:    Direct Assignment
NameServer: DNS004.FORD.COM
NameServer: DNS003.FORD.COM
Comment:
RegDate:    1988-06-15
Updated:    1999-12-07

TechHandle: ZF4-ARIN
TechName:   Ford Motor Company
TechPhone:  +1-313-390-7095
TechEmail:  dnsadmin@ford.com
```

The listing explicitly states that the address belongs to Ford Motor Company.

The Whois method works quite well, but information it provides cannot always be trusted: an IP address can be assigned, for example, in Germany, to an ABC company, but be used in Nigeria by con-letter writers. A somewhat more reliable method is using programs like Trace Route, which trace the path from your location to the specified server. Some of these programs can display the packet progress on a map, and you can see where it winds up visually.

But the packet tracing method can also be fooled. Hackers can fake packet progress information and the packet's geographical destination that is shown will not correspond to the actual physical location of the server.

5.4.2. A Chain of Proxy Servers

A more reliable way to hide your IP address is to use a chain of proxy servers. This will make figuring out your real address much more difficult. With your requests going through two proxy servers, hackers will have to break into both of them to look at the log files and find out your address. This will also add some extra trouble for the secret service, but is still unlikely to stop them. If the secret service sets its sites on getting to a hacker, believe me, they will even get him if he is hiding behind 10 proxy servers.

A chain of proxy servers is created differently than a chain of SOCKS servers; therefore, we will consider them separately.

For starters, let's consider the classical HTTP proxy. Look at the Internet Explorer setting in Fig. 5.9. You cannot see any means for building a chain of proxies there. All you can do here is specify one proxy server for each protocol.

Fig. 5.9. The Internet Explorer **Proxy Settings** window

To create a chain of proxy servers, you will have to use special programs. In order to be a part of the virtual tunnel of proxy servers, a server must support the SSL (Secure Socket Layer) protocol. This protocol encrypts the packet data, thus providing a protection against intercepts, or, rather, against the reading of intercepted data.

To find out whether the proxy supports the SSL protocol, you can use the same site I recommended above for checking proxy servers (**www.atomintersoft.com/ products/alive%2Dproxy/online%2Dproxy%2Dchecker/**), or do it manually. The manual check is performed by using the proxy to access any site supporting SSL. (The addresses of such sites start with **https://**.) Most often, the SSL protocol is used by payment-processing sites. Some mail services also use them — **www.hotmail.com**, for example. If the page loads through the proxy server, this means it supports SSL.

One of the programs for creating HTTP Proxy or SOCKS servers is SockChain, which can be obtained from the **www.ufasoft.com/socks/** site. It is easy to use, and the information concerning configuring its settings can be found on the developer's site.

5.4.3. Anonymous Services

Many web users desire anonymity when surfing the web, and this drives up the demand for this type of service. As we all know, where there is demand, there must be supply. This supply is met by several Internet companies, offering their users total anonymity. The following is a list of the most popular of these services:

❏ Anonymizer (**www.anonymizer.com**). This is probably the oldest company of this type.
❏ Private Web Access (**www.bell-labs.com/project/lpwa**). This service is run by Lucent.
❏ Onion Router (**www.onion-router.net**). This service is run by the research center of the US Navy.
❏ Freedom Network (**www.freedom.net**). The service is run by Zero Knowledge System.

The first three services are the most popular, but their reputations have been damaged over their time in business, and it is not now very difficult to get the needed IP address from them. This has been proven several times by information-technology analysts and computer-security professionals.

Freedom Network was in developing and debugging for two years, and offers the most reliable anonymous services. The peace of mind, however, will cost you $60.00 a year and require the installation of a special program. This program lets you create several pseudonyms to use for your different needs. The service sends your requests through a chain of servers (similar to using Proxy and SOCKS chains), each of which hides the sender's address. This makes it impossible to re-construct the paths of your packets and determine their actual source.

The packets are also encrypted. The encryption is very reliable, because this is a company in Canada, where, unlike in the United States, the length of the encryption key is not restricted.

The fact that the secret services of the United States and Canada expressed their interest in the company can serve as indirect proof of the reliability of the service. The company does not violate the laws of either country, but this degree of anonymity can be taken advantage of by hackers for illegal activities, and it will be difficult to find them out.

This is a lamentable state of affairs, because attention like this could lead to the company folding, or at least decreasing the level of encryption protection. The company may also start keeping operation logs and provide them to the secret services. This type of anonymity is as good as none, and is hardly worth $60.00 a year.

5.4.4. Telltale Cookies

Suppose that you have visited some site that offers several choices of how it can be viewed, and configured the viewing parameters to suit your preferences. Since it took you some time to do this, you would not want to go through the same procedure anew when you visit the site again. This is one of the reasons cookie files were invented.

Each web site has the ability to save to the user disk certain information in a strictly defined file format. This file can be accessed only by the site that placed it and the user.

In addition, some web servers keep logs of all of your activities, and then use the information to peddle you all kind of stuff, or peddle the information to other peddlers. When you enter a site, the server can determine the site you had been before, and when you leave the site, the server can determine where you have gone. In this way, user profiles are created, a circumstance that does not fill me with anything resembling happiness. I am opposed to having my actions monitored, especially where it concerns the sites, on which I am registered and which contain my personal information, such as my name, birthday, and address.

You can prevent servers from collecting information on you by performing the following steps before going web surfing:

❏ Disable cookies. Some sites, however, require cookies to be enabled if you want to use their services. In this case, I recommend that you simply move on to another site, since there are plenty of alternative sites nowadays. I personally do not disable cookies, as they make web surfing more convenient, but I do follow the rest of the rules.

❏ If your browser home page is configured as blank, click the **Home** button before entering a site; otherwise, enter *about:blank* in the browser address field. This way, you will load an empty page before entering the new server, and the latter will not be able to determine where you had been before. It is even better to shut Internet Explorer down, and then restart it.

❏ When registering, I never divulge my real personal information, unless it is really necessary. Accurate personal information needs to be provided in Internet stores or services to pay for merchandise and to enable them to deliver it. It may also be needed when registering software. Most other servers do not need your actual personal information. So, when you are registering for a free mail box, simply make up all your personal information.

All personal information that you leave on web sites can be stolen, or simply misused. Your mail box will then be flooded with spam, offers to see Anna Kournikova, and other similar junk. Some of this spam can even be of interest to you, because it is based on your interest profile that the senders compile using information on the nature of the sites and pages you have visited. But junk mail cannot be welcome, because of its unsolicited nature.

Other than spamming you, your personal data can be used in many other ways that aren't exactly desirable.

5.4.5. Anonymity in Local Network

Just as you can be identified by your IP address on the Internet, on a local network you can be identified by the physical address of the network card installed on your computer: Media Access Control (MAC) address. This is a 48-bit number that is assigned to each network adapter by its manufacturer. The number is unique, and each manufacturer has a range of addresses that it can use.

When you access a computer located on the same network segment, it is addressed by the MAC address, even if you entered its IP address into the address field. The important thing to know here is that a MAC address can be faked, despite the fact that it is hard-wired in the network adapter by the manufacturer. In Linux, this can even be done using standard system tools, without any special software. In Windows, a special program is needed to do this. This is not a big problem, however, as such programs can be found easily on the Internet.

Where I work, Internet traffic is tracked by MAC addresses. It seems that the administrators know that IP addresses can be faked easily, but they think that this cannot be done with MAC addresses. I am not going to tell them how wrong they are for the very simple reason that, after I installed the Phantom MAC program on my computer, the Internet traffic of my boss rose sharply, while mine dropped.

Just like faking an IP address, a faked MAC address must be unique for the given network. This means that you cannot grab the address of the computer you want to appropriate when it is on the network, as this will cause a conflict. The network equipment will not be able to determine, which address is the real one.

So, network administrators should be aware that, in order to prevent unauthorized access, in addition to the user login name and password, the authorization process must also verify the user's IP and MAC addresses. Only then can they have some semblance of certainty that their network is secure. Why just a semblance? Because logins and passwords can be stolen, and then the miscreant can use the traffic of the user whose login and password he or she has stolen. To plug this security hole, each address must be assigned its own switch port. Then, even if a hacker fakes an address, he or she will not be able to use the network, unless the hacker also manages to get connected to the necessary switch socket.

Using IP and MAC address to authorize access is a mistake that many administrators make. Most of them know that an IP address can be faked easily, but not too many are aware that the same can also be done with MAC addresses.

5.5. Anonymous Mail

Sometimes you might not want the recipient of a message to be able to tell where it came from. For example, you want to play a prank on a friend, or simply do not want your address getting into the wrong hands.

This problem is solved in two easy steps. The first step is to configure your browser to work through an anonymous proxy server. The next step is to get a mail box under an assumed name on one of the numerous free mail servers out there. Now, neither your real name nor your IP address will show in your messages.

Several years ago, when free mail servers were few and far between, there were special services for sending anonymous mail. But they operated on the same principle of hiding the IP address and letting the users state any personal data. So, when anonymous proxy servers and free mail boxes became commonly available, the need for those services disappeared.

5.5.1. Faking the Sender Data

Suppose that you want not just to hide your real address, but to make the sender believe that the message is from some other person, joeblow@hotmail.com, for example. This can be done easily using any insecure SMTP server. SMTP (Simple Mail Transfer Protocol) is used for sending e-mail and it is insecure by default. Administrators of the numerous Internet mail services prevent users from sending mail using false addresses in one of the following methods:

❏ A message can be mailed only if the sender's address is the same as the service's address. That is, you will not be able to send a letter with joeblow@hotmail.com in the **From:** field from a mail.com service, because the domain names are different.

❏ The user has to check his or her mail box before sending a message. The mail is checked using POP3 protocol, which is protected by a password, and the server saves the IP address of the computer, from which the check was made for a certain period of time. During this time, e-mails can be sent from this address. This means that if you have no password for the joeblow@hotmail.com address, you will not be able to check the mail. Any attempts to send mail will also fail, because the server will check for a login and password to match those used to check the mail via POP3 protocol.

But this is no problem, and we can do without these servers. Providers often have their own SMTP servers open to all customers. They are necessary to speed up the sending of mail. So, instead of using a SMTP server on a free mail service, which may be located on a different continent, you can use one such an SMTP server run by an Internet provider. You can use the nearest one: your provider's.

Most of these SMTP servers run only one check: The sender must be connected through this provider. This means that, if this protection is enabled, you will not be able to connect using one provider and send mail from another provider's SMTP server. You can find out the address of your provider's SMTP server by calling its support service.

Now, create a new Outlook Express account. Open the **Tools** menu and select the **Accounts** item. In the **Internet Account** window that opens, click on the **Add** button. Select the **Mail** item in the submenu that appears. This will open the Internet Connection Wizard to create a new mail account. Let's consider what needs to be done at each step of the wizard.

1. Specify the name that will show in the **From:** field. Enter here the name of the person from whom the letter is supposed to be. If you happen to have a letter from this person, the best thing would be to use the exact form of the sender's name as shown in the **From:** field. For example, if the sender's name is shown

as *John Doe <johndoe@hotmail.com>*, you have to use the part before the e-mail address, that is, *John Doe*.

2. Specify the sender's e-mail address. This will be *johndoe@hotmail.com*.

3. Specify the incoming and outgoing mail servers. You need to know the login and password for the incoming mail server. While the login usually presents no problems (this is usually the part of the e-mail address before the @ character), the password is a problem. Since you are not interested in receiving mail on this account, you can enter anything in this field. Specify an SMTP mail server as the outgoing mail server. This can be your provider's SMTP server, or any other SMTP server.

If your provider has no SMTP server, or if you want to conduct mailings (but not spammings, which are illegal), you can take advantage of the Postman program (**www.cydsoft.com**) or any other mailing program that has an SMTP server.

The following are instructions for mailing messages using the Postman program. Start the program, open the **Options** menu, and select the **Program options** item. In the **Properties** window, select the **Build-in Mail Server** tab, and enter the e-mail address that the sent messages are supposed to be from (Fig. 5.10). Save the changes by clicking the OK button.

Next, create a new group of addresses, to which to send messages. Start with executing the **Group/New group** command sequence. Enter the group's name, and click on the **OK** button. You could use the default address group, but it is better to leave it for other mailings and create a separate group for anonymous mailings, *Anonymous Mail,* for example.

Select the group, and create an account for an e-mail recipient. Start by executing the **Recipient/New Recipient** menu sequence. In the window that opens, enter the e-mail address. You don't have to fill out the rest of the fields. Save the changes.

Select the e-mail account, to which a letter needs to be sent, and execute the **Recipient/Send e-mail to selected users** menu sequence. This will open a simple text editor window. Type the text of the message here, and click the **Send personalized e-mail** button (the second one on the left on the window's toolbar) when done. This will open a window, in which you will need to specify how to send the message. Select the **Use built-in mail server** option and click **OK**.

At first, it may seem that a large number of operations need to be carried out in order to send a letter using Postman. This is not actually the case, because half of the operations are needed to configure the settings and only have to be performed once.

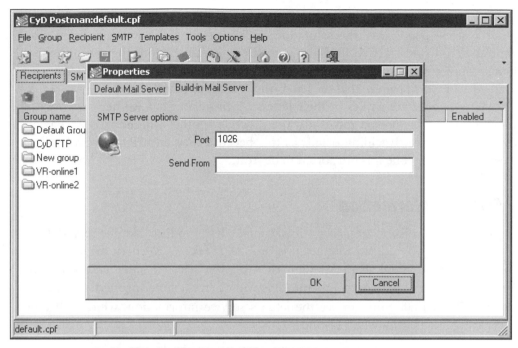

Fig. 5.10. The Postman program **Properties** window

5.5.2. A Genuine Fake Message

Your fake message should be written in the same style used by the supposed author of the message. If he or she makes some common mistakes, you should also copy them in your message, because drastic changes in the style catch the eye immediately, and your fake message will be found out for what it is.

Pay special attention to the salutation and the complementary closing parts. Use the same style that the supposed author of the message does. For example, his or her messages could use the following template:

Hi, recipient name:

Message Body

Best regards,   *Joe Blow*

Try to copy all the details down to the last space. If the supposed author of the letter inserts a line after the salutation, before starting the message body, you should also do this. Try to find out as much as possible about the person whose letter you want to fake. But this is a social engineering issue, because you must make the recipient believe that the letter was actually sent by Joe Blow.

Many people use smiles in their letters. Each person has his/her own way of making them. One person might just use :), while another will use :))))))). Pay attention even to such trifling details as this because they create the overall feel of a letter from someone it is purported to be from.

5.5.3. Service Information

Despite all of our labors at trying to make a fake letter to look like the real McCoy, it is rather easy to find out whether it is real. All it takes is to check the service information. In Outlook Express, right-click on the selected letter and select the **Properties** item in the context menu. This will open the letter properties window. On the **Details** tab, you can see the letter's service information, which will look something like that shown in Listing 5.3.

Listing 5.3. Letter service information

```
Return-Path: <vms@tin.it>
Delivered-To: info@cydsoft.com
Received: (qmail 60106 invoked by uid 89); 20 Sep 2004 00:59:11 +0400
Received: from unknown (HELO tomts4-srv.bellnexxia.net) (209.226.175.10)
   by mx2.valuehost.ru with SMTP; 20 Sep 2004 00:59:10 +0400
Received: from HSE-Toronto-ppp130995.sympatico.ca ([64.228.69.82])
   by tomts31-srv.bellnexxia.net
   (InterMail vM.5.01.06.10 201-253-122-130-110-20040306) with SMTP
   id <200310.VQG998.tomts-srv.bellnexxia.net@HSE-Toronto-
ppp130.sympatico.ca>;
    Sun, 19 Sep 2004 14:31:10 -0400
Message-ID: <006201c49ed8$bd91ecbb$afbafb30@sjeph>
Reply-To: "=?windows-1251?B?U2hvcDR1?=" <lk@tin.it>
From: "=?windows-1251?B?U2hvcDR1?=" <vms@tin.it>
To:  =?windows-1251?B?wOPg7+jp?= <gz@mail.ru>
Subject: =?windows-1251?B?IsLF183bySIg9O7t4PDo6iE=?=
Date: Sun, 19 Sep 2004 22:11:30 +0400
Organization: =?windows-1251?B?Qmx1ZWxpZ2h0?=
```

```
MIME-Version: 1.0
Content-Type: multipart/related;
        boundary="-----=_NextPart_000_001E_01C2AA85.597C61B6"
X-Priority: 3
X-MSMail-Priority: Normal
X-Mailer: Microsoft Outlook Express 6.00.2800.1081
X-MimeOLE: Produced By Microsoft MimeOLE V6.00.2800.1081
```

The `Received:` parameters list all of the servers the letter traveled through, and the letter's source IP can be figured out by way of these IP addresses. The `X-Mailer` parameter contains the information about the mail client used to send the letter. If your mail client is different from the one used by the supposed author of the message, this fact is easily noticed.

Fortunately, not too many users check the service information, or even know that this can be done. Most of those who stumble upon it by accident are unlikely to be able to make anything out of it anyway. You, however, can make use of it to determine whether the letter was really sent by the sender shown in the **From:** field. Just compare the message, about which you have doubts, with a message you know for certain was sent by this person. If the message is really a fake, its service information will be different than the service information for the real letter.

5.6. Network Security

Everything in the worldwide web is interrelated. The anonymity, which we considered in the previous sections, is the starting point for security. If your computer is not seen on the web, no one will try to break into it. The recommendations for protecting against viruses that were considered in *Chapter 4* are also valid for the Internet security. The type of secure computer that we described earlier makes your web surfing safer.

But the list of already described security measures is far from exhaustive. There are several more rules that you should follow to maximize the security of your web travels. Only then will you be able to enjoy your work on the Internet without having to worry about the big bad hackers.

5.6.1. Plugging up the Cracks

In *Section 4.7*, we considered how users can access open computer resources via the file and printer sharing service. A little bit later, we will learn how a network can be scanned for open resources. For security reasons, you have to decide whether you really need open resources. If you work on a local network, the file and printer sharing service will be installed by default, even if you do not open the particular resources, but simply use the server's services. If you do not exchange information with anyone, it would make sense not only to disable this service in the connection properties, but to remove it altogether. This way, potential trespassers will not be able to take advantage of this vulnerability. It simply won't exist.

We also considered security principles in *Chapter 4*, where we learned how services that are not in use can be disabled. This not only optimizes the system's operations, but also enhances its security. For example, I have seen many home computers with Microsoft Internet Information Server installed. (This server is a part of the standard Windows 2000/XP installation package). What in the world do you need a web server for on a home computer?! This is a question that sends most users into deep contemplation, with no meaningful answer to be found. Remove all network components that are not in use from your computer and your computer will become impervious to invasion by way of these potential holes: No hacker is so good that he or she can use loopholes that don't even exist.

Only those services that are necessary for normal computer operation should be installed. For example, at work I sometimes have to work with a local MS SQL Server database on my computer. But I have to do this seldom, normally using the database on the main network server. So, in order not to open unnecessary ports and not to load the system with unnecessary services, I removed the SQL Server from the startup menu group. I start it manually when I need it.

Consequently, by optimizing the system, you increase it reliability, stability, and, most importantly, security.

5.6.2. Passwords Keeping

In addition to making passwords complex or, even better, impossible to pick using the dictionary method, they need to be properly stored. We have already offered several recommendations on how to hide passwords on the local hard disk. You can use my recommendations, you can store all your passwords in your head, or you can devise your own secure method for storing passwords.

Wherever you store your passwords, do not trust this task Windows and Internet Explorer. Even though, as I have already mentioned, their security measures are pretty good, nothing is certain but death and taxes. If a hole is to be found in one of these measures, you can kiss your privacy good-bye.

Many sites and forums recognize your computer and allow you to enter without having to type your password in every time. They save your access parameters in cookie files on your hard drive, and automatically extract them every time you visit the site. We have already pointed out that cookies can be read only by the site that left them and, at first glance, such an arrangement seems acceptable from the point of view of security. But it is acceptable only if you don't care about losing your passwords. In most cases, cookie files and the passwords that are stored in them are not encrypted. The programmers feel that it's too much bother. Consequently, anyone with access to your computer can check the necessary cookie file, find out the password stored there, and wreak havoc wherever that password gains them entry.

5.6.3. BugTraq

To tell the truth, there aren't that many real hackers in the world. Most break-ins are perpetrated by teenagers who have nothing better to do and who want to try their skills somewhere. This sort of hacker is not too strong on the theory or programming, and mainly uses ready-made techniques designed and perfected by real

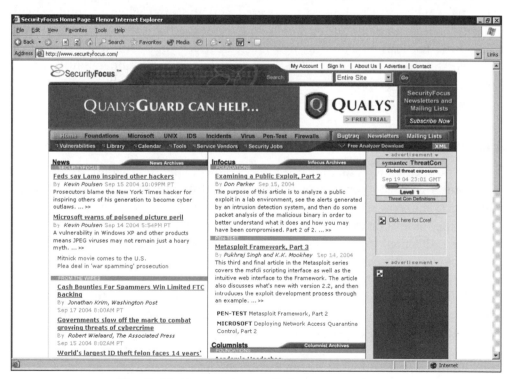

Fig. 5.11. The **www.securityfocus.com** site

hackers. This means that you should keep track of new break-in techniques and newly discovered vulnerabilities. I personally use the **www.securityfocus.com** site for this purpose (Fig. 5.11). They regularly publish information about new security holes, how to use them, and how to protect against their use.

Discussion concerning the need for sites like **www.securityfocus.com** has been around for a long time. On one hand, they allow administrators to protect their systems by learning about new vulnerabilities. On the other, hackers can also use this information for diametrically opposite purposes. I don't see any problems with sites of this type and, what's more, believe they are a good idea. The problem is that most administrators simply do not visit these sites, so they only learn of new weak spots when their site/network/server has been broken into. Even if you consider a security hole discovered back in 1990s, there are still computers and servers on the Internet, on which this hole remains unplugged. If I had my way, all of the administrators involved would be sent packing — with no severance pay.

If you think that regularly updating your system can make it impervious to break-ins, you are sadly mistaken. A considerable length of time may pass between the time a new security hole is discovered and the time when an update with a patch for it is released, during which your computer can be compromised. Any hacker who has learned about the new hole can attack your computer successfully. To keep this from happening, you must learn about new vulnerabilities before hackers do and undertake your own security measures to keep your computer secure until official patches comes out.

5.6.4. Firewalls

There is no such thing as too much security. I only use the Internet for e-mail and to view some web pages. For these activities, the security provided by regular updates and visits to the **www.securityfocus.com** site is enough. However, if you spend lots of time on the Internet or work on a network connected to the Internet, you need more powerful protection. If you spend more than eight hours a day on the Internet, and this is not work related, you should seek some dependency counseling.

Everyone who regularly visits mass gathering places on the Internet must protect his or her computer. For example, there is no guarantee that there is not a hacker lurking in the same chat room where you are. In some chat rooms and on some IRC channels, it is possible to learn the IP address of any computer and to attack it. In the days of Windows 95, I regularly heard ghost stories about someone's computer rebooting all by itself while the user was working on the Internet. The current versions of Windows are more secure and, assuming that you follow the security rules described above, the possibility of a successful hacker attack is decreased. Nevertheless, it remains quite real.

To protect yourself from an Internet hacker attack, you need to observe the following three security basics:

❒ Naturally, refrain from visiting shady places. Hackers seek out their victims to practice and test new break-in techniques on non-moderated chat rooms and IRC channels. All prominent on-line chat sites control the service operation, but not even this can make you safe from running into a scoundrel who is intent on getting into your computer. I never hang around in chat rooms, and my computer has never been attacked by hackers or infected by viruses from such a source. This is even given the fact that I never use firewalls or proxy servers.

❒ If you just can't live without chat rooms, you should hide your IP address. You can hide your real IP with the help of anonymous Internet servers.

❒ Use a good firewall. Firewalls can be software or hardware implemented. A software firewall is an acceptable option for a home computer in terms of the price and protection provided.

Starting with the XP version, Windows has a built-in firewall that provides the most necessary functions. This is better than nothing, but not quite enough to provide you with a complete feeling of security. I recommend that you use a more sophisticated firewall. I will not recommend any specific software, but will give brief descriptions of a few of the most popular firewalls.

❒ *Sygate Personal Firewall.* This is a quality firewall that has all the functions a home computer needs, as well as a convenient interface. The software is freeware for home users and provides protection against hackers, Trojan horses, and DoS attacks. The developer's site address is **http://smb.sygate.com**.

❒ *McAfee Personal Firewall* offers good functionality at a reasonable price. The McAfee company has been developing security software for home computers for a long time, and their firewall provides reliable protection against attacks. The developer's site address is **http://us.mcafee.com**.

❒ *Norton Personal Firewall.* Norton used to be associated with Norton Commander, but now numerous diagnostic, security, recovery, and repair programs for computers and everything having to do with computers and programming are offered under this brand name. This firewall offers, perhaps, the most security features for home computers, but is difficult to use and configure. The inconvenient interface and sluggishness of the software produced by Symantec today are, in my opinion, their biggest drawbacks, which also contributed to the demise of the legendary Norton Commander. The developer's site address is **http://www.symantec.com**.

Before you install a firewall, familiarize yourself with its features. Only install the program if you are satisfied with them. The important thing is that these features have been implemented properly and that regular updates are available. There have been cases where a seemingly great firewall could not protect against most basic attacks and, moreover, contained security holes itself, due to the poor quality of programming.

To help you with selecting a firewall for your needs, let's consider how they work and what security techniques they employ. Fig. 5.12 shows an example of a network protected by a firewall. All requests to or from the Internet must pass through the firewall. The firewall checks the requests for compliance with certain internal rules and permits them through only if they pass this check. Otherwise, the request packets are simply discarded.

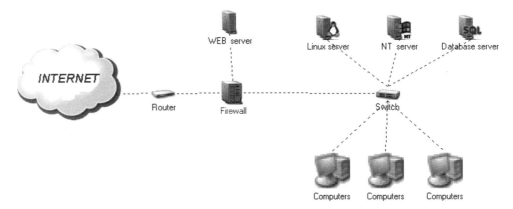

Fig. 5.12. An example of a network protected with a firewall

The following are some of the rules that can be used:

- ❏ *Disallowing the use of certain protocols.* For example, connecting to port 21 can be prohibited. This will make it impossible to use FTP to connect from the Internet and to download or upload files.
- ❏ *Prohibiting connection to certain URLs.* In this case, the users of the local network will not be able to load the forbidden sites, such as porno or warez sites.
- ❏ *Prohibiting connection from a certain range of IP addresses.* For example, if a company does business only with U.S. customers, incoming connections from Asian or African countries can be disallowed. These countries are used for

example only, as most hackers live in Europe or the United States, so this particular ban will not do much good in terms of hacker protection.

❑ *Employing user-identification software* (such as passwords) *or hardware* (such as
Touch Memory, Smart Card, or an encrypted diskette) *means.*

Depending on the firewall used, these rules can be expanded significantly. But
a firewall implementing only those rules just described can not only protect the local network from an intrusion from the Internet, but can also prevent connection
to the specified cites from the local network.

It is not enough, however, to simply install a firewall: The security rules must
be defined and the software must be properly configured. Firewall programs for
home computers are configured practically automatically, because the protection is
mostly needed for attacks from the Internet and by Trojan Horses.

Configuring firewalls for corporate networks is a more complicated business,
and the default settings should not be trusted here. Here, the security rules for the
network must be followed strictly and the firewall configured in strict compliance
with these rules.

5.6.5. Firewall: Not a Heal-All

Don't be lulled into a false feeling of security after having installed a firewall: There
are many ways to circumvent not just a specific firewall, but all of them.

Any firewall is just a security guy at the front door. But the front door is never
the first choice as a point of entry for a burglar. Burglars usually opt for the back
door or a window. For example, Fig. 5.12 shows a protected network and the front
door: the Internet connection through a dedicated computer acting a firewall. But
if one of the network computers happens to be equipped with a modem, this will
create a backdoor to the network without any doorman standing on guard around
the clock. That is, without the firewall protection.

I have seen servers, in which Internet access was permitted from only a certain
list of IP addresses. The administrators believed that this measure would protect
them from hackers. They were mistaken here, because an IP address is easy to fake.

At one time, I worked at a company where Internet access was controlled by way
of IP addresses. My monthly Internet traffic was limited to 100 MB, while my neighbor had unlimited access. To conserve my traffic, I did not download large files, but
only viewed web pages. When I needed to download something, I did the following:

❑ Waited until the neighbor's computer was not in use, for example, when the
owner went to lunch.

❏ Slightly pulled the network cable on the neighbor's computer out of the network card socket to break the connection.

❏ Assigned my computer the IP address of my neighbor and downloaded all that I wanted to download.

❏ Having finished, returned the IP addresses and the network cable to their regular places.

In this way, I was able to download all that I needed over a month. I then upgraded the process by installing a proxy server on my neighbor's computer, and then did all of my downloading through this. I was not selfish, so I shared this good thing with my coworkers, and we all connected to the Internet through this IP address with unlimited traffic.

With modern firewalls, simply switching the IP address will not help you to get into the system. The identification techniques they use now are much more sophisticated than simple IP address checking. Switching the IP address may only provide more privileges within the system, and even this is only the case if the network is not configured properly. But it will not help you to get into the system. But administrators worth their salt will not allow such machinations even within the network, using MAC addresses and access passwords to assign the access rights.

A firewall is a program that runs on a computer under the control of the operating system (a software firewall) or on a physical device (a hardware firewall). But, in either case, this program is written by humans, who, as we all well know, are prone to error. Just like with the operating system, the firewall needs to be updated regularly to repair the programming bugs that are inevitably present in all software.

Let's consider port protection. Suppose your web server is protected by a firewall with only port 80 enabled. Well, that's all the ports a web server needs! But this does not mean that other protocols cannot be used. A technique called tunneling can be used to create a tunnel to transfer data of one protocol within another protocol. This was the technique used by the famous Loki attack, which made it possible to send executable commands to the server within ICMP packets of the Echo Request type (this is a regular Ping query) and to return responses within ICMP packets of the Echo Reply type (Ping reply).

A firewall is a tool for protecting data, but the main protector is the administrator, who must constantly keep watch over the system security and prevent, detect, and ward off any attack. When we were discussing virus protection, I said that the reason a new virus can infect systems protected by antivirus software is because the software is not yet aware of the new virus. The same applies to attacks. A new type of attack can penetrate the firewall because the firewall can only recognize those attacks, for which it has algorithm samples in its database. To be able to process a non-standard attack, the system must be monitored by the administrator, who will be able to notice and react to any unusual changes in the main parameters.

A password or a device like Touch Memory or Smart Card is often needed to pass through a firewall. If the password is not protected, all of the money invested in the firewall will be wasted. Hackers can obtain the password in one of a number of ways and use it to penetrate the firewall. Many systems have been broken into in this manner.

Passwords must be strictly controlled. You must control each account. For example, if an employee with high system privileges quits, his or her account must be disabled immediately and all of the passwords, to which the employee had access must be changed.

I was once called to a company to restore data on its server after they fired the administrator. He considered the termination of his employment unfair and, a few days later, destroyed all the information contained on the main server without any problems. Even the well-configured firewall did not stop him. This happened because the firewall was configured by the malefactor himself. This type of thing should never be allowed to happen, and the firewall must be configured in such a way so that not even a network administrator can break through.

I always recommend to my clients that only one person must be trusted with the highest level firewall password. In a corporation, this should be the chief of the information-processing department. In no case should it be a regular administrator. Administrators come and go, and there is a chance of forgetting to change some password after the next administrator leaves.

5.6.6. Firewall: As Close to Heal-All As You Can Get

From all that was said above, you may get the impression that firewalls are waste of money. This is not the case. If the firewall is properly configured, constantly monitored, and uses protected passwords, it can protect your computer or network from most problems.

A quality firewall provides many levels of checking access rights, and a good administrator should never be limited to using just one. If you use only the IP address check to control Internet access, you can start looking for a bank loan to pay your Internet bill, because this address can be faked very easily. But a system, to which the access is controlled by the IP address, MAC address, and password, is much more difficult to compromise. Yes, both MAC and IP addresses can be faked. To make sure, individual computers can be tied to specific port switches. In this case, even if the hacker learns the password, he or she will have to use it at the computer, to which it is assigned. This may require some ingenuity.

The protection can, and must, be multilevel. If you have data that need protecting, use the maximum number of protection levels. There is no such thing as too much security.

Imagine your average bank. Its entrance door will be much stronger than your average house or apartment door and equipped with an alarm system to boot. A firewall is akin to such an improved door protecting against small-fry hackers, which is what most of hackers are. But it will not protect against a professional hacker, or at least not for long. In addition to protecting the premises with a good door, banks keep their money in safes, which are themselves are placed into vaults.

Money kept in a bank can be compared to secret information stored on a server, and it must be provided with maximum protection. This is why banks keep their money in safes equipped with sophisticated locks that take thieves a long time to open. While they are at, there's more than enough time for the cops to arrive on the scene.

To extend the bank safe analogy to servers, here the role of the safe is played by encryption. So, even if a hacker manages to bypass the firewall and get to the data on the server, it will take too much time to decrypt them. He or she can be nabbed while still sitting at the desk. But even if the hacker carries the safe away to crack at his or her leisure, meaning downloading the data to decrypt them without being bothered, the chances are that the information will become obsolete by the time it can be decrypted. The important thing here is that the encryption algorithm and the key are sufficiently sophisticated.

5.6.7. Virtual Private Network

One of the ways to protect data is to transfer them by way of virtual private networks (VPN). Imagine a company with a network of branches. Branches are located far away, and the least expensive way to connect all of their networks to the main office network is to use the Internet. To secure the traffic, the data transferred over the virtual channel is encrypted (Fig. 5.13).

Today, such networks can be created without any problems. At a glance, everything looks just great. Both sides are protected by a firewall, the traffic between the firewalls is encrypted, so the system is impenetrable. This is not quite the case! There is still a chance that a back door will be created. Suppose that the branch office wants Internet access not to organize the VPT, but simply to view sites. Of course, this traffic can be routed via the main office, but this will cost a pretty penny. Any request for a page will have to go not directly to the Internet, but first to the main office over a paid channel, and then from the main office to the web server over another paid channel. So, all requests must travel through two paid channels, and a double toll is paid for each megabyte. In addition, the VPN channel becomes overloaded, because, in addition to the corporate traffic, regular Internet-access traffic is also encrypted.

Fig. 5.13. An example of a virtual private network

Fig. 5.14. The branch office with two Internet connections

To save money, most companies open a separate Internet access channel directly from branches. The logic is that a separate Internet connection can be created, because the branch office is already protected by the firewall (Fig. 5.14). Everything would be fine here if the same attention was paid to security at the branches as at the main office. In most cases, however, branch-office networks do not even have their own administrator, and if there is one, he or she is usually not as experienced as the administrator at the main office. It is much easier, then, for hackers to break into a branch office network. And, because trusting relations are established between the branch and the main office, a hacker who breaks into the branch office network will be able to obtain access to the company's main servers over the VPN without the headache of decrypting the data between the two offices.

5.6.8. The Internet as Foe

When I was running a Q&A column in Hacker magazine, I was once asked a very good question: Is it possible to launch U.S. nuclear rockets via the Internet? This is not possible, of course, but not because the computers controlling rocket launch are well protected. No security system is infallible, because anything created by man is bound to have some imperfection. We will always overlook some fine detail and, according to Murphy's Law, this detail will be a security hole to let hackers in.

We have all heard about some large site or another with excellent security, into which someone has broken. How many break-ins are not even made public because the company fears the damage to its image? Any computer system can be broken into and I personally would never trust a computer to control even a kitchen tap, let alone the nuclear arsenals of such countries as the United States or Russia. These countries cannot afford to connect computers that control strategic weapons to the Internet. Should they be foolish enough to do something this stupid, any hacker too smart for his or her own good could start a nuclear war.

Data of strategic importance must be stored on computers not connected to the Internet. I was once called to check the security of a software development company. The bosses were extremely concerned about the safety of their source codes and not a single computer was equipped with floppy drives, other recording devices, or Internet connections. All of the computers were connected to a local network and only one of them had a floppy drive and a read/write CD-ROM drive, to exchange data with other computers. In this way, the source codes could circulate only within the local network with only one potential leak source, making this network an easy one to control.

Consequently, if you have super secret information, the only 100-percent guarantee of keeping it secret is isolating the computer, on which it is stored, from the worldwide web. This may make you think that the Internet is some sort of evil. Not so. If the rocket launch panel were put in an easy-accessible place, sooner or later some modern day Herostratus would press the button. (But for whom would he preserve his name?) There aren't too many people of that stock in the world, and the launch panel may remain unused for 10 years, (maybe 20 or 30) but it is bound to be used as intended some day. The Internet is like a very busy highway, as so many people use it nowadays. And this multitude of users is bound to produce a person who, because of inexperience, inadvertence, foolishness, or malice, will do something harmful to those with whom he or she shares the net.

People tend to consider information as something harmless, and do not realize what damage can be inflicted by its improper or unauthorized use. It may be greater than that caused by a nuclear bomb. Consequently, the security measures to protect information must be more stringent to prevent its unauthorized use.

It is very seldom, though, that information saved on home networks requires extreme security measures for protection, while corporate networks are not considered in any significant depth in this book. But I decided to elaborate on this real life example because it may be of help to you in your future work or studies.

At home, it is enough simply to hide your computer. Computers most often are broken into by inexperienced hackers who want to learn something new. Hiding your computer within the network environment is often enough to isolate it from amateurs of this type. This can be done by executing the following command:

```
net config server /hidden:yes
```

Now, your computer cannot be seen in the network environment. But this does not mean that it cannot be accessed. If a hacker knows your IP address, he or she can access your computer directly from both the local network and the Internet, by simply typing it into the browser address field.

5.6.9. The Enemy Inside

Some of the most difficult break-ins, or rather misuses of information, against which you need to protect, are those carried out by insiders, that is, by those people who already have access to the resources. The circle of such people includes company employees, your neighbors, parents, or relatives.

Let's consider an example concerning parents. They might know your password for the computer because you gave it to them yourself. But if your father takes a dim view of flunking a math exam, he may simply delete all of the games from the computer to help provide with more time for your studies. This sort of an "inside job" cannot be protected against, especially if your father knows something about computers himself.

I already cited the case of the disgruntled network administrator. People in his position know all of the passwords and security settings, so it is very easy for them to enter the system, even after they have been fired. These are just facts of life, with which we have to deal. One way to protect your data in situations like this is to change passwords regularly, as well as whenever an employee is let go, regardless of the reason.

Some people just like doing some nasty things to their coworkers by deleting or corrupting their work. In my experience, this is perhaps one of the most common break-ins. Another reason to fool with other people's data could be a desire to cover your own mistake. To cover their own behind, someone might doctor or delete data saved by another worker.

5.7. Scanning for Open Resources

In order to be able to see shared folders and files on another computer, you must have the client for that computer's operating system installed on your computer. For example, if you want to see computers in the network running under Windows, you need to have the Client for Microsoft Windows network service installed on your computer. For a computer's folders and files to be accessible to other computers on the network, the computer needs to have the File and Printer Sharing for Microsoft Networks component installed. If this service is not installed on the remote computer, you will not be able to access its files.

Both services are installed in the connection properties window. Execute the **Start/Control Panel/Network Connections** command sequence, and right-click on the necessary connection. Select the **Properties** item in the context menu that appears. The list of all installed services for this connection will be displayed on the **Networking** tab in this window. If the Client for Microsoft Windows service is not installed, you will not be able to scan the resources. To install the service, click on the **Install** button, select the service in the **Select Network Component Type** window that appears, and click on the **Add** button. In the **Select Network Client** window that opens, select **Client for Microsoft Windows** and click on **OK**. If the client is already installed, make sure that its check box is marked in the connection's **Properties Window**.

Let's consider how hackers can penetrate your computer if you have shared folders that aren't protected by passwords. In order for a computer to be accessed from the Internet, the **File and Printer Sharing for Microsoft Networks** service must be enabled for the internet connection.

Shared resources on other computers cannot be accessed through an Internet connection unless it has this service enabled.

Now, we need to find a computer on the Internet with shared folders. We will be helped in this task by the following two programs:

❏ ipconfig — This program determines local IP addresses.
❏ CyD NET Utils — This program scans a range of addresses for shared resources.

First, start the ipconfig program and determine your own IP address.
The output produced by the program should be similar to the following:

```
Windows IP Configuration
 Ethernet adapter Local Area Connection:
```

```
Connection-specific DNS Suffix  . :
IP Address. . . . . . . . . . . : 192.168.8.57
Subnet Mask . . . . . . . . . . : 255.255.255.0
Default Gateway . . . . . . . . : 192.168.8.1
```

If you have more than one network adapter installed on your computer, the IP address will be shown for each card. In this case, there is only one adapter — `Ethernet adapter Local Area Connection` — and only one address — 192.168.8.57.

Each Internet provider is assigned its own IP address range, which, in most cases, is determined by the first three digit groups of the address.

These three groups of digits are the network number. The last group of digits determines the computer number. Actually, the network number depends on the subnet mask.

The subnet mask determines, which of the digit groups belong to the network address and which belong to the computer address. Let's take, for example, the address 192.168.8.57 and the subnet mask 255.255.255.0. The first three groups in the mask are the same: 255. This means that the first three groups in the address represent the network address. The fact that the last group in the subnet mask is zero tells us that the last group in the address is the computer address. Let's take another example: the address 192.168.8.57 and the subnet mask 255.255.0.0. Analogous to the previous description, 192.168 is the network address, and 8.57 is the computer address in the network. Internet providers most often have addresses, to which the masks 255.255.255.0 or 255.255.0.0 can be applied.

Each network address is unique, and the provider assigns computer addresses as it sees fit within the network address range. For example, they may be assigned dynamically for dial-up customers and statically for customers connecting via a dedicated phone line. For example, the AOL network address is 11.x.x.x (the subnet mask being 255.0.0.0). The first group, the number 11, is the actual network address for AOL, so no other network can have this address. The addresses in the range determined by the last three groups can be distributed among the computers in the network as AOL deems necessary. The network address of another provider may be 192.168.x.x (the subnet mask for this network being 255.255.0.0). Here, the actual network address for the provider network is 192.168. The last two groups are used for addressing computers within the provider's network.

To provide an analogy, the network address is like an apartment building address, with the computer addresses much like the apartment numbers in the building. Which parts of the address are used as the network address and which as computer addresses is determined with the help of the subnet mask.

Consequently, in our example, the computers in the provider's network are numbered from 192.168.8.1 to 192.168.8.254. This is the range that we are going to scan. Launch the CyD NET Utils program (Fig. 5.15), and select the **Share scanner** item from the **Utils** menu. In the **Share Scanner** window that opens, enter 192.168.8.1 in the **From address** field and 192.168.8.254 into the **To address** field. Press the **Scan** button to start the scanning. During the scanning process, the address being currently scanned will be displayed in the status line.

If the program finds an open resource, it will display its address, for example, \\192.168.8.1\ftp. Its contents can be viewed by entering it in the browser's address line and pressing the **Enter** key.

The advantage of using CyD NET Utils to scan for open resources is that, before scanning a given address, the program checks whether it exists, using the `Ping` command. It takes a lot of time to scan for open resources in Windows, and it makes no sense to waste this time on a non-existent address.

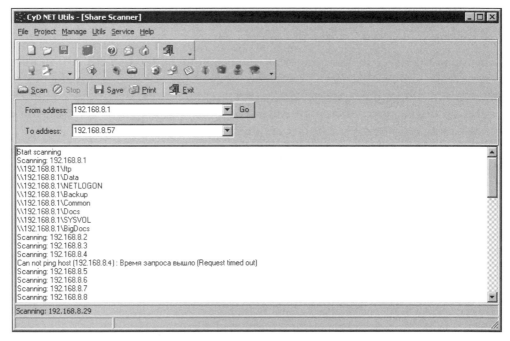

Fig. 5.15. Scanning resource using CyD NET Utils

On the other hand, this is also a drawback. Today, many firewalls intercept the `Ping` command, so the program may not scan an address that actually does exist.

Personally, I don't consider this to be a serious shortcoming. The developer logically assumed that if a firewall is installed and configured not to let `Ping` commands through, then the odds are that it will cut off all attempts to connect with open resources. This is so in 99.99999 percent of cases.

5.8. Hacker Attacks

It is impossible to provide a general formula that can be used for all break-ins.

Each case is different and requires an individual creative approach that depends on the system and its security configurations. Computer systems are most often compromised by taking advantage of software errors, and each administrator can have different software on his or her network.

Why do attacks on computers continue to increase with each passing year? The information about the holes and vulnerabilities in a computer system used to be stored on Bulletin Board Systems (BBS), and only a few people with special privileges had access to it. So it was these hackers who carried out attacks with impunity, because their level of education and experience was high.

The way things stand now, any information about vulnerabilities — holes, bugs, etc. — can be found in any corner of the Internet. Now anyone can be a hacker. I would like to ask the freedom of information fighters how this came to be? Unlimited freedom always leads to destruction in the end. I guess that the urge to destroy is in the blood of all of us. Most of us suppress this, just like we do many other primitive desires, but some give in and use publicly available information to become crackers.

When breaking into a system, hackers pursue one or a combination of the following goals:

❏ *To obtain information.* The system is broken into to obtain information that is not available to the general public. Such break-ins are usually directed at stealing business or financial secrets, software source codes, confidential data, etc. They are usually carried out by professional hackers, fulfilling an order or for personal gain.

❏ *To modify or destroy data.* All Internet or intranet servers are susceptible to this type of attack. They can be carried out not only by professional hackers, but also by amateurs, including disgruntled employees.

❏ *Denial of Service (DoS).* The purpose of this attack is to render the server's service unavailable, without actually destroying any data. These attacks are mainly carried out by amateurs whose only goal is to do damage.

❏ *Zombification.* This type of attack has become common of late. The purpose of the attack is to get the server under the hacker's control (in parlance, to turn it into a zombie) in order to use it to attack other servers. For example, carrying out a DoS attack most often requires powerful resources (a powerful processor, broad bandwidth Internet access, etc.), which are generally not available on home computers. To carry out such an attack, a hacker first takes over a poorly protected Internet server that has the necessary resources, and then uses it to carry out the attack itself.

Attacks can be classified into the following two groups, based on the manner by which they are executed:

❏ *Local attacks.* These attacks are executed with the intruder having physical access to the computer being broken in. This sort of attacks is not that difficult to protect against, as all that is necessary is to restrict physical access to the server by, for example, placing it into a limited-access room and guarding it.

❏ *Remote attacks.* These are carried out remotely via networks from a physical location other than that where the computer being broken into is located. This type of attack is the most difficult to protect against. Even the installation of the best firewalls and monitoring and logging software cannot guarantee complete security. Proof of this can be seen in the many break-ins suffered by some of the world's best-protected Internet servers (Yahoo, Microsoft, NASA, etc.).

When designing our defenses, we must understand the techniques used by hackers to break into computers. Only then will we be able to prevent unwanted intrusions and protect our computers. Let's consider the main attack techniques employed by hackers and how they are used. In order to understand the process better, we will look at it from the standpoint of the perpetrator.

We will not consider social engineering, however. This subject deserves a separate book, and it makes no sense to only graze the topic.

5.8.1. Research

Let's suppose that you want to break into a particular server to test how well it is protected. What should you start with?

There is no clear-cut answer to this question. Any break-in is a creative process and requires an individual, creative approach. There are no set rules or ready-made templates. However, a few practical recommendations to follow can be provided.

The first thing to do is test the system's vulnerability by scanning its ports. What for? To find out what services (daemons in Linux) are installed in the system. Each open port is a service program installed on the server, to which you can connect and have it doing certain things for you. Port 21, for example, is used by the FTP service. If you manage to get connected to this port, you will be able to download files from and upload files to the server. You will have to have the corresponding privileges, however, in order to be able to do this.

First, you need to scan the first 1,024 ports. Many of them are used by standard services like FTP, HTTP, Telnet, etc. An open port is just like a locked entrance to the server. The more entrances of this type there are, the greater are the chances that the lock for one of them will succumb to picking and swing open to let you in. This is why I recommend removing all unused services from the startup group.

A good administrator leaves only the most necessary ports open. For example, if your server is only used to serve web pages, but not e-mail, there is no need to keep the mail servers open. The only port that a web server needs is port 80, so only it should be left open.

A good port scanner not only reports the open port numbers, but also the names of the services using them. Unfortunately, the service names are not real, but only those for the server installed on the port. Thus, the name of port 80 will be given as http. It is good if the scanner can save the scanning results to a file and even print them out. If your scanner does not have these features, you will have to write down all the information yourself and save it. You will need this information for your future exploits.

After scanning the first 1,024 ports, you can then move on to scanning the rest. Standard services are a rare occurrence in this port range. Why bother scanning them then? Well, there is always the chance that someone has already visited this area and left an open door, or installed a Trojan horse on the server. Most Trojan horses keep open ports in the range above 1,024. So, if you are a server administrator, an open port in the above the 1,024 range should make you sit up and take notice. If you're a hacker and stumble on an open port in the range above 1,024, you should find out what Trojan horse server is installed on it and find a client for it to control the machine.

This will be all you need to do to break into the server. By using the Trojan horse installed by a stranger, you obtain access to the server without any great effort on your part. Unfortunately, life is rarely a bowl of cherries and discoveries of this kind are the exception rather than the rule. In most cases, you will have to do all the dirty work yourself.

After scanning, you will know, which doors there are on the server that you can use. But this is not enough, as the doors also have to be opened. This will take a much greater effort.

Identifying the Server's Operating System

Scanning ports is just the very first stage in breaking in. It is kind of like casing a place before a break-in. And there remains the most important thing to do before attempting the actual break-in: determining the operating system installed on the machine. The specific version of the operating system would also be a welcome piece of intelligence, but we can live without this specific piece of information in the beginning.

I recommend the Shadow Scan program (**www.rsh.kiev.ua**) for determining the operating system. I won't say that this is the best program on the market, but it is not among the worst options either.

In addition to determining the operating system, the program can also determine, which services are installed. This can be of great benefit to you in your hacking endeavors. Suppose you have learned that the network server has a web server installed and you have also discovered that the operating system is Windows. It would be a fair guess that the web server is Microsoft Internet Information Server (IIS), but this is not a sure bet. There is another, quite powerful, server that can run under Windows: Apache. Since different servers require different break-in techniques, the first thing we are interested in as hackers is exactly which server is sitting on port 80. There are other web servers than IIS and Apache, but these two are the most popular.

The only shortcoming of Shadow Scan is that earlier versions of the program sometimes produce the famous blue screen of death when attempting to determine the server's operating system. Happily, this bug appears to have been taken care of in the latest version of Shadow Scan.

How do we determine, which operating system is in use? This can be done in one of the following ways:

❑ *By examining the implementation of the TCP/IP protocol used.* Different operating systems implement the protocol stack in different ways. The program simply analyzes the responses to requests from the server and draws conclusions about the operating system installed based on these analyses. In most cases, the answer is vague, with only the general type of operating system provided, Windows or Linux, for example. The exact version of the operating system cannot

be determined in this way, because the protocol stack is implemented in virtually the same manner in Windows 2000, Windows XP, and Windows 2003, so
the responses these versions provide to the queries are the same. So you can
find out that the server runs under Linux, but not under which particular version. Different versions of the same brand of operating system have different
vulnerabilities, so just knowing the basic operating system brand is only half of
the information you need to break into the server.

☐ *By examining responses from various services.* Suppose the victim's computer allows autonomous FTP access. All you need to do is connect to the server and
check the system prompt. The default invitation prompt looks something like
this: "Welcome to the X.XXX client FTP Version of FreeBSD Server."
The message might reflect the true state of things. On the other hand, it also
might not.

☐ *If the invitation prompt reflects reality,* the administrator is still wet around the
ears. An experienced administrator will always change the default welcome
message. And a really canny administrator can make the welcome message
show something different altogether. For example, the Windows NT 4.0 server
can be made to display a Linux welcome message. This will lead an unsophisti-
cated hacker to waste lots of time using Linux vulnerabilities to break into
a Windows NT server. Therefore, don't put too much trust into the welcome
message. Try to ascertain the type of operating system by other methods.

☐ *Social Engineering.* One of the ways to obtain information about services installed
on a hosting company's server is to send the administrator a letter asking for this
information. Administrators and the support-service personnel usually divulge
this information freely, but they sometimes provide information that is nowhere
near the truth. Sometimes, this information will be available on the server's main
page, but it should still be verified.

In order not to be fooled, always pay attention to the services used on the
server. For example, a Linux server will not serve ASP pages. Although things like
this can be faked, this is not often done. To make an ASP page run under Linux,
PHP script files are saved with ASP extensions and redirected to the PHP inter-
preter. So it looks like the server serves ASP files, but these are actually PHP scripts.

As you can see, the defending side goes to great lengths to make life as difficult
as possible for hackers. Most inexperienced hackers believe everything they see and
spend lots of time trying to break in using methods that have not got the slightest
chance of success. Consequently, breaking in becomes too expensive a proposition,
and the hacker gives up.

The hacker's task is to untangle all of the false leads left by the administrator and determine exactly what system he or she is dealing with. Unless this preliminary task has been completed successfully, any further actions would be like looking for a needle in a haystack. The hacker will not even know, which commands to use or what executable files can be infiltrated onto the server.

Using Scripts

Well then, now you know, which operating system is running the server, which ports are open, and which services are sitting on these ports. You should write down all of this information either in a file or on paper. The important thing is that it should be convenient to work with.

Do not overlook the importance of recording all information collected. Even computers malfunction sometimes, while the human brain does it regularly. And, in accordance with Murphy's law, the most important things are usually the first to be forgotten. But make sure that you destroy all the records after the break-in. This will prevent them from falling into wrong hands, such as hackers who may be looking to break into your system, or police looking for some evidence to use against you in court.

All done? This concludes the research section. Now you have enough information to attempt a basic break-in using the vulnerabilities in the server's operating system and services. The information about which vulnerabilities to use can be found by regularly visiting the **www.securityfocus.com** site. Information about new vulnerabilities is updated often on this site, and it is a longstanding and well-known fact that most servers (70 to 90 percent, depending on the source) simply are not patched. Therefore, you should use all known vulnerabilities on the victim and hope that something works.

If the server is well patched, you will have to wait for new holes to be discovered and exploits for them written. (An exploit is a program written to take advantage of a specific vulnerability.) As soon as you see a new vulnerability has been discovered and an exploit for it written, download the exploit and use it before the administrator patches the hole.

Automation

Practically every day, computer security professionals discover vulnerabilities, holes, and gaps that you could drive a truck through in various systems. All of this information is published in BugTraq reports on various servers. One site, on which these reports can be found, as already mentioned, is **www.securityfocus.com**. But, besides new examples, there are plenty of old vulnerabilities that may not have been patched on the server you are trying to break into. But how can you find out exactly which vulnerabilities a given server has? Isn't there a better way than downloading all of the exploits and trying them manually? Of course, there is. There is a great variety of programs to test a server for vulnerabilities automatically, the most common of these being SATAN, Internet Scanner, NetSonar, and CyberCop Scanner.

I will not recommend any specific program. There is no utility that has a database of all existing vulnerabilities. So download various programs and test the server using them all. This way, your chances for a successful break-in become much greater. I do recommend, however, that you use software from Internet Security System (ISS, **www.iss.net**), because their scanners (Internet Scanner, System Scanner, and Database Scanner) use all three scanning techniques. (We will discuss these techniques later.) The ISS personnel work closely with Microsoft and regularly update their vulnerabilities database. But, despite the fact that this company's products are some of the best on the market, I recommend that you use at least one other scanner from a different company.

Internet Security Systems has developed a suite of utilities named SAFEsuite. The suite contains not only system security-testing utilities, but also intrusion-detection utilities and utilities for checking the configuration of the main server operating systems.

Security scanners are similar to antivirus programs: They only protect against known threats. New vulnerabilities will not be detected until the program is updated. For this reason, I don't recommend that you rely on automatic security scanners alone. You should supplement them by checking manually for the latest vulnerabilities described in BugTraqs.

Automatic scanners are good for performing an initial scan for old vulnerabilities. If you are a system administrator and detect vulnerabilities in your system with a scan, you should update the software component containing the vulnerability or check on one of the security sites (e.g., **www.securityfocus.com**) for ways to neutralize the vulnerabilities discovered. Almost always, the description of the remedy for the vulnerability is provided along with the description of the vulnerability itself. The way to neutralize the vulnerability may also be suggested by the scanning program if it has it in its solution database.

Why can't we be certain that the server has no vulnerabilities, even after the most exhaustive and effective scanning provides an empty result? In addition to new vulnerabilities, server configuration is also a factor. Each server is configured differently and, under certain conditions, a vulnerability that can be easily detected manually may be overlooked by an automatic scanner.

Each scanner employs individual techniques and means, and vulnerabilities missed by one scanner may be detected by another. Computer-security professionals like to use the apartment analogy. Suppose that you came to visit a friend and ringed the doorbell, but nobody opened the door. This, however, does not mean that there was no one at home; the owner, for example, may not have heard the doorbell, or the doorbell may have been out of order. But if you had called on the phone, the owner might have answered. Or it might be the other way around: Your friend could miss the phone call but hear the doorbell.

To return to automatic scanners, one scanner is like a phone call, while another is like a doorbell. They both produce results, but with different server configurations one may be better than the other.

There are three methods of automatic vulnerability detection: scanning, probing, and imitation. When scanning, the utility collects information about the server, scans the ports to find out what services are installed, and, based on these scans, produces a report on potential vulnerabilities. For example, a scanner can check a server and discover that port 21 is used by the FTP service. After the scanner attempts to connect to the port, the server issues an invitation prompt, by which its type can be determined (provided that the prompt has not been modified). The scanner then checks its database for vulnerabilities for the given server version and, if it finds any, produces a corresponding message.

Automatic scanning is far from being an exact science and can be fooled easily. Conversely, there may simply be no vulnerabilities on the given server. Some vulnerabilities can only be detected with certain configurations, and will not be noticed with others.

During the probing process, the utility does not scan the server for open ports, but instead scans its programs for vulnerable code. This process is similar to the way that antivirus programs that scan all programs for virus code work. The same thing takes place here, except that the object of the search is vulnerable code.

This is an effective method, but the same type of error (e.g., a buffer overflow) can be present in programs written in different languages. The scanner will not detect this kind of error.

The imitation method consists of the utility imitating attacks that it contains in its database. For example, the FTP server may produce the buffer overfill error when a certain command is executed. The scanner will not try to detect the server version, but will execute the command instead. This, of course, will hang the server, but you will know for certain whether the server has this particular vulnerability.

This method is the lengthiest, but also the most reliable. If the utility can break into a service, then a hacker can do so as well.

If you have a new FTP server installed that is unknown to scanner, it will be tested for errors that other FTP servers contain. Different programmers very often make the same errors. Simple scanning will not detect these vulnerabilities for the basic reason that they are not listed in the database for the given version of the FTP server.

Always disable the firewall when conducting a system scan. It may block access and the scan may not examine the necessary service. In this case, it will report no vulnerabilities, even when a vulnerability does exist. These vulnerabilities, of course, are not that critical, as they are protected by the firewall. But, if a hacker finds a loophole in the firewall, they will become critical.

Give the scanner everything it needs. For example, some people think that remote scanning, where the scanner imitates an attack over the network, is the most effective. While this may be true, it raises a question about how much time it will take to check the strength of the account passwords. A lot! And checks like registry and file-system scans will simply become impossible. This is why local scanning may be more productive and reliable.

In remote scanning, the scanner only attempts to enter the network. This type of analysis can be used to evaluate the server's capability to withstand outside attacks. But, statistically, most break-ins are inside jobs (carried out by disgruntled employees or unscrupulous users), where the perpetrator already has some access rights and manages to enlarge them and obtain access to the areas he or she is not supposed to see. Hackers can also obtain an account with minimal access rights, which they can then raise by taking advantage of vulnerabilities in the access-rights assignment procedures. Consequently, you should perform both remote scanning, in order to detect loopholes that can be used to enter the system, and local scanning, in order to detect configuration errors that can be used to expand access privileges.

Automatic scanners not only scan programs for vulnerabilities, but also accounts for the password strength. Scanner utilities contain a database of the most often used account names and passwords and try to use them to enter the system. If an attempt is successful, the utility informs the user that the password being employed is too simple. Passwords of this type must be changed, because hackers can use the same method and learn the account parameters with ease.

Both hackers and administrators can use security analyzers. Hackers use them to detect vulnerabilities that can be used to penetrate the system, while administrators use them to close such vulnerabilities. If you are an administrator, your task is to find and patch the vulnerabilities before they are found and used by hackers.

5.8.2. Breaking into a Web Server

Breaking into a web server involves its own specific considerations. Breaking a server that allows execution of CGI, PHP, or other scripts requires a different approach than for other server types. The break-in is started by scanning the server for vulnerable CGI scripts. It may be hard for you to believe, but research conducted by various companies indicates that there are many vulnerable scripts employed on Internet sites.

The reason scripts are vulnerable is that pages are programmed by people, who have an inherent propensity to error. Novice programmers very seldom test the incoming parameters, hoping that the users won't change the page code or the URL, through which the data necessary for executing certain actions are passed to the server. But we have already considered in this chapter how to modify page code and fake IP addresses to jack up counters. This was possible because the programmers relied on visitors being conscientious. They shouldn't.

One popular program for site control — PHP-Nuke — contains the parameter vulnerability problem. The program is a collection of scripts used to create a forum, a chat room, and a news service on the site, and to control the site's contents. All script parameters are passed through the URL string of the browser, and the error was located in the ID parameter. The developers assumed that only a number would be passed in this parameter, but did not check if this was actually the case. A hacker who knows the structure of the database (which is not that difficult to learn, as the source codes for PHP-Nuke are public) can easily place a SQL request to the database server in the ID parameter and obtain the passwords for all visitors registered at the site. The information is encrypted, but, as we will see later, it is not difficult to decrypt it.

The problem is aggravated by the fact that some programming languages (e.g., Perl) were not intended for use with the Internet. They contain some functions for manipulating the system and, if a programmer inadvertently uses them in his or her work, hackers can take advantage of them to obtain control over the system.

All programming languages have functions that have the potential for misuse, but some languages have more than others. The only more or less secure language is Java. But it places such a drag on system resources that web masters are very reluctant to use it. Even this language, if used by an unskillful programmer, can leave gaps that, to hackers, like wide-open hangar doors with welcome signs hung above them.

Thus, an ignorant programmer is the biggest vulnerability. Because of the shortage of professionals in this area, anyone who completes a crash programming course becomes a programmer. Many such "accelerated programmers" do not have the slightest idea about computer security, which is not something that is about to become a point of complaint for hackers.

So your main task is to make sure that there are a couple of good CGI scanners in your toolkit. Which CGI scanner should you get? This is not a huge issue, as having any variant is better than having nothing at all. Even the worst scanner can find vulnerabilities, about which even the best hackers are unaware. It just may happen that it will find this vulnerability on a server you are trying to break into. Additionally, you should become a regular visitor to the **www.securityfocus.com** site, where they regularly put out descriptions of the latest vulnerabilities for various web site programming languages.

Breaking a Web Site Using a Search Service

Over the past 10 years, the Internet has grown to such dimensions that it has become impossible to find something there without a good search system. The first search systems simply indexed Internet pages by their contents, and then used the received database for searches. But searches of this type produced only very approximate results. Conducting a search on the word "bow" will produce results for bow ties, archery weapons, ships, and a variety of other subjects. Most languages have words that have double or multiple meanings, which makes searching by these words difficult.

The problem lies not only in words with multiple meanings. There are many commonly used expressions that are difficult to use in searches. To solve this problem, many search systems started using more complex search algorithms and now allow for the use of various search parameters. One of the today's most powerful search systems is Google (**www.google.com**). It offers many options to make a search more precise. Unfortunately, most users do not even know that these capabilities exist, let alone use them. Hackers, on the other hand, have learned how to use the various search parameters very well.

One of the simplest ways to use a search system to break into a server is to use it to find a closed web page. Some sites have areas that can be accessed only through a password. An example of such a site is a paid resource, where the protection is based only on checking a password when entering the system, but individual pages are not protected and Secure Socket Layer (SSL) is not used. In this case, Google can index the pages on closed sites so that they can be found by the search system. You just need to have an exact idea about the information that is stored in the file and to compose the search criteria as precisely as possible.

In Search of Indexed Secrets

Google can be very helpful in unearthing important information not intended for public viewing, but which has become accessible to the Google indexing engine because of a mistake by the administrator. For the search to be successful, you need to specify the correct parameters. For example, the results of entering `Annual report filetype:docs` in the search line will be all Word documents containing the words "annual report."

The number of documents found will likely be too great, so you will have to narrow the search criteria. Persevere and you will succeed.

Searching for Vulnerable Sites

Suppose that you have found out that there is a weak spot in some site-management system. What is a site-management system? There are many payware and freeware software packages written in different languages for creating a website without requiring any knowledge of the conventional tools used to build website, such as HTML, CGI, ASP, PHP, and other technologies. Packages of this type can contain ready-made forums, guest books, news pages, etc. There are packages for building, for example, forums. The forum-building tools *phpbb* and *ikonboard* are very popular and are widely used on the Internet.

So, if a hole is discovered in some site-building or forum-building program, all Internet sites built using this program become vulnerable. Most site administrators do not subscribe to news postings and do not update their scripts. Therefore, you just need to find a site built using the package with the vulnerability and use an exploit to break in.

How can you find sites or forums containing the vulnerability? It's very easy. The script used on the site can most often be determined by the URL string. For example, when viewing a section of a forum created using the Invision Power Board tool, this string contains the `http://www.sitename.ru/index.php?showforum=4` code. The text `index.php?showforum=` will be contained in the URL of any forum built using the Invision Power Board engine. To find sites of this type you need to conduct a Google search using this text:

```
inurl:index.php?showforum
```

There can be other forum engines that use this text. To winnow them out, you can add some text to the search parameter. For example, by default, each page of the Invision Power Board forums has this text at the bottom: `Powered by Invision Power Board(U)`. The text, of course, can be changed by the administrator, but in most cases it is left as is. So, if you add this text to the search string, you can be certain that the search results will only contain pages for the needed forum. Try to execute the following search:

```
Powered by Invision Power Board(U) inurl:index.php?showforum
```

You will see more than 150,000 sites running forums built using this engine. Now, when a vulnerability is discovered in Invision Power Board, you can easily find a victim to exploit it. Not all administrators will rush to patch this hole, while some will not patch it at all.

Try to run a search for `inurl:amdin/index.php`. You will find so many interesting things that it will take your breath away. Such references are often used for some site-administration tasks. Experienced administrators protect them with passwords, so most of them will be inaccessible. But some of them can be accessed, and what can be done with them is only limited by your imagination.

5.8.3. Brute Force

When your attempts to hack into a server using basic brain power have failed, you can always fall back on the brute-force method. No, brute force does not mean that you will have to grab the site administrator by the throat, knock the administrator's head against the wall, and demand that the password be surrendered. Brute force simply means trying different passwords until you hit on the right one.

Let's look at the statistics again. Every security-research project reaches the same conclusions regarding the passwords people use: Most beginners use names of their pets, birthdays, phone numbers, and examples of this type as their passwords. A well-compiled password dictionary can let you break into practically any system, because there are inexperienced users everywhere that use this type of password. And if these users happen to have high privileges, hackers can have a real field day! This is why I always recommend using strong passwords.

Are you still skeptical? Then let me remind you about the famous Morris worm, which used the dictionary method to brake into systems. Its own dictionary contained fewer than 100 words. In addition to its own dictionary, the worm used the dictionaries from the compromised computers. But those did not have too many passwords in them either. Using such a primitive algorithm, the worm was able to spread through a huge number of the Internet computers. This was one of the largest scale infections ever! Yes, it happened a long time ago, but the level of professionalism for the average user has not grown since then. There are many experienced users, but there are many more green beginners.

The dictionary method is often used to pick passwords to mail boxes, FTP servers, etc. This is a rather lengthy process and, if you have a strong password, hackers will not be able to pick it, even using the best dictionary.

But even if you have a password created following all of the security rules, you should not rest on your laurels. Hackers can use real brute-force password picking: trying every possible combination of characters. This will take them a lot more time, but they will succeed in the end. In order to make sure that this does not happen, you need to install an attack-detection system. A good firewall will have no problem detecting attempts at password picking. Make sure that your firewall has this function.

Before you get down to picking a password using the dictionary method yourself, you need to compile a good dictionary of login names and passwords. For this, it is very important that you know, for which system you are trying to pick the password. For example, if you are after a Windows server, you should include *Administrator* in the names list. For *nix systems, you should definitely have *root* in the name list, but all logins like *Administrator* can be removed, because there are no such user names in *nix systems.

This is how hackers usually go about compiling their dictionaries. Having what is known to be a good login name makes password picking easier. To make the hackers' job more difficult, you should rename the default account names. If you use a strong password, you can choose a simple name — one that is easy enough to keep in your head.

A good idea would be to include default logins and passwords for various services in the dictionary. Administrators often forget, or simply don't bother, to change the passwords for services that are installed and running, but are not used. Windows administrators are more likely to suffer from this syndrome. This has to do with the fact that the knowledge level of the professionals working with this operating system is much lower than that for other operating systems. For example, I have seen many cases of MS SQL Server 7.0 with the default account "sa" not protected by a password. This is probably the reason why Microsoft intends to remove this account in the next version of the server and, in the SQL Server 2000, issues warnings at every step about the need to set a password.

Sometimes, however, using strong passwords can backfire on you badly. If you forget the password or misplace the piece of paper, on which you wrote it down, you will not be able to enter the system yourself. In this case, you will have to pick the password using one of the methods you know. The task may be made somewhat easier by the fact that you have some idea of what the password may be, thereby narrowing down the search.

Of the parole-picking programs, I would recommend the Software Scan or CyD NET Utils. They have very good dictionary generators and the password-picking algorithms for all of the main protocols for the corresponding services.

5.8.4. Local Networks

Hacking a local network is easier than hacking the Internet for the following reasons: The computers are connected via a high-speed connection (10 Mb/sec and higher), the traffic of the other network computers can be monitored, fake servers can be created, and firewalls are seldom used, because they are mostly used as a shield between the local network and the Internet. Let's consider the most popular local network-hacking techniques.

Traffic Monitoring

Local networks have certain inherent features. For example, if a local network is built using a coaxial or twisted-pair cable and hubs to connect the computers, all the network traffic passes through all the computers in the network. Why can't you see this traffic? Because the operating system and the network card are joined in a conspiracy and do not show you traffic that is not yours. If you really want to read other people's network traffic, you can get yourself a sniffer program and monitor all of the data that passes through your network card, even if they are not intended for you.

The sniffer trick will not work on the Internet, and you will see only your own traffic. To be able to monitor the Internet traffic of other participants, you would have to hack into the provider's server and install your sniffer there. This is a rather involved undertaking, fraught with the danger of being discovered and kicked out. Therefore, sniffers are generally used only on local networks.

How come that you can see other people's traffic on a local network, but not on the Internet or switched local networks? There are several ways, in which the computers in a local network are interconnected. In the earlier networks, computers were connected by coaxial cables to a common bus (Fig. 5.16), which could be additionally closed into a ring (with the computers on the bus ends connected to each other). When the computers at the bus ends exchange data, all packets pass through the network adapter of the computer (or computers) between them.

Coaxial cable is used very seldom as the network medium nowadays, because such a method of connection is not very reliable, and its rate is limited to 10 Mb/sec.

Fig. 5.16. Bus network topology

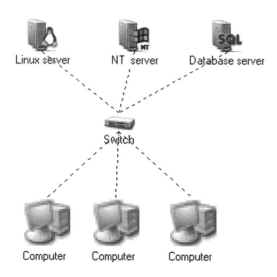

Fig. 5.17. Star network topology using a hub or a switch

Since the early 1990s, the preferred network configuration has been the star-connected topology (Fig. 5.17). In this case, the network computers are connected at the central point via a hub or a switch. If the central connection device is of the hub type (also known as a multiport repeater), all of the packets that it receives from one of the computers are simply resent to the rest of the network computers. If the central connecting device is of the switch type, the packets are delivered only to the recipient, as the switch has built-in routing capabilities.

Switches usually route MAC address-level packets. This type of addressing is used to exchange packets only in local networks (even if data are sent to an IP address). In the Internet, packets are sent using IP addressing. Far from all switches can handle this type of addressing. In this case, a more intelligent device is needed to send packets to the right place: a router. Like switches, routers send packets only to the computer, to which they are addressed, or to another router that knows where the addressee computer is located.

Consequently, switches in local networks and routers on the Internet make sniffing difficult, as sniffers must be placed directly on the switches or routers.

Intercepting packets is only half of the business: The information contained in them is in a form difficult for humans to interpret. It is mostly just fragments of larger data blocks that have been broken into parts to be transmitted.

Today, you can get any type of a sniffer, as well as add-ons for it, on the Internet. Different versions are optimized for different tasks, so you should select the one in line with what it is in particular that you are trying to do. If you are after passwords, you need a sniffer that can isolate registration information from general network traffic. This task is not actually that difficult because, unless the SSL protocol is used, all passwords are sent to the Internet in open text, just like all other information.

The advantage of using sniffers when attempting a break-in is that they do not interact with the computer being attacked, which means that they are very hard to detect. In most cases, it is simply impossible to know that your traffic is being monitored by someone.

I was once hired to figure out the protocol used by a software package to communicate with a device. The company paid big money for the device, which was intended to take readings from goods produced and send this information to the computer. However, the standard software supplied with the device was not suitable for the company's needs. The libraries for writing custom programs that were available at the device vendor's site did not have the source codes and could not be used to write the necessary utility. To solve the problem, I was asked to determine the protocol used by the device to communicate with the computer.

The communication was conducted via usual network interface using TCP/IP. I connected the sniffer to the network and analyzed all the packets that the device was exchanging with the standard program. Then I wrote a simple example to make sure that I got it all right, and finally presented the information I had obtained to a company representative. The company was out some money (and I was in) for the simple reason that they did not know how to monitor the traffic and I did.

It's too bad, though, that sniffers cannot modify packets. They can only observe the transmitted data, and cannot intervene in the process.

Fake Addresses

It has already been mentioned that firewalls allow or disallow user access based on a set of rules. But it is not always convenient to disallow all accesses to all ports. For example, access to the management programs can be disallowed for all IP addresses except the one used by the system administrator. Anyone trying to enter the restricted area from a different IP address will be stopped by the firewall.

At first glance, the defense seems perfect. This would, indeed, be the case, were it not for an attack technique called "spoofing." This attack is carried out by faking the address of an authorized user to enter the server under attack. Older firewalls and cheaper contemporary examples cannot detect a faked address in packets. A good firewall should ping the computer trying to connect to ascertain that it is turned on, and that it is actually this computer that is requesting the connection to the restricted resources.

Fake Servers

Attacks using fake servers or services are much easier to carry out in local networks than on the Internet. For example, the following well-known fake ARP record attacks can be performed only on local networks.

As you already know, when a computer is addressed by the IP address, its MAC address is determined first, and then the message is sent to this address. But how can the MAC address be determined when we only know the IP address and do not know the network interface used? This is done with the help of Address Resolution Protocol (ARP), which broadcasts a request for the computer with the specified IP address to all computers in the network. Only the IP address is provided in the request packet, with the unknown MAC address given as FFFFFFFFFFFFh. If there is a computer with the specified IP address in the network, it answers with a packet in which its MAC address is specified. ARP operates transparently to the user.

If there is no computer with the specified IP address on the given network segment, a router may reply by sending its own MAC address. In this case, the computer will exchange data with the router, which will resend the packet into another network segment or to another router until it reaches its destination.

But what if the computer that answers is not the specified computer but, instead, an impostor with a different IP address? When sending packets on a local network, computers do not use IP addresses, but go by MAC addresses. So the packets will be sent to whichever computer claims that its MAC address corresponds to the specified IP address, regardless of what its real IP address is. The hacker's task, therefore, is to intercept an ARP request and answer it in place of the intended recipient. In this way, a connection can be taken over.

Suppose that a network computer makes a request to be connected to the server. If we intercept this request and emulate the server's password request, we will find out that computer's password for entering the network. The problem with this method is that it is almost impossible to implement manually. This requires writing a corresponding program, which means that you need to have programming knowledge.

There is another point worth mentioning. After the computer associates a MAC address with the IP address, IP/MAC association is stored in the local cache. This cache can be controlled with the help of a Windows utility called *arp*. Because this is a command-line utility, it is not very convenient to work with. The already-mentioned CyD NET Utils program has a graphic interface and is more convenient to use. Launch the program and select the **IP ARP** item from the **Manage** menu. This will open a window, in which you can view the contents of the ARP table and add and delete records.

When an ARP record is added manually, it becomes static, and can only be removed manually. An ARP record added automatically is dynamic and, after a certain period of time, is removed by the system.

DNS requests can be intercepted and substituted in the same way as ARP requests. Where ARP is used to convert IP addresses to MAC addresses, DNS converts symbolic site addresses into IP addresses. The nature of the task is the same: to place a computer on the line to intercept DNS requests and to supply fake answers to them. In this way, several infamous large-scale break-ins have been carried out on the Internet.

The reason for faking an IP address by a hacker could be redirecting the traffic to him or herself in order to filter it for passwords or to redirect the traffic to another server. If all of the traffic of a DNS server is redirected to a single web server, the latter will not be able to handle it all, and will either start answering requests very sluggishly or hang altogether. But this question belongs to the DoS attacks area, which will be discussed later.

5.8.5. Trojan Horses

Using Trojan horses is the most stupid and unreliable method to employ against network administrators, but it is good enough to use against regular users, because they are easier to fool. Although there are network administrators that are probably in over their heads, very few will fall for this trick. But who says that there are only administrators on networks? There also are plenty of regular users with high access privileges and trusting souls. They are the ones you can horse around with, so to speak.

A Trojan horse program consists of two parts: a server and a client. The server needs to be installed on the victim's computer, one way or another, and started.

Most often, a Trojan horse program places itself into the startup folder, starts automatically with the system, and runs surreptitiously in the background. With the server part planted on the victim's computer, you use the client part to communicate with the server and make it do all kind of things, like rebooting the computer, checking its hard drives for interesting information, etc.

But how do you plant a Trojan horse on someone's computer? The most common way is to send it via e-mail. Simply give the executable file of the server part some intriguing name, attach it to the message, and send it to the victim. The message text should be persuasive enough for the victim to launch the attached file. This is the same method used to insert viruses. If the user falls for your ruse and launches the server part, it will be as if this computer were on your own desk.

How should you name the attachment so that the victim will not become suspicious? We already talked about this when considering the system security. By default, Windows 9x/NT/2000/XP operating systems do not show extensions of registered file types. So if you name the attachment as Anna_Kournikova.jpg.exe, the extension (EXE) will be hidden, and a large number of users will think that they are dealing with a picture. To make sure that the real extension will not be seen, you can even name the file as follows: Anna_Kournikova.jpg...........exe. In this case, the real extension will not be seen, even if the system is configured to show the registered file type extensions.

I used this method successfully on two occasions to infiltrate a Trojan horse into my friends' computers via the e-mail. The first time I did it on a bet, when a friend of mine said that I could not slip a Trojan horse into his computer. The other time I wanted to play a joke on another friend of mine. To effect the penetration, I used a very interesting and effective method. I already mentioned the danger of opening e-mail attachments, especially when the e-mail is from a stranger. Most experienced users do it very carefully, screening attachments on viruses before opening them.

So, in order to sneak a Trojan horse into a victim's computer, you have to make him or her download and install the executable file. To this effect, I sent my friend an e-mail, in which I advertised freeware software that could be downloaded from a site that I had set up especially for this purpose. The important thing is that the program be of interest to the user. For example, if the intended victim is into graphics, the bait could be a new graphics effect.

The message itself should look like spam. No matter how much we say that we do not read spam, we do read it, or at least glance through messages of this type. If the first sentences of the message get the victim interested, the victim will do what you are asking for without fail. If the first message gets sent to trash, don't get discouraged. Keep on trying. However, if a third message does not produce the desired effect, it might mean that the mark filters e-mail or that your offer is of no interest to him or her. So you should start offering a new program and write a new letter.

To keep the victim from becoming suspicious, the site must look as professional as possible, with a description of the offered program and screenshots. This information can be lifted off the actual site of some lesser-known company or individual programmer.

Despite the fact that both of my friends are very familiar with all methods of infiltrating viruses into computer systems, both of them took the bait. Of course, I sent the server part of the Trojan horse with an anonymous mail to keep from being found out. In this way, I made sure that the file would be launched despite the fact that the victims knew me.

The method described is complicated and requires spending a good deal of time and effort to prepare, set up the site, to place the server part of the Trojan horse in it, etc.

If the Trojan horse program is intended to steal passwords, it can send them in a file to an e-mail address specified in advance. The address can be figured out easily by professionals (by examining the Trojan horse), but this is as far as they will get. Professional hackers are not stupid, and send their wares from mailboxes they register on free mailbox services under assumed names. When a mail box is created and checked for mail only through an anonymous proxy server, figuring out the owner is next to impossible (assuming that no secret service agency becomes interested in the case).

Trojan horse programs are so popular because, by following a few simple rules, the perpetrator will likely remain anonymous. In addition to all of this, today's Trojan horse programs are very easy to use. Nowadays, you don't have to be a programmer to create your own Trojan horse. You can make use one of the constructors aplenty that are available on the Internet. The most famous of these is Back Orifice, which has been used in perpetrating countless break-ins.

The server part of Back Orifice installed on the victim's computer allows the hacker to perform the following actions on the remote computer:

- ❑ Access the hard disks
- ❑ Edit the registry
- ❑ Execute programs
- ❑ Monitor passwords
- ❑ Copy the screen contents
- ❑ Control processes, including the reboot

But the most powerful feature of this particular Trojan horse is that plug-ins (of which there are many varieties offered on the Internet) can be added to the source code and compiled into the executable file, thus providing additional control features.

The danger presented by the Trojan horses is confirmed by the fact that most new antivirus programs check not only for viruses, but also for Trojan horse programs. For example, antivirus programs identify Back Orifice as a Win32.BO virus.

5.8.6. Denial of Service

The most stupid attack thought up by hackers is the Denial of Service (DoS) attack. The essence of such an attack is that the hacker attempts to make the server stop answering requests for pages. How can this be done? This is often achieved by making the server enter an endless loop. For example, if the server does not check whether incoming packets are in the proper format, the hacker may send it a request that will lead the server to service this request endlessly, leaving no processor time for servicing other requests and, thus, denying service to other clients.

A DoS attack can be executed in two ways: by exploiting a bug in the server program or by overloading the communication channel or the resources associated with the server. The first method requires that the server contain a vulnerability and that you know what it is. The most often used vulnerability is the buffer overflow error.

The procedure for executing a buffer overflow DoS attack is as follows. Suppose that you want to send the string "HELLO" to the server. To accept this string, the server software allocates enough memory to store five characters. The program code may look like this:

```
Program code
A buffer to store five characters
Program code
```

If the program has no provisions for checking the actual size of the data it receives and writes to the data buffer, the buffer is subject to overflow. If a user sends 100 characters instead of just 5, when all these character are written to a buffer intended to hold only five characters, the other characters will be written into the program code area overwriting the code. This means that the program code will be corrupted and will not be able to execute as intended. The program will most likely hang. The server then stops responding to client requests and you have carried out a successful buffer overflow DoS attack.

Consequently, the computer was not broken into, no information was touched, but the computer has been put out of network service. The DoS attack is even easier to execute in a local network. All you have to do is replace the IP address of your machine with the IP address of the machine under the attack. This will result, in the best case, in the machine under attack becoming inaccessible or, worst case, in both machines becoming inoperable.

To execute a resource-overload attack, little or no knowledge is needed about the machine under attack. Here, the stronger machine wins. Resources on any computer are limited. For example, a web server can organize no more than a certain number of virtual channels to communicate with clients. If the number of clients exceeds the limit, the server becomes inaccessible. All you have to do to execute this attack is write a program whose only function is to keep on opening connections. Sooner or later, the connection limit will be exceeded, and the server will not be able to open new connections.

If there are no programmed limitations on resources, the server will process as many requests as it can. In this case, either the communication channel or the server can be attacked. The choice of the target depends on which is weaker. For example, if a 100 Mb/s channel is serviced by a Pentium 100 server, it is much easier to kill the computer than to overload the communication channel. But if, on the contrary, a relatively powerful server is sitting on a narrow bandwidth channel, it is easier to overload the channel.

How can a communications channel be overloaded? Suppose that someone enraged you in a chat room. You find out his or her IP address and learn that the offender uses a simple 56 Kb/s dial-up Internet connection. Even if yourself use the same connection, you can overload the smart alec's channel with no problem. You do this by sending an endless stream of large packet-size ping requests to his or her IP address. The victim's computer will receive these packets and will have to answer them. If you send enough packets, receiving the ping requests and answering will be the sole activity on the part of the victim's computer, leaving no channel capacity for anything else and effectively taking your offender out of the chat room. If your channel capacity does not exceed the victim's, you will not be able to do anything but to send and receive large ping packets. If you think this price is acceptable to take revenge, go ahead and have fun.

CyD NET Utils can be handy tools for executing ping DoS attacks. Launch the program and select the **Ping server** item in the **Utils** menu. In the window that opens, select the **Options** tab (Fig. 5.18). In the **Number of packages** field, set the number of packages to send to some very great quantity, in multiples of thousands. The **Time out** field can be set to 1. In this way, the program will not wait for a response, but will send a ping packet every second. Set the **Size of packets** field to some large number again, say 10,000, to send a large volume of data in one packet. Now you can send the ping command to the IP address you have chosen.

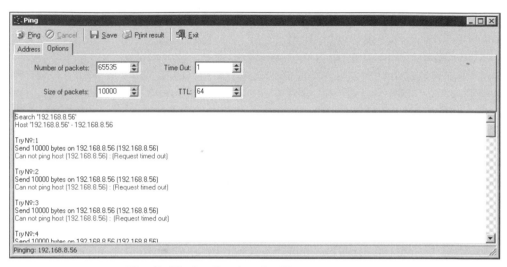

Fig. 5.18. Configuring the Ping command

In this way, you can overload the victim's Internet channel only if your own channel bandwidth is greater than, or at least the same as, the bandwidth of the channel under the attack. If your connection bandwidth is narrower that the victim's, you will be able to load only a part of his or her channel, the maximum being determined by your own channel bandwidth. The rest of the channel will be available and the victim will be able to use it. On the other hand, his or her communications will be sluggish and you will achieve at least something.

If you decide to attack a server, mind that your communications channel will be much narrower than the server's total bandwidth, and you will have to determine a weak spot in order for the attack to be successful. Suppose that the server offers a service for downloading files from other sites and saving them in its storage. To overload the communication channel of such a server, you may request the simultaneous download of several large files. The server will devote most, if not all, of its bandwidth to carrying out your request and, during this time, will leave other clients without service. Your own Internet connection will not be affected at all by this process.

A wide bandwidth channel is not needed to overload a server's processor. All that is necessary is to send it a very time-intensive request. Suppose that you want to attack a server that offers on-line translation services for site pages. In this case, you find a page containing lots of text (e.g., a book, a technical manual, or an RFC) and send the server a bunch of requests to translate it. In addition to the server having to load its channel to download the book, it will have to load its processor to translate it. Sending about 100 requests a second to translate, for example, the King James' Bible will surely put the server out of commission. If the server is equipped with protection against multiple requests for the same material, you can send it several large books.

Denial of service attacks are considered quite easy to defend against: The server software must control and limit the number of requests that can be submitted from one IP address. But this is only in theory, and a check of this type will only protect you from inexperienced hackers. An experienced hacker will have no problem with counterfeiting IP addresses and flooding the server with packets supposedly issued from those addresses. This makes the situation even worse for the server, because, if the attack is conducted over TCP/IP protocol, the server will have to establish a connection for each of those requests.

If a hacker sends a large number of requests to establish connections with different IP addresses, the server will send acknowledgements to those addresses and wait for further actions from the computers at those addresses. Since, in reality, there no such addresses, waiting is pointless. Consequently, filling the server's incoming connection queue buffer puts the server out of service while it waits for a connection with the nonexistent computer. How long this wait will last depends on the timeout value, which can be as large as five seconds. During this time, the hacker can flood the buffer with new requests and extend the wait. The process can be repeated for as long as desired.

Distributed Denial of Service

DoS attacks are suitable for attacking servers with narrow bandwidth communications channels. Large servers like **www.microsoft.com** or **www.yahoo.com** are difficult to take out with these attacks because they have wide bandwidth channels and super powerful processing resources. No hacker can ever match this bandwidth or these processing resources. However, there is more than one way to skin this cat. To match a large server's bandwidth and processing resources, hackers resort to Distributed DoS (DDoS) attacks.

By "distributed," I mean that the communications channels and processing resources of many users are used to execute the attack. However, there aren't too many users who would volunteer their resources for such purposes. Hackers solve this lack of cooperation problem by taking over users' machines with special-purpose viruses. For example, the Mydoom.C virus searched in the Internet for computers infected with Mydoom version A and B viruses and used them to attack the Microsoft servers. Fortunately, this virus did not manage to take over enough machines to execute a full-fledged attack. The Microsoft administration maintained that the servers were working as usual, but some customers did notice some lag in the servicing of their requests.

It is very difficult to protect against a distributed DoS attack, because the numerous requests are sent by existing computers. It is difficult for the server to determine that these are not bona fide requests, but are, instead, directed at taking the server out of commission.

5.8.7. Password Cracking

When a hacker is trying to break into a system, he or she most often uses one of the following methods:

❑ If he or she already has an account on the server under attack (even if it is just a guest account), the hacker may try to obtain greater privileges.
❑ Obtains the account of a specific user.
❑ Obtains the password file and makes use of the accounts belonging to other users.

Even when hackers manage to obtain privileged system rights, they still strive to get their hands on the password file. Succeeding in this endeavor gives them access to the root account (in Unix systems) and, correspondingly, the rights to the entire system. But the passwords are encrypted and the most the successful hacker will see will be the hash sums produced by irreversible password encryption.

When the administrator adds a new user, the user's password is irreversibly encrypted (most often, using the MD5 algorithm), meaning that the plain password cannot be reproduced from the encrypted form. The obtained hash sum is saved in the password file. When the user enters the password, it is encrypted and compared with the hash sum saved in the file. If the results match, the password entered is accepted.

Because the encrypted password cannot be decrypted, it may seem at first that the hash file is of no help. But appearances can be deceiving. Even though the password cannot be decrypted, it can be picked by the brute-force method. There are many programs designed for this task, for example, John the Ripper (**www.openwall.com/john**) and Password Pro (**www.insidepro.com**).

In Windows systems, passwords are also irreversibly encrypted, but are stored in the SAM database. Here, another utility, SAMInside (**www.insidepro.com**), can be used to pick them. Its work is shown in Fig. 5.19.

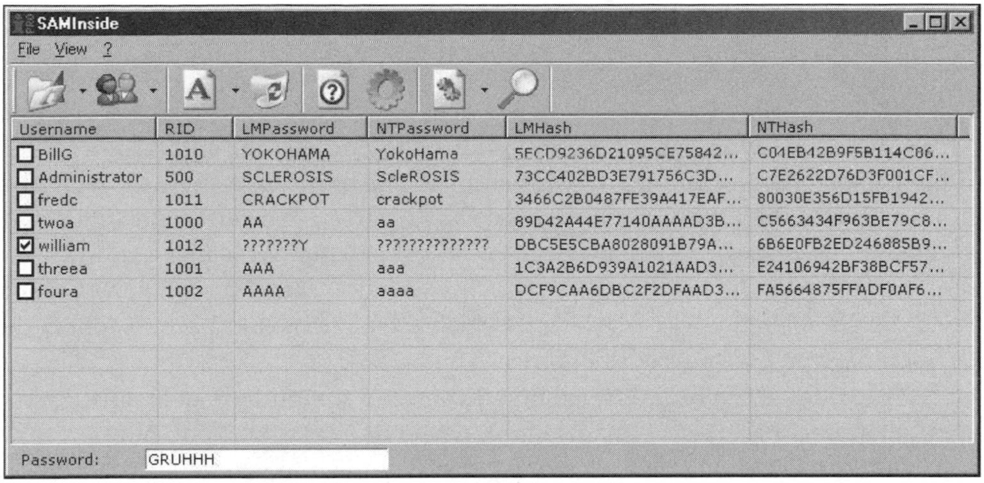

Fig. 5.19. SAMInside in the process of breaking Windows NT passwords

Why can utilities like these be obtained freely on the Internet by anyone, when they can be used for criminal purposes? Any program has negative as well as positive aspects. What should you do when you forget the administrator password or the administrator forgot to tell you what it was when you fired him? Reinstall the system? This will take a long time and is fraught with the danger of lost data. It is much easier to remove the hard drive and to connect it to another computer (or simply load from a diskette), take the password file, and break the necessary password.

In Windows 9*x*, passwords are stored in files with the PWL extension. These files have no protection at all and the passwords can be stolen easily. Whereas in Windows 2000/XP, the SAM password database is protected from direct access, here a password file can simply be copied from the victim's computer. Once the hacker has the file in his or her possession, the passwords can be extracted with the help of the PWLInside program (**www.insidepro.com**).

Specific User

To obtain the rights of a specific user, hackers most often employ the following techniques:

❒ *Social engineering.* This is a quite simple and time-effective method. It is not guaranteed to produce results, however.
❒ *Trojan horses.* This method is easy to use but, like social engineering, is not guaranteed to produce results if the target computer is not infected.

❑ *Password picking.* This is the most difficult method and may take the perpetrator years to hit on the right password, the end result being no meaningful results.

To make use of social engineering, you need to possess the contact information of the person whose account you want to hijack. If this is an e-mail address, then you could send this address a message asking the target, in a not too obvious way, to divulge the password. The message could masquerade as a message from the administration of the server that needs this data for some verification. Or you could place a reference to a fake site, to which the target would have to supply the account name and the password in order to enter.

A Trojan horse can be infiltrated into the target's computer in at least two ways. First, if we have the target's e-mail address, we send the executable to him/her as an e-mail attachment and hope the mark is curious enough to launch it. Another way is to provide a reference to a web page, from which the user could download the executable him/herself. Again, we need to send an e-mail with such a reference and a good come-on to make the user go to that reference and download the Trojan horse.

The chances of success depend on the degree of the victim's professionalism (being able to recognize the bait for what it is) and on your skill in circumventing that professionalism and enticing the mark to take the bait.

Picking the password may be the quickest method, if the password is not difficult. But it can also take the longest if a strong password is used. Hackers only break Pentagon computer-system password in five minutes in the movies. In real life, the process takes at least a few hours, usually days, and quite often months.

When a hacker is trying to break into a system, all of the available methods can be employed. There is good chance that one of them will produce results.

There is another method that has not been mentioned directly here, but was treaded in relation to system security earlier: system services. Each service has rights of a certain account and, if commands are executed in the name of the service, their rights will be those of the account, under which the service operates.

Most administrators don't want to bother getting involved into the fine points of service configuration and give all services the greatest administrator rights. Giving a service rights that are too limited (for example, those of a guest account) may result in its failing to work. Some server programs need to access the registry or the system folders. If this is forbidden, the service will simply not start. It is often difficult to find the cause of a service going on strike, especially if detailed documentation describing the program's security policy is not available. On the other hand, most services simply do not need significant privileges.

When a hacker wants to obtain administrator rights, he or she may try to discover a vulnerability in a service with these rights. If such a vulnerability is found, the perpetrator can use it to penetrate further into the server.

So, in order to deprive hackers of extra loopholes, the rights of services must be limited to those that are necessary for their proper operation — and nothing more. Then, even if a miscreant finds a vulnerability in some service, it will be difficult to use it to get into the system if the service does not have sufficient privileges.

For example, an account can be created for the FTP server that has access only to certain folders, which are already available over the network to the FTP clients. Most often, however, FTP servers do not need access to system folders. If your server uses the registry or writes to the system files, just say no here, because its security leaves a lot to be desired. Most services do not need access to system folders (or, at least, should not have this access, even though some not-too-bright programmers give it to them).

If you are a programmer who develops server products, do not get into system areas unless it is really necessary. Limit the server operations to the folder, in which the user installs the program. If your server does not access dangerous resources, it cannot be used to access the system. This means that your program will not make it onto industry lists of vulnerable services, which will improve its market standing.

The list of potential recommendations for programmers could be extended to infinity, but we are considering the computer from the user's point of view, and will not go off too far on this tangent.

5.8.8. No Operating System Is Safe

There is a perpetual discussion about which operating system is more secure against break-ins, Windows or Linux? The argument for Linux is that, supposedly, Windows systems are broken into more often. The argument is flawed, because the operating system that is broken is the one that a perpetrator needs to break to achieve his or her purposes. If hackers need to break into a bank's server, they will work on it, regardless of what operating system it runs under. Whether it is Unix or Window will make no difference to the malefactor. The only thing to prevent either system from being broken into is a professional administrator implementing proper security policies.

Both systems are equally susceptible to being compromised. I would say that the results to a great degree depend on the professionalism of the two sides: the cracker and the administrator. A break-in is somewhat similar to the Trojan war. While hackers are attacking the operating system fortress, looking for cracks and vulnerabilities in its walls, the defender — the administrator — is beating off the attackers by making his system as secure as possible. If the administrator commits an error, the hacker wins. If the hacker makes an error, the administrator and the secret service win.

Security is a function of the administrator's professional skills. Performing most of the administrative tasks in Windows does not require the level of skills as required by the same process for Unix, so Windows administrators tend to be less qualified than their Unix counterparts. Administering Unix systems requires more skill but, because these systems are much more difficult to administer, even skilled administrators sometimes make gross errors. Thus, Windows-type operating systems combine the ease of administering with inexperienced administrators, while Unix-like systems combine experienced administrators with the difficulty of administering. In the latter case, because of the difficulty of the process, even experienced administrators sometimes make blunders.

As we already know, not just the operating system, but also its services can be broken into. In this case, the developer of the operating system cannot be held responsible. For example, when an Apache web server running under Windows is broken into, this is not a fault of Microsoft, who took no part in its development. So developers of operating systems cannot be blamed for all computer system break-ins.

Why are there so many computer-system break-ins today? At its inception, the Internet was designed as an open system and the issue of break-ins was simply not considered. There are no means for ensuring security, data and user authenticity, etc. in the TCP/IP suite of protocols, which is the main Internet protocol. This circumstance is the explanation for most break-ins.

The new version of the protocol, IPv6, has the built-in means to provide more security, improved authentication, etc. The protocol was designed a few years ago but its implementation has been moving along rather slowly, and when it will finally replace TCP/IP is difficult to predict. All that remains is to hope that its security features will not already have been rendered obsolete by the time it finally arrives.

5.8.9. Conclusion

The above review of hacker attacks does not claim to being exhaustive. I did, however, try to provide the most essential basic information. At the same time, I did not describe any specific break-in methods. Doing this could be considered as a call to action, while the purpose of this book is not to add to the already overly large roster of hackers. My goal is to show how hackers see the computer and how they use it. This should help you to learn more about the computer and make your computer more secure.

We mainly considered only theory, rather than practice. To implement the break-ins described above, you would need specialized programs and, for certain tasks, you would have to write custom programs yourself. This falls into the hacker programming area.

Why is it so often easy for hackers to break into servers? This is due to several reasons, some of which are the following:

- The open nature of network traffic. By default, network traffic is not encrypted and can be read easily.
- Errors in the server's operating system and application software, and the failure to update them in a timely manner.
- The difficulty of organizing secure interconnection between different types of networks.
- Faulty configurations of the operating system, application software, and security software.
- Scrimping on security professionals and the security systems.

For the last factor, taking the cheap road with regard to security professionals is the greatest evil. Only a professional with many years of experience can protect a system from being compromised. Many people rely on their own knowledge or configure networks themselves in order to learn how to do it. You, however, should learn on systems specifically intended for this purpose and leave business systems to be serviced by professionals.

5.9. Hide and Seek

The foundation of any attempt to cover up activity in an area where it shouldn't be taking place is the use of anonymity principles, which we considered earlier in this chapter. Malefactors usually hide their real IP addresses by using long chains of anonymous proxy servers. The most sophisticated hackers even resort to using zombie computers. In the context of Internet hacking, a zombie is a computer that has been cracked and taken over by a hacker for the purpose of using it as a second-stage attack beachhead. A zombie is much easier to find than the hacker who uses it, because the hacker usually has a complete control over the zombie and can delete any information that could be used to establish his or her identity (e.g., security and activity logs).

What do hackers do after they gain access to a system? This all depends on the goals they are pursuing. If the purpose is to destroy information, covering up their tracks is not the highest item on hackers' to-do lists. Taking over a powerful server for further use as a zombie is a different business altogether.

5.9.1. Long-Term Takeover

If a hacker wants to take over a system for a long time, he or she needs to create a hidden door to provide entry to the system at any time. It is too inconvenient to use the vulnerability every time. Besides, this can be noticed easily. It is much better to have some hidden entryway.

Having penetrated a system, hackers most often open a shell on some port that allows them to execute commands on the system or place a Trojan horse within. Administrators check open ports on their systems very seldom, especially those above 10,000, as this is a pretty boring process.

An original solution is to raise the privilege level for a compromised account. Once again, administrators are too lazy to keep an eye on existing accounts and react only when new accounts are added. For example, it will take most administrators a while to notice that a guest account has been given the rights to read and write to the system folder. Some will never notice.

Giving privileged rights to a guest account was only used as an example. If you have the choice of accounts to edit, pick an account that does not stand out too much, one for a rank-and-file accountant, for example. The guest account is edited too much by administrators themselves and is under much closer scrutiny than the accounts of common network users.

During my career as a network administrator, I once noticed that some records were missing in the server operation log. This was not due to records having been deleted, but simply to the fact that the log would be disabled at certain times and nothing would be written to it at all. Having analyzed the times, at which the log was disabled, and the recent records, I discovered that it would be disabled practically right after the same user entered the system. As it turned out, a hacker raised the privileges for this account. In order to keep his exploration of the system in the guise of this user, who did not have rights for this, from being logged, the hackers would disable the log during each of his visits.

Cleaning the log files is the main modus operandi for a hacker wishing to remain in the shadows. Regardless what lengths a perpetrator may go to in hiding his or her IP address, he will be traced back, or at least searched for, if it is discovered that someone unauthorized has entered the system. However, if there is no indication that the system was entered by unauthorized entities, there is no one to look for. Even if the administrator does notice that the system might have been visited surreptitiously, and starts looking for the unwelcome guest, the chances of tracing down the perpetrator are practically nil. With the log cleared, there is nothing to trace. This is why hackers will try to erase all the traces of their visits to a system. Since these traces are left in the security logs, the latter get cleared.

I drew another conclusion from the missing-log-records incident. Like other system administrators, I find reviewing logs a drag. I did not install special monitoring software, nor was I using the standard monitoring tools. There is too much traffic going through my server. It is not that easy to notice traces of hacker activity among all the heaps of log records, so I simply did not look into the log at all.

The hacker who broke into my system was very careful and disabled the logs during his or her visits. On the other hand, he or she was not too experienced, because it would have been better for the intruder to simply clear the records of clandestine activities without disabling the log. Had the intruder not touched the security log, I would have never noticed his visits.

Short visits are highly unlikely to be noticed, so it is not worth bothering with clearing the logs. It is better to take a care to hide the IP address. In this case, the transaction log will not be of much help to the administrator or secret services if they cannot determine the IP address of the party that left the tracks. When visits are infrequent and short, this is very difficult to accomplish.

5.9.2. Hit and Run

If all a hacker wants is to get into the system for a short time to get something done (e.g., delete or steal files), he or she does what was planned, deletes the tracks to the extent possible (e.g., clears the transaction logs), and exits the system, never to return. This type of hacker is the most dangerous because, if they are not sure that simply clearing the logs is good enough, they may erase or format the entire disk.

Many servers employ log mirroring systems, where copies of the transaction logs are stored on another disk. When hackers destroy the main system disk in attempts to cover their tracks, they don't realize that this does not achieve their purpose. All of their escapades are logged in the reserve log copy and can be found out using these records. The first thing that needs to be done is to look for and clear the reserve log copy. Only then should the main log be cleared.

Some hackers are only out to wreak havoc and destruction and don't care about clearing transaction logs. They simply destroy all the information before leaving the system. Fortunately, these represent the minority. Most hackers understand that a good administrator will do everything possible to find a miscreant. Consequently, they realize that they stand a better chance of remaining unknown by covering up their tracks than by destroying all of the information on the disk.

The shorter the time hackers spends in a system, the more difficult it is to find them out. But if a visit is a long one, the hacker will unwillingly leave lots of tracks of his or her activity, even when simply viewing the contents of the server without changing anything.

5.9.3. You Can Run but You Can't Hide

If you steal some candy from a store and the shortage is discovered, it is unlikely that anyone will spend a lot of time looking for the thief. The expense of recovering the loss in this case will simply be incommensurable with the loss itself. However, if you steal the blueprints for some secret military equipment, take my word for it, the government will spare no expense in finding you.

The same applies to computer-system break-ins. If you change the main page for some mom-and-pop company, the chances are good that no one will go after you. However, if you steal a good chunk of money from a bank or penetrate military networks, they will definitely be looking for you.

Some hackers think that encrypting their hard disk covers them and that the law-enforcement agencies will not be able to find any proof of their illegal activities. This is a mistake. Suppose that you stole some merchandise and hid it behind a steel door with seven locks. Do you really believe that the police will not get to them? Of course they will. Having obtained a search warrant, the police will demand that you hand over the keys. If you refuse, they will simply destroy the locks. Any attempt to impede their actions will be considered obstruction of an investigation and will only put you in still hotter water.

There is also no way to prevent a computer from being searched. Even if you insist that all this police business has given you amnesia and you have forgotten the keys, the government can employ huge resources to break the password. If it turns out that you are in possession of stolen goods, you can be sentenced to some extra time at the government's expense. Everyone knows that cooperating with the prosecution may help you receive a shorter sentence, while interference will, at best, leave it unchanged or, at worst, prolong it.

5.10. The Unthinkable Has Happened

The event any computer administrator or user dreads most is the discovery that his or her system has been penetrated. What should be done in such a case? Most administrators and managers attempt to conceal this fact and do not undertake measures to find out who the culprit is. They simply try to get rid of the unwelcome guest.

The first thing many administrators do is disconnect the malefactor's session and, only then, start trying to figure out how the system was penetrated. This is the wrong approach, because you will not be able to trace the path of the penetration. Most often, the most that you will be able to discover is the account used by the invader, and to change its password.

But what if the hacker was able to use the account because of a script error? In this case, the hacker can simply repeat the same steps, obtain a new password, and use it until the new penetration is noticed — assuming that it is.

The best-case scenario is that where your server performs only one specific action. For example, a web server is installed on one machine and a mail server on another. In this case, it is easy to determine a vulnerable spot, which can be one of the following:

☐ *A vulnerability in the operating system of a service.* Check all recent BugTraq reports and make sure that you have all the updates installed.
☐ *A user password.* A non-protected user password that can be picked by a hacker.
☐ *Monitoring.* The hackers might have obtained the password with the help of a sniffer program in the case of a local break-in.
☐ *A vulnerability in the system configuration.* You have not configured the system or a service properly, which made restricted resources accessible, or enabled a user to obtain privileged rights.

These are the most common errors, although we already know that more sophisticated and complex break-in methods exist. But sophisticated break-ins are only executed by professionals. There actually aren't that many of these around.

Local break-ins, within a local network, are the simplest to deal with. You simply report the miscreant to the management, punishment is meted out, and no more local break-ins take place for a while. People have always suffered from the excessive curiosity and this vice has to be controlled somehow.

In the case of a remote break-in, you start at figuring out the responsible party by determining his or her IP address. Having determined the IP address, cut the hacker's system rights. If the hacker has given privileged rights to a regular account, you should lower these privileges to prevent the hacker from doing harm to the system. Now you can begin your cat-and-mouse game with the intruder.

If the hacker is disconcerted by having these rights reduced, and attempts to get them back again, you will have the opportunity to discover the method used for this. This is done by monitoring the moves the hacker makes by the IP address and the account used. You should see all of the actions he or she carries out and, in this way, determine how the restricted server areas are penetrated. Your task is to determine the hole, through which the hacker penetrated the system, and to close it up.

If you see that a resource overload DoS attack is being carried out against your server, you should configure your firewall to reject packets from the nodes emitting intensive traffic. Unix-type systems, such as Linux or FreeBSD, are equipped with efficient firewalls that can stop anything. Windows only acquired this attribute recently, and its functions and features are still in the development stage.

If, for some unfathomable reason, your server is not equipped with a firewall, you will be reduced to watching helplessly as your server is flooded with trash packets. When the load approaches 90 percent of the server's capacity, I would recommend breaking the connection for a short time (about 2 minutes) to wait out the attack. If the server hangs, it may take much longer than this to reboot and put it back into service. If it is necessary to maintain uninterrupted communications and disconnecting from the network is impossible, we can only sympathize with you, because communications cannot remain stable at the 90-percent-load level. You should have installed a firewall as a simple matter of security policy. It is too late to do it with an attack underway.

The only protection from traffic monitoring is encrypting your traffic. If your server software is equipped with encryption capabilities, they have to be enabled and configured in advance. There is nothing an administrator can do to protect against fake DNS server or fake ARP request attacks. In this case, only updating the system with a corresponding protection patch or disabling the vulnerable services altogether can help.

Some attacks can be carried out targeting specific vulnerabilities, through JavaScript executed in the browser, for example. In this case, you should immediately disable JavaScript and leave it disabled until a browser update fixing the vulnerability becomes available. Do not wait until a hacker takes advantage of an error in a program and penetrates your computer.

But the worst thing for an administrator is an attack aimed at destroying the data when there are no backup copies. I personally make monthly backup copies of the main data folders on my computer, where the source codes for my programs, various documents, mail, etc. are stored. In this way, in the event of hard disk failure or the deletion of its contents performed by a virus or a hacker, the most I will lose is a month of work.

But some administrators do not back up their data at all. I worked for a manufacturing company once whose computer network administrators did not even think about this issue. Only the domain controller computer was backed up on a regular basis. The file, mail, web, and database servers were backed up only when someone felt like it, which was often as infrequent as once a month or less. This lackadaisical attitude toward backups on the part of the network administrators could have resulted in the loss of all the information that had been accumulated over the course of a number of years and, as a result, of millions of dollars. Losing the database could have even bankrupted the company.

Defense here is similar to fighting hackers, where the one who reacts to the changes in the situation faster wins. The enemy is constantly on the attack, and you have to keep your system security in tip-top shape at all times, and react to any actual or potential threats in the most expedient manner. Hackers usually attack en masse when a new vulnerability in some software is discovered. This is also confirmed by the fact that 90 percent of hackers are young men using other people's techniques. As soon as someone discovers a new attack technique, the whole hacker army rushes to try this technique personally. Some of them do it with malicious intent, but most of them just want to play pranks. But even the most innocent prank can turn out to be fatal for a company if important information is destroyed inadvertently.

If you are a server administrator, you must have all of the necessary tools for detecting remote attacks in your arsenal. A simple firewall will suffice for a home computer, but you need additional tools for monitoring the system for a corporate server. The earlier you notice an intrusion, the fewer undesirable consequences the break-in will produce.

5.10.1. Backing Up and Restoring

You have to be prepared for the event that your computer system is compromised, as no computer system is immune against this scourge. Being prepared means that you have a clear action plan for this contingency. Only in this way can you react rapidly to a break-in. One component of preparedness is having worked out potential defenses against various intrusion versions. You should have a practical mastery of the following skills:

❑ Restoring the operability of the operating system, including restoring all configuration files. If a hacker leaves a back door, restoring all configuration files will place the system into the state it had been prior to the break-in, which may close the back door.

❏ Restoring databases and all work files. Hackers often destroy data or files. You should be able to restore the destroyed data. While restoring work files is as simple as replacing the corrupted or destroyed files with their backup copies, restoring databases is often not this easy.

To satisfy the two requirements above, you must devise and strictly adhere to a backup copying policy that will allow the destroyed data to be restored rapidly and with minimal losses. There are three main strategies for carrying this out. These are the following:

❏ The files that are modified infrequently and slightly can be backed up at long time intervals. Should the latest modifications be lost, their insignificance means it will not take too much time to restore them manually.

❏ If data are changed often, but the changes are not significant, then only the changes can be backed up. (An example of such changes for databases is the transaction log).

❏ If data are changed often and significantly, the best thing to do is to make a complete back up.

You should make backup copies every time there are significant changes in the data or the system configuration.

The main files should be backed up daily, and not to the local hard disk, but to removable media like CD-R/RW, DVD, Zip drive disks, etc.

Backup copies made on rewritable media should be kept for a month. The media can be reused only after this period of time. It is good practice to store monthly backups permanently. In this way, you will always be able to examine the configuration files for the certain time period and roll back the system in case of a faulty configuration.

Backup copying makes it possible to protect not only against malicious intrusions, but also against system and permanent-storage device (i.e., hard disks) malfunctions, which may result in data loss. Backup copies can also come in handy for restoring data lost due to human or program errors. When the lost information cannot be recovered by standard recovery methods, the only way to save the day is to restore it from the backup copies.

The backup process can be automated to take place at a certain time. This makes the operator's job easier, but does not guarantee the integrity of the information being backed up. I was once asked to restore a system after a crash. The server's data were automatically backed up at the end of every workday to the same file in a network folder. This means that only a one-day rollback was possible. The error that caused the data loss took place 12 minutes before the backup and was noticed only 15 minutes later, three minutes into the backup process. So the old backup copy was destroyed and the new one contained the corrupted data. Thus, the automation, because it was misconfigured, did more harm than good.

System administrators should work out all possible data-restoring mechanisms in advance. You should have a test system, on which you should practice all the aspects of restoring data lost due to various causes and on various scales.

Backup and restore can be performed in different ways, depending on the application software or the database server used. You should familiarize yourself with the backup program's features and, only then, select the option most suitable for you.

Conclusion

Reading this book may leave some people with the impression that the defending side (the administrators) is helpless against the attacking side (the hackers). This is not the case. It is not that difficult to create effective protection. You just need to understand how your server or computer can be broken into, and strictly adhere to the security rules. Any violation of these rules can bring unhappy consequences.

Most break-ins (up to 90 percent) are committed by teenagers who do not have the requisite skills and knowledge to find and exploit new vulnerabilities themselves. Instead, they make use of the already known vulnerabilities (learning them from BugTraqs, for example) and use exploits devised by other, more professional, hackers. This does not require any special knowledge or skill on their part.

If all users and administrators updated their system and application software regularly, the number of break-ins would fall by 90 percent. In order for this to happen, the knowledge level of all users and administrators needs to be raised, or a method to update the software automatically found.

If all users restrained from launching message attachments, the number of virus infections would go down by 99 percent. Most viruses cannot launch on their own, and are launched by users themselves. The exceptions to this are those viruses that use operating system vulnerabilities to launch themselves. But even these viruses can be made less of a threat by updating the system regularly. Most often, enough time passes between the discovery of a vulnerability and the writing of an exploit for it to allow for the updating of any application or system software.

Nevertheless, even 10 percent of the break-ins that are perpetrated nowadays are too many. This number can be reduced by introducing the new IPv6 protocol, which is more secure and meets today's Internet requirements. The important thing is that the introduction be carried out rapidly, before the technology becomes obsolete.

I hope that, in the future, we will not have to exchange passwords unencrypted as we do currently. It's high time to use PGP or SSL for encrypting passwords. This would eliminate the eavesdropping threat, as the intercepted data would be useless.

If the administration of your company scrimps on network security, you have to take care of making your computer secure yourself.

Appendixes

Appendix 1: Contents of the UIRile

```
<style resid=framess>
    element
    {
        background: argb(0,0,0,0);
    }
    element [id=atom(contentcontainer)]
    {
        background: rcbmp(100,6,#FF00FF,0,0,1,0);
    }
    button
    {
        background: rcbmp(112,6,#FF00FF,0,0,1,0);
        borderthickness: rect(8,8,0,8);
    }
</style>

<style resid=toppanelss>
    element
    {
        background: argb(0,0,0,0);
        fontface: rcstr(1);
```

```
    }
    element [id=atom(toppanel)]
    {
        background: argb(0,0,0,0);
    }
    element [id=atom(divider)]
    {
        background: argb(0,0,0,0);
    }
    element [id=atom(product)]
    {
        animation: alpha | s | mediumslow;
    }
    element [id=atom(toppanel)]
    {
        foreground: rgb(239,247,255);
    }
    element [id=atom(welcome)]
    {
        fontstyle: italic;
        fontsize: rcint(44) pt;
        fontweight: bold;
        padding: rect(0rp,0rp,22rp,0);
        contentalign: topright;
    }
    element [id=atom(welcomeshadow)]
    {
        foreground: rgb(49,81,181);
        fontstyle: italic;
        fontsize: rcint(44) pt;
        fontweight: bold;
        padding: rect(2rp,3rp,20rp,0);
        contentalign: topright;
    }
    element[id=atom(help)]
    {
        fontsize: rcint(45) pt;
        padding: rect(140rp,141rp,0,0);
        contentalign: wrapright;
    }
</style>

<style resid=bottompanelss>
    element
    {
        background: argb(0,0,0,0);
    }
    element [id=atom(bottompanel)]
```

```
    {
        background: argb(0,0,0,0);//gradient(argb(0,57,52,173),
argb(0,0,48,156), 0);
        fontface: rcstr(2);
    }
    element [id=atom(divider)]
    {
        //background: rcbmp(126,6,#FF00FF,0,0,1,0);
        background: argb(0,0,0,0);
    }
    element [id=atom(options)]
    {
        padding: rect(25rp, 20rp, 25rp, 20rp);
    }
    button
    {
        fontsize: rcint(42) pt;
        foreground: black;//white;
        cursor: hand;
    }
    button [mousefocused]
    {
        fontstyle: underline;
    }
    button [keyfocused]
    {
        fontstyle: underline;
    }
    element [id=atom(instruct)]
    {
        contentalign: wrapleft;
        padding: rect(18rp,0,0,0);
        fontsize: rcint(43) pt;
        foreground: white;
    }
</style>

<style resid=leftpanelss>
    element
    {
        background: argb(0,0,0,0);
        fontface: rcstr(1);
    }
</style>

<style resid=rightpanelss>
    element
    {
```

```
            background: argb(0,0,0,0);
        }

</style>
<style resid=hotaccountlistss>
    element
    {
        background: argb(0,0,0,0);
        fontface: rcstr(3);
    }
    logonaccount
    {
        cursor: hand;
        animation: alpha | log | fast;


    }
    logonaccount [logonstate=1]
    {
        animation: rectangle | s | mediumfast;
        cursor: arrow;
        alpha:255;
    }
    logonaccount [mousewithin]
    {
        cursor: hand;

        alpha:255;
    }
    logonaccount [selected]
    {
        cursor: hand;

        alpha:255;
    }
    element [id=atom(userpane)]
    {
        padding: rect(2rp,2rp,14rp,2rp);
        borderthickness: rect(0,0,0,0);
        bordercolor: rgb(43,102,159);
        fontsize: rcint(45) pt;
    }
    element [id=atom(userpane)][selected]
    {
        background: rcbmp(112,6,#FF00FF,0,0,1,0);
    }

    logonaccount [selected]
    {
```

```
    alpha: 255;
}
element [id=atom(pictureframe)]
{
    background: rcbmp(113,6,#FF00FF,0,0,1,0);
    borderthickness: rect(5,5,5,5);
    margin: rect(0,0, 7rp,0);
    alpha: 96;
}
element [id=atom(pictureframe)] [mousefocused]
{
    background: rcbmp(119,6,#FF00FF,0,0,1,0);
    borderthickness: rect(5,5,5,5);
    margin: rect(0,0,7rp,0);
    alpha: 255;
}
element [id=atom(pictureframe)] [selected]
{
    background: rcbmp(119,6,#FF00FF,0,0,1,0);
    borderthickness: rect(5,5,5,5);
    margin: rect(0,0,7rp,0);
    alpha: 255;
}
element [id=atom(username)]
{
    foreground: rgb(0,0,0);//rgb(101,121,173);
    contentalign: endellipsis;
}
element [id=atom(username)] [mousefocused]
{
    foreground: rgb(0,0,0);
    contentalign: endellipsis;
}
element [id=atom(username)] [selected]
{
    foreground: rgb(0,0,0);
    contentalign: endellipsis;
}
button [class="status"]
{
    background: argb(0,0,0,0);
    foreground: rgb(0,0,0);//rgb(255,255,255);
    fontsize: rcint(46) pt;
    fontweight: bold;
}
button [class="status"][mousefocused]
{
    fontstyle: underline;
```

```
    }
    button [class="status"][keyfocused]
    {
        fontstyle: underline;
    }
    button [class="status"][selected]
    {
        foreground: rgb(239,247,255);
        fontsize: rcint(46) pt;
        fontweight: bold;
    }

</style>

<style resid=accountlistss>
    element
    {
        background: argb(0,0,0,0);
        fontface: rcstr(3);
    }
    logonaccount
    {
        cursor: hand;
        animation: alpha | log | fast;
        background: argb(0,0,0,0);
    }
    logonaccount [logonstate=1]
    {
        animation: rectangle | s | mediumfast;
        cursor: arrow;
    }
    element [id=atom(userpane)]
    {
        padding: rect(2rp,2rp,14rp,2rp);
        borderthickness: rect(0,0,0,0);
        bordercolor: rgb(0,0,0);//rgb(43,102,159);
        fontsize: rcint(45) pt;
    }
    element [id=atom(userpane)][selected]
    {
        background: rcbmp(112,6,#FF00FF,0,0,1,0);
    }
    element [id=atom(pictureframe)]
    {
        background: rcbmp(113,6,#FF00FF,0,0,1,0);
        borderthickness: rect(5,5,5,5);
        margin: rect(0,0,7rp,0);
    }
```

```
    element [id=atom(username)]
    {
        foreground: rgb(239,247,255);
        contentalign: endellipsis;
    }
    button [class="status"]
    {
        background: argb(0,0,0,0);
        foreground: rgb(255,255,255);
        fontsize: rcint(46) pt;
        fontweight: bold;
        contentalign: wrapleft;
    }
    button [class="status"][mousefocused]
    {
        fontstyle: underline;
    }
    button [class="status"][keyfocused]
    {
        fontstyle: underline;
    }
    button [class="status"][selected]
    {
        foreground: rgb(0,0,0);//rgb(239,247,255);
        fontsize: rcint(46) pt;
        fontweight: bold;
    }

</style>

<style resid=passwordpaness>
    element
    {
        background: argb(0,0,0,0);
    }
    element [id=atom(passwordpanelayer)]
    {
        padding: rect(71rp,0,0,0);
    }
    element [id=atom(instruct)]
    {
        fontface: rcstr(48);
        fontsize: rcint(47) pt;
        foreground: black;//white;
        padding: rect(3rp,0,0,3rp);
    }
    edit [id=atom(password)]
    {
```

```
        background: rcbmp(102,6,#FF00FF,0,0,1,0);
        borderthickness: rect(3,3,5,5);
        passwordcharacter: 9679;
        fontface: "arial";
        fontsize: 16pt;
    }
    button [id=atom(go)]
    {
        margin: rect(5rp,0,0,0);
        content: rcbmp(103,3,-1,26rp,26rp,0,0);
        padding: rect(0rp,1rp,0,1rp);
    }
    button [id=atom(go)][keyfocused]
    {
        content: rcbmp(104,3,-1,26rp,26rp,0,0);
    }
    button [id=atom(info)]
    {
        margin: rect(5rp,0,0,0);
        content: rcbmp(105,3,-1,28rp,28rp,0,0);
    }
    button [id=atom(info)][keyfocused]
    {
        content: rcbmp(106,3,-1,28rp,28rp,0,0);
    }
    element [id=atom(keyboard)]
    {
        cursor: arrow;
        margin: rect(5rp,0,0,0);
    }
</style>

<style resid=scroller>

    scrollbar
    {
        layoutpos: ninebottom;
    }

    scrollbar [vertical]
    {
        layoutpos: nineright;
    }

    viewer
    {
        layoutpos: nineclient;
    }
```

```
thumb
{
    background: dtb(handlemap(1), 3, 1);
    content: dtb(handlemap(1), 9, 1);
    contentalign: middlecenter;
}

thumb [mousefocused]
{
    background: dtb(handlemap(1), 3, 2);
    content: dtb(handlemap(1), 9, 2);
}

thumb [captured]
{
    background: dtb(handlemap(1), 3, 3);
    content: dtb(handlemap(1), 9, 3);
}

repeatbutton [id=atom(lineup)]
{
    background: dtb(handlemap(1), 1, 1);
    width: sysmetric(2);
    height: sysmetric(20);
}

repeatbutton [id=atom(lineup)][mousefocused]
{
    background: dtb(handlemap(1), 1, 2);
}

repeatbutton [id=atom(lineup)][pressed]
{
    background: dtb(handlemap(1), 1, 3);
}

repeatbutton [id=atom(linedown)]
{
    background: dtb(handlemap(1), 1, 5);
    width: sysmetric(2);
    height: sysmetric(20);
}

repeatbutton [id=atom(linedown)][mousefocused]
{

    background: dtb(handlemap(1), 1, 6);
```

```
        }

        repeatbutton [id=atom(linedown)][pressed]
        {
            background: dtb(handlemap(1), 1, 7);
        }

        repeatbutton [id=atom(pageup)]
        {
            background: dtb(handlemap(1), 7, 1);
        }

        repeatbutton [id=atom(pageup)][mousefocused]
        {
            background: dtb(handlemap(1), 7, 2);
        }

        repeatbutton [id=atom(pageup)][pressed]
        {
            background: dtb(handlemap(1), 7, 3);
        }

        repeatbutton [id=atom(pagedown)]
        {
            background: dtb(handlemap(1), 6, 1);
        }

        repeatbutton [id=atom(pagedown)][mousefocused]
        {
            background: dtb(handlemap(1), 6, 2);
        }

        repeatbutton [id=atom(pagedown)][pressed]
        {
            background: dtb(handlemap(1), 6, 3);
        }

    </style>

    <logonframe resid=main id=atom(frame) sheet=styleref(framess) layout=
borderlayout() layoutpos=client>
    <element id=atom(contentcontainer) layout=borderlayout() layoutpos=
client>

        <element id=atom(toppanel) sheet=styleref(toppanelss) layout=
borderlayout() layoutpos=top height=80rp>
                <element id=atom(logoarea) layout=
verticalflowlayout(0,3,3,2)>
```

```
                <element id=atom(product) contentalign=topright padding=
rect(10rp,0rp,20rp,20rp)/>
                <element id=atom(help) contentalign=wrapright width=1rp
padding=rect(0rp,0rp,40rp,0rp)/>
            </element>
            <element id=atom(msgarea) layout=verticalflowlayout(0,0,0,2)>
                <element layout=filllayout() width=384rp>
                    <element id=atom(welcomeshadow) content=rcstr(7)/>
                    <element id=atom(welcome) content=rcstr(7)/>
                </element>
            </element>
        <element id=atom(divider) layoutpos=bottom height=2rp/>
    </element>

    <element id=atom(bottompanel) sheet=styleref(bottompanelss) layout=
borderlayout() layoutpos=bottom>
        <element id=atom(divider) layoutpos=top height=2rp/>
        <element id=atom(options) layout=borderlayout() layoutpos=client>
            <element layout=borderlayout() layoutpos=left>
                <button id=atom(power) layout=borderlayout() layoutpos=
top accessible=true accRole=43 accName=rcstr(11)>
                    <element layoutpos=left content=rcbmp(107,3,-1,
26rp,26rp,0,0) />
                    <element id=atom(label) layoutpos=client margin=
rect(2rp,0,0,0)/>
                </button>
                <button id=atom(undock) layout=borderlayout() layoutpos=
top margin=rect(0,2rp,0,0) accessible=true accRole=43 accName=rcstr(14)>
                    <element layoutpos=left content=rcbmp(108,3,-1,
26rp,26rp,0,0)/>
                    <element id=atom(label) layoutpos=client margin=
rect(2rp,0,0,0)/>
                </button>
            </element>
            <element id=atom(instruct) layoutpos=right content=rcstr(25)
width=325rp/>
        </element>
    </element>

    <element id=atom(contentcontainer0) layout=flowlayout(1,3,2,3)
layoutpos=client content=argb(0,0,0,0)>
        <element id=atom(leftpanel) sheet=styleref(leftpanelss)
layoutpos=left>
        </element>

        <element id=atom(rightpanel) sheet=styleref(rightpanelss)
layout=borderlayout() layoutpos=left width=920rp>
```

```
            <element id=atom(divider) layoutpos=left width=1rp/>
            <scrollviewer id=atom(scroller) sheet=styleref(scroller)
layoutpos=client xscrollable=false margin=rect(0rp,0rp,0rp,0rp)>
                <selector id=atom(accountlist)
sheet=styleref(accountlistss) layout=verticalflowlayout(0,3,3,2)/>
            </scrollviewer>
        </element>

    </element>

</element>
</logonframe>

<logonaccount resid=accountitem id=atom(accountitem) layout=filllayout()
accessible=true accRole=43>
    <element id=atom(userpanelayer) layout=borderlayout() height=80rp>
        <element id=atom(userpane) layout=borderlayout() layoutpos=top>
            <element id=atom(pictureframe) layout=flowlayout(0,2,2)
layoutpos=left width=58rp height=58rp>
                <element id=atom(picture) />
            </element>
            <element id=atom(username) layoutpos=top/>
            <button id=atom(status0) class="status" layoutpos=none/>
            <button id=atom(status1) class="status" layoutpos=none/>
        </element>
    </element>
</logonaccount>

<element resid=passwordpanel id=atom(passwordpanelayer)
sheet=styleref(passwordpaness) layout=borderlayout() height=80rp>
    <element layout=borderlayout() layoutpos=bottom>
        <edit id=atom(password) layoutpos=left width=163rp/>
        <element id=atom(keyboard) layoutpos=left/>
        <button id=atom(go) layoutpos=left accessible=true accRole=43
accName= rcstr(100)/>
        <button id=atom(info) layoutpos=left accessible=true accRole=43
accName= rcstr(13)/>
    </element>
    <element id=atom(instruct) layoutpos=bottom content=rcstr(6)/>
</element>
```

Appendix 2: Some Helpful Programs

CyD Careful Observer (**www.cydsoft.com**). The program monitors connections with specified computers. When a connection is broken, a specified action is carried out: a message or an audio signal issued, an e-mail sent, a program executed, the computer rebooted, etc.

CyD NET Utils (**www.cydsoft.com**). This is an excellent collection of easy-to-use network utilities for any hacker or network administrator. Its capabilities include checking the connection with the remote computer (using the Ping command), scanning open ports (checking running services), scanning for open resources, etc.

John the Ripper (**http://www.openwall.com/john/**). This is program for breaking passwords for Unix systems.

Internet Scanner (**www.iss.net**). This is one of the best security scanners. It is a part of the SAFEsuite utility kit, which comprises many security testing and intrusion-detection utilities.

Password Pro (**http://www.insidepro.com/**). This is another program for breaking passwords for Unix systems.

Postman (**www.cydsoft.com**). This is a mass-mailing program. It has a built-in SMTP server, which allows origin e-mail addresses to be faked.

PWLinside (**http://www.insidepro.com/**). This is program for breaking passwords for Windows 9*x* systems.

SAMinside (**http://www.insidepro.com/**). This is program for breaking passwords for Windows NT systems.

SockChain (**http://www.ufasoft.com/socks/**).This is a utility for building chains of proxy and socks servers, thus allowing anonymous work on the Internet.

Shadow Scan (**http://www.rsh.kiev.ua/**). This is a great program, with many options for testing systems for vulnerabilities. The program is a handy tool for collecting system information and for dictionary password breaking.

NT Crack (**http://archivedaru.hypermart.net/winnt_hacking/Ntcrack.zip**). A program for checking NT systems for vulnerabilities. This program is a must-have for anyone intending to break into a Windows server. It is even more useful for those in the business of providing NT security.

NT Bugs (**hhttp://archivedaru.hypermart.net/winnt_hacking/Ntbugs.zip**). This is a rather extensive description of Windows server vulnerabilities. Another must for NT crackers and their counterparts.

LC3 (**http://www.l0pht.com/l0phtcrack/dist/lc252install.zip**). This is the most famous and one of the best programs for those trying to break passwords to NT systems.

Restorator (**http://www.bome.com/Restorator/**). The most famous and most convenient program-resource editor.

Retina Network Security Scanner (**http://www.eeye.com/**). A good security scanner.

Appendix 3: Some Helpful References

www.cert.org. A good web site that has a section with vulnerability descriptions. Updates to the information sometimes occur after a delay, but are very descriptive.

www.securityfocus.com. Another site providing vulnerability descriptions.

www.2600.com. The most famous hacker magazine.

http://www.defcon.org/. The most famous hacker hangout.

www.opensource.org/for-hackers.html. Open source projects for hackers.

www.kaspersky.com. The site of the Kaspersky antivirus lab. Provides exhaustive virus information.

Appendix 4: Glossary

*nix — A common name for Unix-like systems (Unix, Linux, Solaris, etc.).

ASP — Active Server Pages. A Microsoft script language for the Windows platform.

CGI — Common Getaway Interface. Used to develop programs for web servers in such languages as Perl, C, Delphi, etc.

Cookies — This technology allows web sites to store information files to the user's hard drive.

DNS — A service for determining a computer's IP address by its domain name.

Firewall — A hardware or software system designed to prevent unauthorized access to or from a private network. The main operating principle is filtering data packets according to predefined rules.

FTP — File Transfer Protocol.

Hub (concentrator) — A device used to connect computers to a network using twisted-pair wiring. A hub relays all packets it receives to all computers connected to it, regardless of to which of the computers specific packets are addressed.

IP address — A 32-bit device or computer-network address. In the near future, a transition to a new version of the IP is planned that will have a larger address and allow many more network devices to be addressed.

MAC address (Media Access Control address) — This is a 48-bit number that is assigned to each network adapter by its manufacturer.

PHP — A script language for web pages. Lately, this language has been becoming more and more popular because it offers an implementation for all major operating system platforms and is quite simple and easy to use.

RFC (**Request For Comments**) — Documents describing recommendations for implementing various technologies. For example, recommendations for implementing SMTP are described in an RFC and these recommendations should be followed when implementing this protocol in your software. It is not mandatory to follow the recommendations, but it is highly advisable.

Switch — A device used to connect computers to a network using twisted-pair wiring. Unlike hubs, a switch resends incoming packets only to those computers to which they are addressed. This makes eavesdropping on other people's traffic more difficult.

Anonymous access — Access to a server not requiring authorization. When accessing an FTP server, the login is given as Anonymous and any e-mail as the password. The validity of the password is not checked for the Anonymous login, but it does have to have a valid e-mail format. The rights under anonymous access are limited and only open information can be viewed. Changing or deleting information is usually not allowed.

Datagram — A packet of data sent to a network. A connection does not need to be established to send a datagram, and no acknowledgement of its successful arrival is provided.

Daemon — A server program working in the background. This name is used in *nix environments. There, the names of such programs are usually appended with the "d" character.

Let's imagine a web server daemon. This must be a program that is loaded into the memory and is listening to some port — port 80, for example. As soon as it detects that a client has connected to this port, the daemon start accepting requests from the client and answering them. The equivalent of daemon in Windows is a service.

Checksum — A number calculated according to a certain algorithm and used to determine the integrity of data.

Port — Every network program opens a free port for itself when it starts. Some ports, however, are reserved for specific purposes. Thus, port 21 is reserved for FTP, port 80 is reserved for HTTP, etc. Now, imagine a situation, in which two services are launched on a server: FTP and HTTP. This means that there are two programs running on the server that can be connected to over the network. If you want to connect to the FTP service, you send your request to the computer address to port 21. When the server receives this request, it determines that this request is addressed to the FTP service and not to the HTTP (web) service by the port number.

So network ports are virtual entities that cannot be seen. Without ports, computers would not be able to determine, to which service network requests are addressed.

Services — The same thing as daemons, only for Windows platform machines.

Exploit — A program that exploits some vulnerability. Exploits written for *nix platforms may come as source codes. In this case, they have to be compiled before use.

A Trojan horse — A program that is surreptitiously installed on the target's computer and allows its owner to control this computer. These programs most often consist of two parts: a client and a server. The server is installed on the victim's computer. Then the client is used to connect to the server and make it perform certain operations on the remote computer.

There are Trojan horses with the server part only. In this case, when the victim starts the program, it carries out certain actions (e.g., searches the hard drive for passwords and then sends the passwords it finds to a predefined e-mail address) and may self-destruct afterwards.

CD-ROM Description

Folder	Description
\Chapter1	Programs described in Chapter 1 that can be used to embellish Windows and Internet Explorer.
\Chapter2	Files used in Chapter 2 examples.
\Chapter2\Login	Windows XP login programs.
\Chapter4	The CyD Archiver XP program for making archives inaccessible.
\Chapter5	Programs and files used in Chapter 5 examples.
\Soft	Demonstration programs from CyD Software Labs and the Restorator program. Most of these programs were used to prepare the materials in the book.

IMPORTANT

The StyleBuilderInstall.exe and StyleXPInstallFemale.exe programs located in the Chapter1 folder work only under Windows XP.

IMPORTANT

We recommend that you do not launch programs located in the Chapter2\Login folder without installing them on the system first. The installation instructions for them are described in *Chapter 2*.

The DivX511Bundle.exe file shows a video about A-List Publishing books. To watch this file, install Standard DivX Codec(FREE), available for free download from **http://www.divx.com/divx/**.

Index